Shakespeare on European Festival Stages

RELATED TITLES

Shakespeare and the 'Live' Theatre Broadcast Experience
Edited by Pascale Aebischer, Susanne Greenhalgh and
Laurie E. Osborne
978-1-3501-2581-0

A Year of Shakespeare: Re-living the World Shakespeare Festival
Edited by Paul Edmondson, Erin Sullivan and Paul Prescott
978-1-4081-8814-9

Shakespeare and the Challenge of the Contemporary:
Performance, Politics and Aesthetics
Francesca Clare Rayner
978-1-3501-8215-8

Directing Shakespeare in America: Historical Perspectives
Charles Ney
978-1-4742-8969-6

Shakespeare on the Global Stage: Performance and Festivity
in the Olympic Year
Edited by Paul Prescott and Erin Sullivan
978-1-4725-2032-6

Shakespeare on European Festival Stages

Edited by
Nicoleta Cinpoeş,
Florence March and
Paul Prescott

THE ARDEN SHAKESPEARE
LONDON • NEW YORK • OXFORD • NEW DELHI • SYDNEY

The Arden Shakespeare
Bloomsbury Publishing Plc
50 Bedford Square, London, WC1B 3DP, UK
1385 Broadway, New York, NY 10018, USA
29 Earlsfort Terrace, Dublin 2 Ireland

BLOOMSBURY, THE ARDEN SHAKESPEARE and the Arden Shakespeare logo
are trademarks of Bloomsbury Publishing Plc

First published in Great Britain 2022
Paperback edition published 2023

Copyright © Nicoleta Cinpoeş, Florence March, Paul Prescott and
contributors, 2022, 2023

Nicoleta Cinpoeş, Florence March, Paul Prescott and contributors have asserted
their right under the Copyright, Designs and Patents Act, 1988, to be identified as
the authors of this work.

For legal purposes the Acknowledgements on p. xvi constitute an extension of
this copyright page.

Cover design: Charlotte Daniels
Cover image: Poster of the 2019 edition of the festival Printemps des comédiens,
Montpellier (France). Photograph by Werner Jeker. Permission by festival
Printemps des comédiens

All rights reserved. No part of this publication may be reproduced or transmitted
in any form or by any means, electronic or mechanical, including photocopying,
recording, or any information storage or retrieval system, without prior
permission in writing from the publishers.

Bloomsbury Publishing Plc does not have any control over, or responsibility for,
any third-party websites referred to or in this book. All internet addresses given
in this book were correct at the time of going to press. The author and publisher
regret any inconvenience caused if addresses have changed or sites have ceased
to exist, but can accept no responsibility for any such changes.

A catalogue record for this book is available from the British Library.

Library of Congress Cataloging-in-Publication Data
Names: Cinpoes, Nicoleta, editor. | March, Florence, 1970-editor. | Prescott, Paul, 1974-editor.
Title: Shakespeare on European festival stages / edited by Nicoleta
Cinpoes, Florence March and Paul Prescott.
Description: London; New York: The Arden Shakespeare, 2022. |
Includes bibliographical references and index.
Identifiers: LCCN 2021030345 (print) | LCCN 2021030346 (ebook) |
ISBN 9781350140165 (hardback) | ISBN 9781350140189 (ebook) | ISBN 9781350140172 (epub)
Subjects: LCSH: Shakespeare, William, 1564-1616–Stage history–Europe. |
Shakespeare, William, 1564-1616–Dramatic production. | Drama festivals–Europe–History.
Classification: LCC PR3109.E2 S533 2022 (print) |
LCC PR3109.E2 (ebook) | DDC 822.3/3–dc23
LC record available at https://lccn.loc.gov/2021030345
LC ebook record available at https://lccn.loc.gov/2021030346

ISBN: H B: 978-1-3501-4016-5
P B: 978-1-3502-8324-4
ePDF: 978-1-3501-4018-9
eBook: 978-1-3501-4017-2

Typeset by Integra Software Services Pvt. Ltd.

To find out more about our authors and books visit
www.bloomsbury.com and sign up for our newsletters.

This book is dedicated to the memory of Professor Jerzy Limon (1950–2021), founder of the Gdańsk Shakespeare Festival and a prince of European Shakespeare festival stages.

CONTENTS

List of figures ix
Notes on contributors x
Acknowledgements xvi
A note on the text xvii

1 Shakespeare on European festival stages: An introduction *Paul Prescott, Nicoleta Cinpoeş and Florence March* 1

2 Shaping democratic festivals through Shakespeare in southern France: Avignon, Montpellier, Nice *Florence March* 17

3 Shakespeare at the Almagro festivals: Reinventing the plays in Spain *Isabel Guerrero* 37

4 Shakespeare at Four Castles: Summer Shakespeare Festival in Prague, Brno, Ostrava (Czech Republic) and Bratislava (Slovakia) *Filip Krajník and Eva Kyselová* 55

5 Globolatry in Germany: The Shakespeare Festival at Neuss – a dramaturg's perspective *Vanessa Schormann* 75

6   A world's stage for many players: The International Shakespeare Festival – Craiova (Romania) *Nicoleta Cinpoeş* 93

7   Festivalizing Shakespeare in Italy: Verona and Rome *Lisanna Calvi and Maddalena Pennacchia* 119

8   The Gdańsk Shakespeare Festival: Four centuries of travelling theatre in Poland *Urszula Kizelbach and Jacek Fabiszak* 137

9   From a schoolyard play to civic festival: Shakespeare in the Bulgarian village of Patalenitsa *Boika Sokolova and Kirilka Stavreva* 157

10 The Gyula Shakespeare Festival (Hungary): Local, national, European, global *Júlia Paraizs and Ágnes Matuska* 175

11 Unhomely Shakespeares: Interculturalism and diplomacy in Elsinore *Anne Sophie Refskou* 195

12 Shakespeare's Globe in Inđija: A portrait of Itaka Shakespeare Festival (Serbia) *Alexandra Portmann* 213

Index 230

FIGURES

1.1 A map of European Shakespeare festivals in 2020 2
4.1 Jan Tříska as Caliban and Martin Huba as Prospero in *The Tempest* (2009) 66
6.1 Fairies taking over Craiova in *A Midsummer Night's Dream* (2018) 110
8.1 The upper galleries of the Gdańsk Shakespeare Theatre with an open roof (night view) 142
8.2 Photo impression from ShakespeareOFF during the 23rd Shakespeare Festival 146
9.1 Velizar Emanuilov (Demetrius), Nikolai Vladimirov (Lysander), Maria Panayotova (Helena) and audience members at the July 2019 production of *A Midsummer Night's Dream* in Patalenitsa, directed by Terrie Fender 169
11.1 The new stage construction during the theatre concert *Searching for William* by Christian Friedel and Woods of Birnam (HamletScenen, Shakespeare Festival 2018) 196
12.1 Open-air stage, Itaka Shakespeare Festival 219

NOTES ON CONTRIBUTORS

Lisanna Calvi is Associate Professor of English Literature at the University of Verona, Italy. Her main research interests have focused on Restoration and early modern drama and literary culture. She has written a book on Restoration and early-eighteenth-century tragedy (2015) and on James II's devotional papers and *Imago Regis* (2009). She also authored articles on John Dryden (2000), Robert Browning (2002, 2010), Thomas Otway (2007), Edmund Gosse (2009), *The Tempest* and the *commedia dell'arte* (2012), madness and autobiography in seventeenth-century England (2012, 2013), *Romeo and Juliet* on the nineteenth-century Italian stage (2013, 2017), and Shakespearean eighteenth-century adaptation (2020). She co-edited a miscellany on *The Tempest* (2014) and on *Romeo and Juliet* (2016). She has recently edited a collection on *Romeo and Juliet* and its afterlife (2018). She is currently working on a project on Italian nineteenth-century Shakespearean actors with a focus on *Romeo and Juliet*.

Nicoleta Cinpoeş is Professor of Shakespeare Studies at the University of Worcester, UK, where she teaches early modern literature, Shakespeare in performance and screen adaptation, and directs the Early Modern Research Group there. Author of *Shakespeare's Hamlet in Romania 1778–2008* (2010), editor and contributor to *Doing Kyd* (2016) and *Europe's Shakespeare(s)* special issue of *Cahiers Élisabéthains* 96 (2017), she has published articles in *The New Theatre Quarterly*, *Cahiers Élisabéthains*, *Shakespeare Bulletin* and *SEDERI*. For the modernized translation of Shakespeare's *Complete Works*, she has written the introductions to *Hamlet* (2010) and *Titus Andronicus* (2019). She has worked with Shakespeare festivals in the European Shakespeare Festivals

Network for over a decade, and she has organized the ESRA Shakespeare in Performance Seminar series at the International Shakespeare Festival, Craiova, since 2010.

Jacek Fabiszak is Professor in the Faculty of English at Adam Mickiewicz University, Poznań, Poland, where he teaches cultural history and theory. His research interests include English Renaissance drama and its stage, televisual and filmic transpositions. He has published and given papers at conferences on Shakespeare's plays – one of his major publications in this area is *Polish Televised Shakespeares* (2005). His monograph *Shakespeare's Drama of Social Roles* (2001) interprets Shakespeare's Last Plays in light of the theory of social roles and speech act theory. He has popularized Shakespeare's works in Poland, co-authoring *Szekspir. Leksykon* (Shakespeare. A lexicon; 2003) and co-editing *Czytanie Szekspira* (Reading Shakespeare). He has also written on Christopher Marlowe, both his plays and their screen versions.

Isabel Guerrero is Assistant Professor at Universidad Nacional de Educación a Distancia (UNED), Spain. Her research focuses on Shakespeare's presence at theatre festivals of different status, from official to fringe. Her work has appeared in the volume *Romeo and Juliet in European Culture* (2017) and the journals *Cahiers Élisabéthains* (2020), *SEDERI Yearbook* (2017), *Cartaphilus* (2016, 2017) and *The Grove* (2017), among others. She has co-edited two thematic volumes on theatre studies for EDITUM (2017, 2019) and was a founding member of the 1st International Conference for Young Researchers on Theatre Studies (CIJIET, Universidad de Murcia). Beside her academic work, she is also a stage director.

Urszula Kizelbach is Assistant Professor in the Department of Studies in Culture at Adam Mickiewicz University in Poznań, Poland. She specializes in Shakespeare theatre studies and literary pragma-stylistics, in particular the pragmatic and stylistic analysis of early modern drama. She has published a book on power in politics in Shakespeare's history plays, *The Pragmatics of Early Modern Politics: Power and Kingship in Shakespeare's History Plays* (2014). Her latest research concentrates on the pragma-stylistic nature of blunders as a means of literary characterization in Shakespeare's works. She is a contributor to *Reviewing Shakespeare* and she acts as the Polish Ambassador of PALA (Poetics and Linguistics Association), an organization uniting stylisticians, literary scholars and linguists, who promote the knowledge of stylistics in literature in academia. She is an Assistant Editor of *Studia Anglica Posnaniensia*, a quarterly journal published at the Faculty of English at Adam Mickiewicz University.

Filip Krajník (PhD Durham University, 2014) is a specialist lecturer in English Literature in the Department of English and American Studies at Masaryk University in Brno, Czech Republic. His research interests include late medieval and early modern English literature, early modern theatre, and the cultural and intellectual history of dreams in Europe. Currently, he is finishing a manuscript of his first monograph, tentatively entitled *Fearful Slumbers: Dramatising Sleep and Dreams in Shakespeare's Plays*.

Eva Kyselová is a graduate of the Faculty of Theatre, Academy of Performing Arts in Bratislava, Slovakia; she obtained her PhD in Theory and Practice of Theatre Creation at the Faculty of Theatre, Academy of Performing Arts in Prague (DAMU), Czech Republic. Since 2013, she has been an assistant professor at the Department of Theory and Criticism and an external lecturer at the Department of Arts Management at DAMU, teaching courses on the history of world and Czech theatre. Her main research interest is the history of Slovak and Czech theatre and their relations; as a critic, she focuses on contemporary spoken and alternative drama, collaborating with a number of Czech and Slovak theatre journals.

Florence March is Professor in Early Modern English Drama at University Paul-Valéry Montpellier 3, France, and Director of the Institute for Research on the Renaissance, the Neo-Classical Age and the Enlightenment (IRCL) at the French National Centre for Scientific Research (CNRS). Her research currently focuses on Shakespearean stage configurations in twentieth- and twenty-first-century Europe, particularly in festivals, and the relationship between stage and audience or 'pact of performance'. She has published extensively on Shakespeare's structuring function in southern France festivals in journals (*Shakespeare Jahrbuch*, *Shakespeare Studies*, *Litteraria Pragensia*), in a contribution to *The Shakespearean World* (2017), as well as in her monograph *Shakespeare au Festival d'Avignon* (2012). She is co-editor-in-chief of *Cahiers Élisabéthains*.

Ágnes Matuska is Associate Professor in the English Department at the University of Szeged, Hungary. Her main field of research is English Renaissance drama, particularly the changes in the logic and ontology of early modern theatrical representation. Her monograph *The Vice-Device: Iago and Lear's Fool as Figures of Representational Crisis* (2011) suggests a re-evaluation of the Vice character in morality plays. She is currently working on the diverse traditions of the *theatrum mundi* metaphor in Elizabethan England and the ways contemporary understandings of the *topos* influence our readings of the plays. She is editor of the journal *Apertúra: Film-Visuality-Theory* and a recipient of the Folger Shakespeare Fellowship (2007 and 2013) and the Fulbright Research Fellowship (2011).

Júlia Paraizs is currently an independent scholar, living in the UK. She has a PhD in English Literature from Eötvös Loránd University, Budapest (2010) and was a Junior Research Fellow at the Research Centre for the Humanities of the Hungarian Academy of Sciences between 2011 and 2018. She was a Visiting Researcher at The Shakespeare Institute, University of Birmingham and Wolfson College, University of Cambridge and also a Visiting Fellow at Trinity College, University of Cambridge. Her research focuses on Shakespeare in translation with a twin interest in editing and performing Shakespeare. She is the editor of János Arany's classical Shakespeare translations (*A Midsummer Night's Dream, Hamlet, King John*), originally published in the 1860s and of a volume on the cultural significance of Arany's translation of *Hamlet* (2015). She has written theatre reviews on the Gyula Shakespeare Festival, which she has followed since its inception.

Maddalena Pennacchia is Full Professor of English Literature at Roma Tre University and Director of the Silvano Toti Globe Theatre Archive in Rome. She is Director of the Shakespeare's Rome International Summer School and of an audience development programme for high school students in collaboration with the Globe in Rome. She is the author of *Shakespeare intermediale. I drammi romani* (2012) and *Tracce del moderno nel teatro di Shakespeare* (2008); she edited *Literary Intermediality* (2007) and co-edited *Questioning Bodies in Shakespeare's Rome* (2010), *Adaptation, Intermediality and the British Celebrity Biopic* (2014) and *Shakespeare and Tourism* (2019). She also authored a bio-fiction for children, *Shakespeare e il sogno di un'estate* (2009), which was translated into Spanish (2013) and Romanian (2016).

Alexandra Portmann is Assistant Professor in Theatre Studies at the University of Bern, Switzerland. Her dissertation '"The time is out of joint": Shakespeare's *Hamlet* in the Region of the Former Yugoslavia' (2015) deals with the interrelation of memory culture and theatre and was awarded twice (Faculty Prize by the University of Bern and the German Shakespeare Society). She worked as a lecturer at the University of Cologne, Germany and on a mobility fellowship at Queen Mary University of London, UK and Ludwig–Maximilians–University Munich, Germany. Her current research project 'Festivals and Institutional Changes: Perspectives on Transnational Theatre Production' (funded by the Swiss National Science Foundation) investigates professional networks in the performing arts.

Paul Prescott is Professor of English and Theatre at the University of California, Merced, USA. He has acted, adapted and taught Shakespeare in a range of countries and contexts and published widely on Shakespeare in performance. As a dramaturg and adaptor, he has collaborated with a number of companies including the National Theatre of Great Britain, and is co-founder of 'Shakespeare in Yosemite'. He is the author of *Reviewing Shakespeare: Journalism and Performance from the Eighteenth Century to the Present*, the editor of *Othello* (Arden Performance Editions) and co-editor of *A Year of Shakespeare: Re-living the World Shakespeare Festival* and *Shakespeare on the Global Stage: Performance and Festivity in the Olympic Year* (both The Arden Shakespeare).

Anne Sophie Refskou is research consultant at 'HamletScenen', Elsinore, Denmark. Until 2019, she was a lecturer in theatre and performance at the Guildford School of Acting, University of Surrey. Her publications include *Eating Shakespeare: Cultural Anthropophagy as Global Methodology*, co-edited with Vinicius Mariano de Carvalho and Marcel Alvaro de Amorim (The Arden Shakespeare, 2019). She is currently completing a monograph on Shakespeare and compassion in early modern culture.

Vanessa Schormann studied English Literature, History of Art and Theatre Studies at the Ludwig Maximilians University of Munich (LMU), Germany and the University of Kent, England. Since 2002 she has been a Lecturer at the Department of Theatre Studies at the University of Munich (LMU) and works as a Dramaturg for the International Shakespeare Festival at the Globe Neuss as well as for Shakespeare Companies in Germany. She is Director of the Shakespeare Globe Center Germany as well as Director of Education at the Shakespeare Festival in Neuss and a board member of the German Shakespeare Society. As a dramaturg and theatre scholar she has published on the subject of Shakespeare's Globe and its replicas, focusing on the architecture, the actor's use of the space and new discoveries made for Shakespeare's dramaturgy.

Boika Sokolova teaches Shakespeare and Drama at the University of Notre Dame (USA) in England. She has published widely on Shakespeare, his reception in Europe and performance. Her most recent publications are an essay cluster entitled *Operation Shakespeare in Post-Communist Bulgaria* (*Toronto Slavic Quarterly*, 2017), co-authored with Kirilka Starveva, 'The Merchant of Venice East of Berlin' (*Shakespeare Survey 71*, 2018), '"To be/ not to be": *Hamlet* and the Threshold of Potentiality in Post-communist Bulgaria' (2020), co-authored with Kirilka Stavreva, and *Shakespeare's Others in 21st-century European Performance: The Merchant of Venice and Othello* (The Arden Shakespeare, 2021), a collection of essays, co-edited with Janice Valls-Russell. She is currently working on a book on the performance history of *The Merchant of Venice*.

Kirilka Stavreva is Professor of English at Cornell College, USA. She is the author of *Words Like Daggers: Violent Female Speech in Early Modern England* (2015), contributing editor of the e-book series *Major Authors and Movements in British Literature* and *Major Genres, Forms, and Media in British Literature* (2017) and has published numerous articles on European Shakespeare, early modern women's speech, and the scholarship of teaching and learning. With Boika Sokolova, she co-authored the essay cluster *Operation Shakespeare in Post-Communist Bulgaria* (*Toronto Slavic Quarterly*, 2017); they are currently completing a book on key modern performances of *The Merchant of Venice*.

ACKNOWLEDGEMENTS

The editors are very grateful to everyone who has played a role in bringing this book to fruition. To our team of authors who have condensed their expertise and experience into each of the chapters and who have responded so patiently to our editorial prodding. To Lara Bateman, our equally patient and good-spirited editor, and to all of her colleagues at The Arden Shakespeare. To the anonymous peer reviewers who have made valuable suggestions throughout. To the photographers and image-holders who have allowed us to reproduce their images in the following pages and on the book's cover, the latter including: the 2017 production of *Hamlet* at Elsinore (by permission of HamletScenen); AGENTURA SCHOK and photographer Pavel Mára for the Prague Shakespeare Festival production of *Twelfth Night*; the Printemps des Comédiens, Montpellier (© Werner Jeker); the Patalenitsa Shakespeare Festival's productions of *The Tempest*, dir. Rex Doyle, 2014, and *Romeo and Juliet*, dir. Trevor Rawlins, 2015 (both posters designed by Ina Hicheva Dimitrova); the official poster advertising the 23rd Shakespeare Festival in Gdansk (by permission of the Festival); and the poster for the 2018 edition of the Craiova Shakespeare Festival (by permission of the Festival).

We are also grateful to a range of institutions and organizations, including our own universities (the University of Worcester, University Paul-Valéry Montpellier 3, the University of Warwick and the University of California, Merced), but also invaluable organizations such as the European Shakespeare Festivals Network and the European Shakespeare Research Association, at whose conferences we have held a series of illuminating seminars.

Finally, we extend our gratitude to the thousands of people – staff, actors, technicians, volunteers – who make Shakespeare happen on European festival stages. This book is our collective tribute to their labour and artistry.

A NOTE ON THE TEXT

All Shakespearean quotations follow the relevant edition in The Arden Shakespeare Third Series.

1

Shakespeare on European festival stages: An introduction

Paul Prescott, Nicoleta Cinpoeş and Florence March

Dear Reader: you have before you a travel companion, the first of its kind. This book will take you across continental Europe offering an introduction to each of the festival stages that have illuminated the works of William Shakespeare over the last seventy or so years. You will travel across the length and breadth of the continent: from the (mostly) balmy south to the (often) chilly north, from the planes of central Spain, to the Rhodope Mountains of southwest Bulgaria, to the sea-swept Baltic settings of Gdańsk and of 'Hamlet's' castle in Helsingør, Denmark. You will see the widest imaginable variety of theatrical and artistic offering on a range of stages, from castles, parks and historic theatres to black box spaces, streets and bars. You will hear the works of Shakespeare spoken in many European tongues and in languages from far beyond the continent's borders. In short, you have here an analytical map for a Shakespearean Grand Tour. Unlike its eighteenth-century antecedent, this Grand Tour is not devoted to the consumption of ancient and enduring monuments of lost cultures and empires. Rather it is a Grand Tour of the exquisitely ephemeral, a journey to sample fashions, trends

FIGURE 1.1 *A map of European Shakespeare festivals in 2020.*

and innovations in theatre-making as mediated through the lingua franca of live Shakespearean performance.

Preparations for this book began some years ago when, noting the relative paucity of literature on European Shakespeare festivals, the editors held a sequence of seminars on the theme in Paris, Montpellier, Worcester and elsewhere, often at the biennial conferences of the European Shakespeare Research Association (ESRA). These seminars were rich and stimulating in their own right, but also enabled us to identify the resident experts on each of the fourteen festivals featured in this book and commission the following chapters. These chapters are written by scholars who have long-standing relationships with their respective festivals, sometimes as critics or dramaturges or advisors. They write with insight, expertise and local knowledge. A researcher in live arts is first and foremost a lover of performance, although fascinated spectating and distanced analysis may *a priori* seem two stances that are difficult to reconcile. The spectator's pleasure sets off the researcher's desire to work on the performance, which means overcoming fascination (or at least suspending it) to adopt a critical distance. The paradox is certainly one of the difficulties the researcher in performance studies must learn to deal with. In some cases, the spectator's frustration may turn out to be the researcher's good fortune. Failure to fulfil the spectator's desire and meet his or her expectations can provide an analytic counterpoint to study the creative process at work in a theatrical performance. These dialectics between proximity and distance, love and alienation, play out in the following pages. Equally, given the anti-festive pandemic context in which the book was completed, a year of loss and longing and theatre closures, it is perhaps unsurprising that our authors err more towards celebration than critique.

For much of its recent history, the continent of Europe has been preoccupied with the fraught challenge of forging a peaceable consensus in the wake of the catastrophic first half of the twentieth century. Such a cooperative understanding – especially in the context of the growth of what we now call the European Union – depended on the identification and ratification of shared norms, values and definitions. In an analogous spirit of norm-setting and transparency, we will use this introduction to define each of the keywords in the book's title and in doing so offer previews of the places to which each chapter will take us.

Shakespeare

When faced with the challenge to define 'Shakespeare' in a previous work on European Shakespeare, Balz Engler asked 'Does the term refer to a person, to a set of printed texts, to a cultural icon, to a theatrical tradition, or to a combination of all of these?' (2003: 27). The 'Shakespeare' in the following pages has little to do with the historical person and everything to do with the ways in which the printed texts ascribed to that person have been theatrically staged in European festivals devoted in part or in whole to those works. Writing in the same volume as Engler at the turn of the millennium, Angel-Luis Pujante and Ton Hoenselaars described a long historical shift of critical perspective – a shift that their own work greatly encouraged – that had served effectively to decentre what they called 'English Shakespeare'. After this shift, 'it was no longer necessary to regard translations or foreign Shakespeare performances as adaptations or fallings off from the native stock'; Shakespeare was rather 'a quarry for a pan-European lexis or collection of myths' (2003: 24).

It is notable that contributors to this book do not refer with any frequency to the UK or Great Britain. The Shakespeare found here is both pan-European and post-English, a truly globalized phenomenon, floating across cultures and largely untethered to its point of origin. The works have been performed and celebrated for so many decades and even centuries in these continental European locations that the nationality of the author appears to have become almost irrelevant. One of the editors is here reminded of an informal conversation they had with Carlos Cedran, an eminent theatre-maker in Cuba: 'Shakespeare isn't English; Shakespeare is *theatre*.' Across continental Europe 'Shakespeare' also acts as a relatively uncomplicated, post-national umbrella under which to gather theatre-makers from different countries and cultures.

As you will also see in the following chapters, 'Shakespeare'-making happens differently from festival to festival. In the case of the Four Castles Shakespeare Festival in Prague, Brno, Ostrava and Bratislava, 'Shakespeare' signifies native, open-air productions performed in Czech and sometimes Slovak translations. In the cases of the festivals at Gyula (Hungary), Gdańsk (Poland), Craiova (Romania) and Neuss (Germany), 'Shakespeare' signifies a range of international, polyglot productions often curated according to a theme or focused on multiple versions of the same text. At the Almagro Festival in central Spain, 'Shakespeare' is not the raison d'être for the festival and indeed is barely mentioned on the festival website, so 'Shakespeare' means one playwright among many in the European (but specifically Iberian) 'Golden Age'. In the small village of Patalenitsa in Bulgaria, 'Shakespeare' means community theatre made for and mostly by the residents of this remarkable location. In southern France, at festivals in Avignon, Nice and Montpellier, 'Shakespeare' has long connoted a humanist model for an inclusive, democratic theatre, a catalyst for social cohesion, 'a theatre that trusts in man', according to Roland Barthes (1954: 430–1).

Shakespeare/European

As Tony Judt points out, Europe isn't really a geographic continent, 'just a subcontinental annexe to Asia' (2005: xiii). Our focus is on Shakespeare festivals based on this subcontinental land mass. There is no place for the UK or its variety of Shakespeare festivals in this definition of 'European', although British practitioners and companies do figure in the history of some of the continental festivals featured here. It might be tempting to view our choice to exclude the UK through the prism of Brexit: if a slim majority of UK citizens voted in 2016 to take the UK 'out' of Europe, who are we to deny the will of the people (or those people of *their* particular Anglo-nationalist Will)? More pertinently, though, we felt that a single chapter on Shakespeare festivals in the UK could offer only a superficial account, ranging, as it would have to do, from David Garrick's Stratford Jubilee to the present day. Furthermore, this book is structured chronologically and this would have meant opening with the UK chapter, thus setting exactly the wrong tone for a book that wishes to decentre 'English Shakespeare'.

Geopolitics and theatre history ask a common question: 'Who's in and who's out?' In selecting our festivals, we have tried to include every major extant festival at the time of writing. Some smaller, shorter festivals have not made the cut. These include the Bitola Shakespeare Festival (Macedonia) and Shakespeare in Catalonia, both of which run for roughly one week and are – at the time of writing – either still in an embryonic stage of development or (in the case of Shakespeare in Catalonia, 2003–15) apparently suspended or defunct. Shakespeare in Turkey and the Armenian Shakespeare Festival are both of great interest but perhaps belong to a book more closely focused on Shakespeare production and reception in Eurasia. We considered a chapter on the Dubrovnik Festival (founded 1950) which, although not a Shakespearean festival per se, has had a tendency to stage *Hamlet* in Lovrjenac Castle in fits and bursts over the last seventy years. As Ivan Lupić writes, 'It is as if the Festival gets tired of *Hamlet*, but cannot live without *Hamlet*' (2014).

In the event, this book covers nearly every active member festival of the European Shakespeare Festivals Network, which was founded in 2010 in order to help festivals 'exchange information and experience, participate in common projects, and mutually inspire each other for future ventures' ('ESFN' 2021). Although the ESFN currently contains two UK institutions, the York Shakespeare Festival and Shakespeare's Globe (the latter of which is not really a 'festival', given its year-round activities), the vast majority of members are based in Continental Europe, and the contents of this book reflects that preponderance.

Shakespeare/European/Festival

In a fascinating chapter in *The Cambridge Companion to International Theatre Festivals,* Ric Knowles describes a range of non-European Indigenous festivals as valuable 'alternative origin [stories]' that might help us to 'consider festivals as sites of exchange rather than the commodification of cultures ... as being grounded in the land and in Indigenous knowledge systems rather than in the deterritorializing and decontextualizing programming practices of most contemporary Western festivals' (2020: 72). 'Indigenous "festivals"', Knowles suggests, 'have always been about learning how to share territory and resources – how to live together "in a good way"' (73).

Such small-scale, localized festivals do indeed offer an attractive model for the future, especially in the present contexts of the climate emergency *and* global pandemic. But 'living together "in a good way"' is not something Europeans have been very good at for most of the last few centuries and what we might call the European Festival Model is clearly a response to that grim fact. As Erika Fischer-Lichte has argued, Wagner's Bayreuth Festival was conceived in the wake of the failed proto-democratic revolution of 1848/9. The later and equally influential model of the Salzburg Festival can only be understood in the context of the First World War with its co-founder Max Reinhardt viewing the Festival as 'a peace mission' and as a 'place of pilgrimage ... for the innumerable people who long to be redeemed through art following the bloody atrocities' (2020: 89). The number of Europeans who accepted the peace mission offered at Salzburg was wholly insufficient to prevent another war, after which a ruined continent in need of physical and moral reconstruction chose to put its faith in planning, which Tony Judt has described as 'the unofficial religion of postwar Europe' (2005: 66f.). The postwar creation of welfare states meant planned housing, education, health care and transport by interventionist governments, but it also meant planned culture, with the rise of international festivals in particular as one component of the premeditated manufacture of civility. One of the chief architects of postwar Europe, Jean Monnet, reflected: 'Si c'était à refaire, je commencerais par la culture' (qtd in Judt 2005: 701), implying that culture might have been even more central to continental reconstruction than it was. And yet it did indeed play a major role in shaping a post-nationalist vision of an imagined community. As Karen Zaiontz has argued:

> International festivals attempted to repair and, to a certain extent, repress the image of the nation as a generator of far-right populism. The emphasis on 'masterpieces' was an attempt to swerve towards more official, elite forms of nationalism, which also made claims to universalism, and away from the kind of populist nationalism that defined territorial sovereignty in terms of ethnic purity.
>
> (Zaiontz 2020: 15)

Of the festivals featured in this book, only the Avignon Festival and the 'Festivo Shakespeariano' in Verona date from this immediate postwar period, but many still share the model of reparative festivity and its logic of benevolent cultural exchange. The resistance to the cult of 'ethnic purity', for example, was very clearly an impetus for many post-1989 festivals: the Craiova Shakespeare Festival has always embraced Romanian-, Hungarian- and German-speaking theatres from across Romania, while the Shakespeare Festival in (bilingual) Gdańsk often hosts productions from, for example, Lithuania and Germany that draw attention to the city's complex and richly 'impure' pasts. While embracing difference, however, these and other festivals also gesture towards a proto-utopian humanism, one in which, as Hugh Grady has written:

> Shakespeare is presented as a democratic, international, universally available, free good that takes its place in and for an imagined community. Such a community consists of social beings untrammelled by inequality or social conflict, taking pleasure in universal narratives that affirm the desired continuity of love and courage as a means to a happier world.
>
> (2001: 26)

Along with Avignon, the key example here is Edinburgh International Festival, also founded in the aftermath of the Second World War, in August 1947, only a few weeks before the Avignon Festival and with a production of the very same play by

Shakespeare: *Richard II*. In October 2006, Jonathan Mills, the newly appointed director of the Edinburgh International Festival, gave the Sir William Gillies Lecture at the Royal Scottish Academy and reflected that:

> The Edinburgh International Festival owes its origins to the urgent imperative to rebuild a sense of community in a continent that had been torn apart by the tragedy of World War II; to restore faith, to heal the heartache of shattered lives through music, opera, drama, dance, literature, painting; to pick up the fragments of a civilisation shaken to its core by the atrocities of Leningrad or Auschwitz. In the words of John Falconer, Lord Provost at the time, it was to be a festival whose ambition was to 'embrace the world'.
>
> ('EIF' 2014)

This optimistic vision of the healing and peace-making capacity of culture is hardwired into the ethos of festivity and continues to underwrite the philosophy of Shakespeare festival-makers across Europe. In advertising their 2019 season, Ilina Chorevska and Ivan Jerchikj, the artistic directors of the Bitola Shakespeare Festival in Macedonia, invited their audiences to:

> Imagine the world and humanity came to an end, all our civilization, as we know it today [...] it's supposed [i.e. 'we suggest'] that it could be rebuilt and reconstructed solely based on the works of William Shakespeare.
>
> (Chorevska and Jerchikj 2019)

As with Western Europe after the Second World War, so with the former Soviet bloc of Central and Eastern Europe after the collapse of the Soviet Empire in the late 1980s and early 1990s. It is striking that almost half the festivals featured in this book are based in former Soviet bloc countries. Here the paradigmatic case is that of president-playwright Vaclav Havel in Czechoslovakia in 1990. As we learn in Filip Krajník and Eva Kyselová's chapter, one of Havel's first acts on becoming president was to commission Shakespearean performances in the grounds of Prague Castle as part of a wider agenda to reform the civic foundations of a fledgling democracy. In his memoir *Disturbing the Peace*, Havel wrote:

theatre doesn't have to be just a factory for the production of plays or, if you like, a mechanical sum of its plays, directors, actors, ticket-sellers, auditoriums and audiences; it must be something more: a living spiritual and intellectual focus, a place for social self-awareness, a vanishing point where all the lines of force of the age meet, a seismograph of the times, a space, an area of freedom, an instrument of human liberation.

(1991: 40)

Krajník and Kyselová link the formation of the Four Castles Shakespeare Festival in the Czech and Slovak republics with a wider 'espousal of Western culture', towards which both republics pivoted after the fall of Communism (see Chapter 4). Although not necessarily conscious of Havel's initiation of what would become the Four Castles Shakespeare Festival, other festivals would emerge in many parts of formerly Soviet Europe: in Craiova (Romania) in 1994, in Gdańsk (Poland) in 1997, in Patalenitsa (Bulgaria) in 1999, in Gyula (Hungary) in 2005 and in Indija (Serbia) in 2014, each of which festivals has a chapter in this book. Boika Sokolova has written of how, under Communism, Shakespearean theatre provided 'a privately darkened emotional space' that made political dissent possible (qtd by Pujante and Hoenselaars 2003: 21). These festivals have, in their varied ways, brought Shakespeare's works out into the light, making them vehicles for – *inter alia* – an opening of borders and reconnection with a cross-national network of theatre-makers, a celebration of local, regional and national excellence, and (not insignificantly) a pretext for restorative joy. If, according to Dennis Kennedy, Shakespeare was part of a 'cultural Marshall plan' in Western Europe after the Second World War (1993: 81), Shakespearean production in Central and Eastern Europe *during* the Cold War also points at the playwright's enlistment as a 'cold warrior' (Kennedy 2003). In the context of the emergence of multiple Central and Eastern European Shakespeare festivals, it is also possible to think about Shakespeare as a *post*-cold warrior. But then again, history is restless and cosmopolitanism is not inevitable: witness the rise in the 2010s and since of populist and nationalist governments in Hungary and Poland. It may or may not be indicative of a less open future that, as Ágnes Matuska and Júlia Paraizs note in their chapter, the 2020 programme of the international Shakespeare Festival at Gyula was to be a 'Hungarian Shakespeare edition' showing only Hungarian-language productions.

Shakespeare/European/Festival/ Stages

Finally, we would like to introduce the types of stages featured in this book. Given the widely discussed ways in which festivals in general exceed the architectural limits of any given theatre/s and radiate outwards in the process known as 'festivalization', it makes sense to think of 'stages' and 'places' as locked in a relationship that can be symbiotic and/or dialectical.

The visibility and impact of a given festival will vary depending on the size of its location. Some of the festivals in this book – for example, those in Rome, Verona, Prague and Nice – take place in cities with large populations, widespread, year-round artistic provision and a well-established tourist industry. This is not untypical. Marjana Johansson has observed that of the 715 arts festivals belonging to the 'Europe for Festival – Festivals for Europe' association, thirty-seven list only 'theatre' as a keyword, and 'of the thirty-seven festivals, only three are held in cities or towns with fewer than 50,000 inhabitants' (2020: 63). It is striking, then, that five of the Shakespeare festivals in this book take place in towns or cities with fewer than fifty thousand inhabitants, namely: Almagro (pop. 9,000), Gyula (pop. 32,000), Patalenitsa (pop. 1,300), Helsingør/Elsinore (pop. 47,000) and Indija (also pop. *c.* 47,000). Thus Shakespeare festivals are disproportionately likely to occur in a small- to medium-sized town when compared with theatre festivals in general, doubtless because the magnetic pull of the Shakespeare brand can survive relocation to an otherwise small and/or overlooked town or city (just as it has in the United States at 'destination' festivals in Cedar City, Utah, or Ashland, Oregon). The case of 'Shakespeare in Catalonia' might be instructive, a festival which began in the small town of Santa Susanna in the Maresme region of Catalonia, moved to Mataró, the capital of the region, then finally relocated to Barcelona for what appear to have been its last two editions in 2013 and 2015.

Reading across this volume, it is notable that most festivals are synonymous with one or more pre-existing historical spaces. Only two of these are 'genuine' and bespoke classical or early modern theatrical spaces: the Teatro Romano, Verona, and the Corral de Comedias in Almagro, built in 1628, and rediscovered and restored in the 1950s. The most common extra-theatrical stage setting for

European Shakespeare festivals is that of the castle, whether in Prague, Brno, Bratislava, Ostrava, Gyula or Helsingørg. Even if the relevant castle burned down in the nineteenth century and was since rebuilt – as at Ostrava and Bratislava – the contemporary, restored version retains an early modern patina and affect. To these examples, we might add the Villa Stanković, home to the Itaka Shakespeare Festival, which although built in 1930 is sited on the footprint of a Roman villa and was modelled on medieval Serbian castles. When Americans see an empty park, they tend to fill it with Shakespeare; for continental Europeans, the equivalent appears to be a castle. Here, again, a defining influence would appear to be Avignon, a medieval city whose various historic buildings and monuments – most notably the *Palais des Papes* – are repurposed as theatrical venues each summer.

The effects of staging Shakespeare against historic backdrops are complex. On the one hand, such settings can suggest or even enforce a sense of dislocation from the here and now to an essentialized pastness. As Hamilakis and Yalouri write:

> Ancient monuments ... provide the most powerful currency of [a] specific site of symbolic capital, due to their materiality, visibility (especially in case of prominent architectural monuments), authenticity, age and sense of timelessness ... They [are] instrumental in constructing a *topos*, that [is] at the same time within history and outside it. A *topos* structured by specific temporality: a monumental time distinct from the 'social' experiential time of everyday life.
>
> (1999: 125–6)

The same might also be said of some of the pseudo-historical spaces analysed in this book, imitation theatres like the Silvano Toti Globe in Rome or the Neuss Globe in Germany. The spectacularly remodelled Shakespeare Theatre Gdańsk, while technically sophisticated and highly flexible in its various configurations, also firmly gestures backwards, to the playing space that hosted visiting troupes of English actors to the influential Hanseatic merchant city in the seventeenth century.

Given the preponderance of such historical and pseudo-historical spaces in European Shakespeare festivals, one might expect a tendency towards conservative, nostalgic or 'traditional' spectacles.

In fact, though, these festival stages host a great variety of aesthetic practices and trends, up to and including the types of post-dramatic productions routinely seen in non-festive settings in, for example, well-subsidized regional theatres in Germany. In interculturally experimental productions such as Arianne Mnouchkine's *Richard II* (1982) at Avignon, or Ong Keng Sen's *Search: Hamlet* (2002) at Elsinore, the creative team clearly pushed back against the layered weights of architectural and theatrical history in ways that were both playful and profound.

It is also the case that these 'official' festival sites are often counterpointed by 'off' or 'fringe' festivals. A festival is a complex form in itself since it is a 'meta-event', that is, a macro-event 'encompassing a series of single events that are linked by various factors' (qtd in Hauptfleisch et al. 2007: 6). Such a form becomes even more complex when festivals interact with fringe festivals (Almagro, Avignon, Craiova, Gdańsk) or come to embed micro-festivals within their structure (*Le Printemps des comédiens* in Montpellier, which frames *Le Printemps des collégiens*, a Shakespeare school festival, or Shake-Nice! which hosts another school festival, ShakeFreestyle). Whereas some festivals focus on one specific venue, others owe their complex morphology to the proliferation of venues in the city (Craiova, Montpellier, Nice), on its outskirts and even in the neighbouring towns and villages (the Tricity of which Gdańsk is part, or the ways in which the Avignon festival radiates across the city's suburbs and outlying conurbations).

Conclusion

The challenges of putting together a book of this type mimic the challenges of the European political project in miniature. As editors, we were anxious to strike a balance between standardization and self-determination, especially as this is the first volume that brings together Shakespeare on festival stages across Europe. Thus, all of the chapters are consistent in offering information about the foundation, location, repertoire and ethos of the featured festival. But how that information is structured and conveyed differs from chapter to chapter and according to what cultural and theatrical work 'Shakespeare' performs in each individual instance. Many contributors choose to focus on symptomatic productions or editions of their festival. Anne Sophie Refskou's chapter offers two case studies of very different site-specific *Hamlet*s to analyse the haunted space that is Elsinore. Ágnes Matuska and Júlia Paraizs focus on three pivotal moments in the history of the Gyula Shakespeare Festival in order to delineate its local, European and global dimensions. Other writers take a deep historical perspective, setting the foundation of their festival within the *longue durée* of their nation's relationship to Shakespeare. As Filip Krajník and Eva Kyselová note in their chapter, 'as for many other European peoples, Shakespeare holds the status of a national author and the history of productions of Shakespeare's works in the Czech lands closely follows the trajectory of Czech cultural (and, by extension, social and political) history'. Similarly, Vanessa Schormann argues that the long history of German appreciation and adulation of Shakespeare helps explain the advent of the Neuss Globe and the phenomenon she describes as 'Globolatry', the celebratory fetish of Shakespeare's theatre. Both stances are recognizable in the International Shakespeare Festival in Craiova, whose evolution from a venue for theatrical celebration and exchange to a locus of Shakespeare-making – for the stage, as well as in translation, in criticism and in the classroom – Nicoleta Cinpoeş charts in terms of the festival's agency in cultural policy, civic regeneration and social inclusion. Other chapters plunge us, evocatively and experientially, into the present day: both Boika Sokolova and Kirilka Stavreva (on Bulgaria) and Alexandra Portmann (on Serbia) begin their chapters with accounts of the landscape through which the Shakespearean tourist moves to reach their destination, a reminder that a festival will alter our mood and shift our perspective long before we become official spectators. Finally, two of the book's chapters employ a comparative methodology: Florence March surveys the Shakespeare-rich region of southern France and unpicks the artistic and philosophical strands that link quite different festivals in Avignon, Nice and Montpellier. Across the Mediterranean, in Italy, Lisanna Calvi and Maddalena Pennacchia invite us to compare and contrast the Festival Shakespeariano in Verona and the summer season of the Silvano Toti Globe in Rome and the dialogues that take place between these events and the cities that host them.

Whatever their narrative and analytical approach, all of the authors in this volume are united in their desire to share their subject with a new audience, to put their festival on the map. While many Shakespeare festivals in the English-speaking world have become tourist shrines in their own right and have been the focus of sustained critical attention and regular reviewing; European Shakespeare festivals are, comparatively, a more recent addition to the global circuit and have been relatively untouched by Shakespeare studies. We hope that this book will help embed them in the cartography of contemporary performance.

This book was completed while much of the European continent was under lockdown. Just as in Shakespeare's time, theatres have been closed for a year and festivals have been either cancelled, postponed or have sought to use digital technologies to reach their spectators. In the current sanitary, economic, social and cultural crisis, European festivals reassert the idea that Shakespeare is a common language and a means symbolically to (re)open the borders. By celebrating Shakespeare on European festival stages, we celebrate a humanist, democratic, inclusive model of theatre-making. In the specific, global context of the Covid-19 crisis in which it is issued, this book not only aims to fill a knowledge gap in the history of European festivals – and that of world Shakespeare festivals – it also reasserts the crucial role of live arts in post-traumatic reconstruction and resilience. These festive qualities of optimism, ingenuity and perseverance were all embodied in the life and work of Professor Jerzy Limon, founder of the Gdańsk Shakespeare Festival, to whose cherished memory we dedicate this book.

References

Barthes, Roland ([1954] 1993), 'Pour une définition du théâtre populaire [For a definition of theatre for all]', in *Œuvres complètes*, ed. É. Marty, vol. 1, Paris: Le Seuil, 430–1.
Choreska, Ilina, and Ivan Jerchikj (2019), 'Bitola Shakespeare Festival 2019', https://narodenteatarbitola.com/en/bitola-shakespeare-festival/bsf-2019/ (accessed 13 March 2021).
'EIF' (2014), 'History of the Festival', https://www.eif.co.uk (accessed 14 September 2014).
Engler, Balz (2003), 'Constructing Shakespeares in Europe', in A. Luis Pujante and Ton Hoenselaars (eds), *Four Hundred Years of Shakespeare*, Newark: University of Delaware Press, 26–39.

'ESFN' (2021), 'About Us', http://esfn.eu/about-us (accessed 13 March 2021).

Fischer-Lichte, Erika (2020), 'European Festivals', in Ric Knowles (ed.), *The Cambridge Companion to International Theatre Festivals* Cambridge: Cambridge University Press, 87–100.

Grady, Hugh (2001), 'Modernity, Modernism and Postmodernity in the Twentieth Century's Shakespeare', in Paul Yachin and Kathleen McLuskie with Christopher Holmes (eds), *Shakespeare and Modern Theatre: The Performance of Modernity*, 20–35, London: Routledge.

Hamilakis, Yannis, and Eleana Yalouri (1999), 'Sacralising the Past', *Archeological Dialogues* 6 (2): 111–35.

Hauptfleisch, Temple, Shulamith Lev-Aladgem, Jacqueline Martin, Willmar Sauter, and Henri Schoenmakers, eds (2007), *Festivalising! Theatrical Events, Politics and Culture*, Amsterdam and New York: Rodopi.

Havel, Vaclev (1991), *Disturbing the Peace: A Conversation with Karel Hvíždàla*, New York: Vintage Books.

Johansson, Marjana (2020), 'City Festivals and Festival Cities', in Ric Knowles (ed.), *The Cambridge Companion to International Theatre Festivals* Cambridge: Cambridge University Press, 54–69.

Judt, Tony (2005), *Postwar: A History of Europe since 1945*, London: Penguin.

Kennedy, Dennis (1993), *The Spectator and the Spectacle: Audiences in Modernity and Postmodernity*, Cambridge: Cambridge University Press.

Kennedy, Dennis (2003), 'Shakespeare and the Cold War', in A. Luis Pujante and Ton Hoenselaars (eds), *Four Hundred Years of Shakespeare*, 163–79.

Knowles, Ric (2020), 'Indigenous Festivals', in Knowles (ed.), *The Cambridge Companion to International Theatre Festivals* Cambridge: Cambridge University Press, 70–84.

Knowles, Ric, ed. (2020), *The Cambridge Companion to International Theatre Festivals*, Cambridge: Cambridge University Press.

Lupić, Ivan (2014), 'What's Past is Prologue: Ragusan Shakespeare', unpublished seminar paper presented at the 'Shakespeare 450' conference in Paris.

Pujante, A. Luis, and Ton Honselaars, eds (2003), *Four Hundred Years of Shakespeare in Europe*, Newark: University of Delaware Press.

Zaiontz, Keren (2020), 'From Post-War to "Second Wave": International Performing Arts Festivals', in Ric Knowles (ed.), *The Cambridge Companion to International Theatre Festivals*, Cambridge: Cambridge University Press, 15–35.

2

Shaping democratic festivals through Shakespeare in southern France: Avignon, Montpellier, Nice

Florence March

'True hope is swift, and flies with swallows' wings' (*R3* 5.2.23). These words rounded off the statement issued by Montpellier's international arts festival to announce the cancellation of its 34th edition in June 2020 as a consequence of the Covid-19 pandemic. For the second time in its history, swallows did not herald the actors' spring, the literal translation for the festival's name: *Le Printemps des comédiens*. It was not long before the Avignon summer festival followed in its tracks. 2020 also marked a non-event year for the Shakespeare festival in Nice, *Shake-Nice!*, which came to an end as its founder Irina Brook left the Riviera after resigning from her position at the head of the National Theatre. This chapter focuses on the three southern France festivals founded in Avignon, Montpellier and Nice, respectively in 1947, 1987 and 2015.

In such a context, physical distancing measures induced the Avignon and the Montpellier festivals to imagine new modes of sharing. *Le Printemps des comédiens* launched a web radio which, for ten weeks throughout the first lockdown period, broadcast play readings by actors, spectators' memories of previous festival editions, academic commentaries and a weekly Shakespeare chronicle.[1] The symbolic timing of *Radio Printemps*, which stopped on the eve of the festival's planned opening date, showed that it was not so much meant to replace the event as to support the community of theatre professionals and spectators hard hit by the crisis, to help them make sense of the festival's absence rather than try and fill the gap it created. Theatre must keep quiet, *Printemps*' director Jean Varela argued, as the time had come for mourning and the pandemic had made so many 'Antigone families'.[2] Not only did the metatheatrical reference to Sophocles' tragedy stress the festival's solidarity with families prevented from burying their dead due to sanitary restrictions, it also suggested that this was the moment to reflect on the vital importance of theatre in society.

Avignon proposed a four-pronged answer to the crisis. In July, during the customary three-week period of the festival, 'A Dream of Avignon' consisted in rebroadcasting filmed productions from previous years both on French television and in the Honour Court of the medieval Popes' Palace, the cradle and emblematic place of the event, in front of a limited audience of two hundred. At the same time, the OFF festival organized a cycle of play readings. The third answer was postponed to autumn, when seven of the productions that had been cancelled were rescheduled for 'A Week of Arts in Avignon', thus reviving the very first edition of the festival launched under this name by Jean Vilar in September 1947. The idea was to foreground the original – in all senses of the term – dimension of a reflective event, meant to combine retrospective and prospective dynamics, and avoid the derogatory notion of a 'mini-festival' which might be viewed as a 'consolation prize'.[3] Meant to be an alternative response to the cancellation of the summer festival, the 2020 'Week of Arts' ironically fell under the scope of new sanitary measures to counter the onslaught of the second pandemic wave. They first imposed evening curfew hours, the start time of all shows having to be moved forward by three hours, soon followed by a new nationwide lockdown which curtailed the festival by two days. Yet, as a further step in this resilient process – surviving, adapting, rebounding and strengthening – and in keeping with its festival's twofold specificity as laboratory and showcase for the performing arts, Avignon held a National Festivals Forum to assert the importance of festivals in the French cultural landscape, both at artistic and economic levels,[4] and to help redesign the political pact with local and state authorities.

A dark year for festivals, 2020 has paradoxically highlighted the reparative and transformational potential of democratic festivals in Avignon, Montpellier and, retrospectively, Nice, all three of them envisaged as a public service to the population. The absence of *Shake-Nice!* acted as a ghostly reminder of its cohesive and healing role in the wake of the 2015 and 2016 devastating terrorist attacks in Paris and Nice, the Riviera city being again the stage of a tragic act of terrorism in October 2020. *Le Printemps* and *Shake-Nice!* were both built on the model of the Avignon Festival, which originated in the traumatic aftermath of the Second World War as a contribution to national reconstruction, a response to the urgent imperative to restore France's dignity and rebuild a sense of community. Cultural producers in Montpellier and Nice availed themselves of the legacy of Avignon's founder, Vilar, who believed in the power of arts and culture to heal, nurture and transform. It is no coincidence, then, that Shakespeare's humanist drama and theatre for all people inform the structure and programmes of the three festivals, as well as their political and artistic ethos. This chapter purposes to further explore the nature and function of Shakespeare's seminal role in the origins of the Avignon and the Montpellier festivals, whose focus, unlike that of *Shake-Nice!*, is not exclusively Shakespearean; his continued presence in what have become the main two French arts festivals; and the emergence and impact of the first international Shakespeare festival in France, however short-lived it was. (The independent Avignon OFF and Montpellier's fringe festival, *Warm Up*, which shows exclusively local companies' work in progress, are not part of this study.) Shakespeare's involvement in the foundation, history and ethos of the festivals under survey will be approached along three lines: mapping Shakespeare's presence in southern France festivals; festivalizing Shakespeare through the case studies of three plays (*Richard II*, *A Midsummer Night's Dream* and *The Tempest*) and their emblematic fortune on the Avignon, Montpellier and Nice festival stages; 'Shakespearizing' southern France festivals by shifting the focus from corpus to festivals as multifaceted events in which Shakespeare qualifies as a necessary but not sufficient condition.

Mapping Shakespeare's presence in southern France festivals

Shakespeare's presence in Avignon, Montpellier and Nice derives from the implementation of postwar cultural policies and individual initiatives, all of which aimed to make theatre accessible to all. Vilar thus became one of the leaders of the decentralization policy launched under the Fourth Republic in 1946 to export theatre outside the capital city into the entire country, at a time when culture was considered as a catalyst for national reconstruction and a factor of social cohesion (Wehle 1974: 65). For 'A Week of Arts in Avignon' in 1947, he commissioned concerts of early modern music, an exhibition of contemporary paintings and sculptures and the productions of three plays never performed before in France: *Richard II* by Shakespeare, *L'Histoire de Tobie et de Sara* by contemporary French author Paul Claudel and *La Terrasse de midi*, a rewriting of *Hamlet* by Maurice Clavel, a young French dramatist at the beginning of his career. The programme foregrounded three features that would, from then on, define the identity of the festival: Vilar's intention to promote cultural heritage as well as contemporary creation; the experimental dimension of a festival envisaged as a laboratory as much as a showcase for the performing arts; the founding presence of Shakespeare as a facilitator to address these goals. The Avignon Festival was thus born under the joint auspices of *Richard II* and *Hamlet*, from two Shakespearean productions directed by Vilar himself (March 2018). Incidentally, another production of *Richard II* had already initiated the Edinburgh International Festival in August 1947, a few weeks before Vilar's premiered in the Honour Court of the Popes' Palace. Right from the first edition of the festival, Shakespeare was a catalyst for new texts, whether translations or rewritings. Performed in a heritage site, in a postwar context when the government could not afford to support the decentralization policy by building new venues, Shakespeare became associated with the development of site-specific theatre in Avignon, from which derived new aesthetics. Vilar's minimalist staging of the prison scene – a few props, a red robe, three shafts of light that carved out Richard's cell in the darkness, and the lament of a violin (Wehle 1981: 110) – thus established the so-called 'aesthetic of the three stools' (Guignebert 1953), which both enhanced the actors' art and relied on the spectator's capacity for imagination.

From then on, Shakespeare has been the most frequently performed author in Avignon. Through the years, the festival has spread over the city, venues have multiplied and the independent OFF festival founded in 1966 by André Benedetto has taken to the streets. The 'city festival' has given rise to a 'festival city' (Johansson 2020: 54) where Shakespeare's presence crystallized both as a result and an agency of the decentralization policy: a major actor of the centrifugal movement from Paris, Shakespeare led to a centripetal dynamic in Avignon, which in turn inspired other initiatives along the French Mediterranean coast.

Although *Le Printemps* was launched in Montpellier in 1987, its roots can be traced back to 1958 when André Crocq, a pioneer of popular education and youth instruction in a professional corps established by the government at the end of the Second World War, organized the first drama summer school of a long series in Pézenas, known as Molière's town, near Montpellier. Ironically hinging on *A Midsummer Night's Dream*, a comedy by the British – not the French – champion of democratic theatre, the summer school met with such success that Jean Bène, the President of the *Conseil départemental de l'Hérault* – the Council of the Hérault district of which Montpellier and Pézenas are part – commissioned Crocq to set up and run the *Centre Culturel du Languedoc* (Languedoc Cultural Centre). After Crocq's death in 1980, the *Conseil départemental* pursued its policy of 'cultural solidarity' (Archives: 2102W/100) by founding *Le Printemps*, whose editions have foregrounded Shakespeare as a common thread and have featured *A Midsummer Night's Dream* more often than any other play. Four decades after 'A Week of Arts in Avignon', *Le Printemps* enforced the decentralization policy on a local scale, in the Hérault district. The shows programmed in Montpellier toured in twenty of its surrounding towns and villages, until the costs occasioned were judged to be prohibitive. Yet, over the past few years, at the instigation of its director Jean Varela, the festival has been progressively reviving the tradition in neighbouring towns.

Also heir to French postwar cultural policies, *Shake-Nice!* was launched by Irina Brook, with the support of Peter Brook, in January 2015, shortly after she was appointed the head of the National Theatre in Nice (TNN), one of the thirty-eight state-funded theatres established in the aftermath of the Liberation as part of the decentralization policy and whose mission it is to address wide local audiences. *Shake-Nice!* took place every year for three weeks in January and February, except for its fifth and last edition in 2019 which was moved to April, the month that marks both the birth and death of Shakespeare, as a symbolic obituary of the festival and a hope for its revival. Brook's Shakespeare festival allowed her to export the theatre outside the TNN's institutional building, implementing decentralization at the scale of the city. In 2015, *Le Tour complet du cœur* (a complete picture of the heart) opened the festival's first edition; this one-man show, inspired by the (more or less) complete works of Shakespeare, was performed under a marquee tent on the esplanade in front of the playhouse. The title of the production, the nomadism associated with the tent, the position of the esplanade overlooking the city, all symbolically ushered in Brook's plan to reorganize the theatregoing community by bringing together spectators with heterogeneous backgrounds, so as to provide a mirror image of Nice's socio-cultural diversity and bridge the gap between the disparate areas of the city (March et al. 2016).

All three festivals succeeded in fostering local, national and international dynamics. *Shake-Nice!* immediately joined the European Shakespeare Festivals Network founded in 2010 to encourage artistic and educational collaborations. *Le Printemps* has recently developed a strategic partnership with China. In the medieval city of Avignon, Shakespeare played a key role not only in the creation of the festival but, since his theatre connected tangible and intangible heritage through site-specific productions, in defining it as a 'destination festival' (Engle et al. 1995: 17) for audiences from France and abroad. From decentralized theatre to international festivals, Shakespeare acted as an incentive to cross boundaries and open borders.

How has Shakespeare's presence thematically and structurally informed each of the festivals under study? What kind of dialogue has his theatre entertained with other dramatic corpora in Avignon and Montpellier?

Festivalizing Shakespeare: three case studies

While Shakespeare occupies a prominent place in Montpellier, the other cornerstone of the festival is Molière, the French seventeenth-century man of the theatre who spent several years in Languedoc and to whom the very first edition of *Le Printemps* was dedicated. Shakespeare and Molière are the two pillars on which *Le Printemps* has always rested to promote art theatre for all. No French playwright can claim to rival Shakespeare in Avignon. Racine was never a favourite under Vilar's leadership of the festival, for his classical tragedies were not deemed to address an all-inclusive audience. Racine thus had to wait until 1975 to make his official entry in the Honour Court of the Papal Palace, four years after Vilar's death. In 1953, a crisis pitted Vilar against the organizing committee of the festival in charge of the budget, which pressed him for a Racine production in the Honour Court of the Popes' Palace. Vilar resigned from his function and when called back by the Mayor of Avignon, he retaliated by staging *Macbeth* in 1954. The opposition of these two emblematic figures of the theatre crystallized the debate on the nature of democratic theatre, as if in a parody of Stendhal's essay on *Racine et Shakespeare* (1823) in which the early modern playwright was championed over the French tragedian.

Shakespeare's encounter with Avignon, and particularly the Honour Court, was such a triumph in 1947 that Vilar's production of *Richard II* was programmed again in 1948, 1949 and 1953, alongside his adaptation of the two parts of *Henry IV* in 1950. Pressured to turn the Avignon Festival into a Shakespeare festival, Vilar resisted the temptation for fear of turning Shakespeare into a business, a 'guaranteed income', a 'share capital' (Vilar 1971: 95–7):

> I immediately opposed it ... and I was right. As a matter of fact, those in favour of a Shakespeare festival understood later on and approved of my decision. We should *not* give in to the temptation. The whole spirit of Avignon was at stake. We had to evolve right from the beginning. If we had become a Shakespeare festival, Avignon would never have become what it is, even though we had done a good job. This way, we were able to perform his plays without risking sclerosis.
>
> (Roy 1987: 66)

For Vilar, democratic theatre and Shakespeare's theatre should meet but not merge in Avignon. He aimed to implement a theatre for all people inspired by the Elizabethan model and to imagine new ways of staging the British poet's plays in heritage sites. He wanted Avignon to be the place where classical and contemporary repertoires and stage practices came into contact and rubbed elbows. In this regard, the philosophy behind the non-Shakespeare festivals of Avignon and Montpellier did not clash with Brook's commitment to Shakespeare in Nice. Whereas the Avignon and the Montpellier festivals are independent cultural events, *Shake-Nice!* was embedded in the middle of the National Theatre season running from September to June. As a consequence, Shakespeare became prominent in an otherwise diversified programme. The Shakespeare festival thus interacted with a variety of repertoires, artistic forms and events, which were part of the same overall project, even though they were slightly shifted in time.

Shakespeare has been programmed in forty-five editions of the Avignon Festival out of seventy-five, including the cancelled ones in 2003 and 2020, and twenty-four of his plays have been performed. The histories and tragedies are favourites, for their epic dimension adapts particularly well to the historic medieval buildings that are turned into places of performance during the festival. The Elizabethan and his contemporaries were present in twenty-three editions of *Le Printemps* out of thirty-four, including the cancelled ones in 2014 and 2020. Fourteen plays by Shakespeare have been performed in Montpellier, striking a balance between histories, tragedies, comedies and romance plays, and in 2016 the festival hosted *After Shakespeare*, a thirteen-hour marathon production of the complete – although abridged – plays and the result of an academic interdisciplinary project of University Paul-Valéry initiated by the Institute for Research in the Renaissance, the Classical Age and the Enlightenment (IRCL) to mark the 400th anniversary of Shakespeare's death. The first edition of *Shake-Nice!* also provided festival-goers with an overview of Shakespeare's (more or less) complete works in a four-hour solo performance, *Le Tour complet du cœur*.

Three plays in particular hold special significance for the festivals under study: *Richard II* for Avignon, *A Midsummer Night's Dream* for *Le Printemps* and *The Tempest* for *Shake-Nice!* Historically linked to the origins of the festivals, these founding plays enjoy a specific status due to the way they have continued to inform them over the years. One may wonder how Shakespeare's historical drama, which is frequently said to present a patriotically English – and sometimes decidedly anti-French – view of history could become a vector of French national reconstruction. As this collection of essays shows, after the Second World War Shakespeare was used, not only in France but across Europe, to explore a diversity of national political contexts. Vilar found in the Elizabethan 'theatre of a nation' (Helgerson 1992: 197–8) an essential reference to invent a French civic theatre that would ensure social cohesion through the construction of a collective memory and the critical appropriation of History. His choice of *Richard II*, which initiates two tetralogies dramatizing more than a century of civil war and closing on the advent of a new dynasty, seemed particularly appropriate to the first edition of the Avignon Festival, which bore the promise of a renewal and encouraged faith in the future. After *Richard II*, Vilar staged the two parts of *Henry IV* in Avignon in 1950. And just like Firmin Gémier, who had founded the French Shakespeare Society in 1919 to strengthen the alliance between France and Britain in the aftermath of the First World War, Vilar placed his own project of national reconstruction in a broader context of Anglo-French cooperation. In this respect, the ambivalent role assumed by France in *Richard II* epitomizes the history of its complex relations with Britain. While the play's action takes place during the Hundred Years' War, France is also dramatized as a refuge for exiles, such as Bolingbroke or the French-born Queen herself (March 2018: 60–1).

Vilar's intention to experiment with new forms of theatre in Avignon also accounted for his production of *Richard II*, never staged in France before and for which he commissioned a new translation by Jean-Louis Curtis. The history play helped him negotiate with the Honour Court of the Popes' Palace, a UNESCO World Heritage Centre that had never yet been used as a place of performance. The play's epic dimension appropriately matched the monumentality of the venue. The timeline of the dramatic action coincided with the time when the medieval palace was erected – the fourteenth century. Fraught with rituals and ceremonies, the play also served Vilar's intention to ritualize the theatre, as it was in Ancient times. Eventually, Vilar's minimalist aesthetic, which relied on the spectator's capacity for imagination, left its mark on the festival. The encounter of *Richard II* with the Honour Court in 1947 thus established the ideological and aesthetic foundations of the Avignon festival meant to promote civic theatre and to be a laboratory as well as a ritualized festive event. Two later productions of the history play staged in the Honour Court, respectively by Ariane Mnouchkine in 1982 and Jean-Baptiste Sastre in 2010, experienced contrasting fortunes. Mnouchkine radically defamiliarized both play and venue culturally and geographically, submitting them to Asian influences through references to *Kabuki, Noh* and *Bunraku*, thus avoiding direct comparison with Vilar's founding gesture in 1947 while upholding his festival's experimental vocation. By contrast, Sastre's *Richard II* provided an occasion for reviving the memory of Vilar's mythical production, in effect turning Avignon into a museum or high altar against its founder's intentions, thus failing to measure up to the festival-goers' most demanding expectations (March 2010). Over the years, *Richard II* has become the play against which the Vilarian project for Avignon is regularly assessed (March 2015: 88–90).

In the same way as *Richard II* has become emblematic of the Avignon Festival, the comedy of *A Midsummer Night's Dream* seems to contain *Le Printemps* in a nutshell. Productions and adaptations of the play were programmed in 1995, 1997, 2000, 2003, 2007, 2011 and 2017. Performed every several years in Montpellier's *Domaine d'O*, the park hosting the festival, it is tightly interwoven with its history, reflecting on its evolution while simultaneously reasserting its morphological and ideological constants. Not only does the play dramatize the fundamentals of a theatre for all people that has been at the core of a voluntarist socio-cultural policy in the Hérault district since 1958, but the night action in a wood near Athens also mirrors the conditions of performance in the woods of Montpellier. Composed on a special occasion – perhaps for an aristocratic wedding – and involving interactions between the aristocracy, the gentry and a company of craftsmen, *A Midsummer Night's Dream* crystallizes the vision of theatre as festive celebration, which restores the link between man and nature, and generates social cohesion. The play within the play reasserts the importance of a pact of performance relying on the curiosity and critical sense of committed spectators in a theatre that, at *Le Printemps*, is meant to raise questions as much as to cause aesthetic emotion. It is no coincidence that Crocq chose this comedy for his first summer school in Pézenas in 1958. The free performances given by the trainees in a park, *Parc Sans Souci*, for the town's inhabitants constituted another example of democratic theatre. The craftmen's scenes, in which Shakespeare obliquely acknowledged his debt to amateur theatre while keeping it at a distance through parody, ironically reflected on Crocq's pioneering work in popular education and then on the Montpellier festival dedicated to actors (The Actors' Spring), of which they were both a figuration and a disfiguration. Following in the footsteps of Crocq, *Le Printemps* in partnership with the IRCL at University Paul-Valéry and six schools in Montpellier launched in 2016 an educational programme on 'Shakespeare and Citizenship' in which *A Midsummer Night's Dream* is given a central place. The craftmen's plot, which dramatizes the production of a play by amateur actors, from the first rehearsal to the premiere, implements one of the cardinal values attached to the notion of citizenship: solidarity, meaning the capacity for building a common project, without which there can be no society.[5]

Significantly, the first edition of *Shake-Nice!* was launched under the auspices of *Tempête!*, an adaptation of *The Tempest* by Irina Brook's company. The name of the show extended the metaphor already contained in the name of the festival since Brook wished to shake Nice through Shakespeare. Even the exclamation mark punctuating it was one more sign of its symbolic relevance to the festival. Brook's reading of the opening scene was particularly interesting. Whereas in Shakespeare's text Prospero creates a storm at sea for Miranda and the spectator, Brook displaced it from stage to audience. Prospero pointed binoculars at the auditorium, commenting upon the storm as if it was actually taking place there, so that it was the spectators' own imagination that conjured up the storm, in keeping with the prologue's recommendations in *Henry V*. The audience's commitment to shake things up in the context of the show could not but symbolically apply to the festival itself, celebrating their appropriation of Brook's project for Nice. Badges to be worn by festival-goers carried the quotation 'we are such stuff as dreams are made on' (*Tem* 4.1.156–7). Symbols of inclusion, they contributed to the sense of belonging to the festival's community, as well as highlighting the necessity for commitment inside and outside the playhouse and the need to awaken one's capacity for dreaming. To some extent, Brook's *Tempête!* could be viewed as a *mise en abyme* of *Shake-Nice!* (March et al. 2016).

Festivalizing Shakespeare in southern France means much more than celebrating a great dramatist who has taken on mythic status. Viewed as a model to promote art theatre for all, Shakespeare is a catalyst for creativity, a factor of social cohesion and a vector of emancipation. His potential for transformational power has shaped the artistic and socio-political projects of the Avignon, the Montpellier and the Nice festivals.

'Shakespearizing' southern France festivals

Many of the projects of democratic theatre which developed in Europe in the twentieth and twenty-first centuries relied on Shakespeare.[6] For Dennis Kennedy, Shakespeare qualifies as a 'cultural Marshall Plan' in Western Europe (2009: 81) and as a 'cold warrior' in Central and Eastern Europe (2003), the latter point indebted to the thesis developed by Jan Kott in *Shakespeare Our Contemporary* (1964). Shakespeare's name is thus to be understood in a broad sense: it designates not only the man or the playwright, but a certain idea of the theatre, a certain relationship to the spectator and beyond, to the city and society. This model informed the festivals under study along two main lines: an audience-inclusive ethos and a collaborative relationship with the audience.

Aiming at social cohesion through cultural action, the Avignon, Montpellier and Nice festivals target a widely diversified audience in terms of geographical distribution, social classes and age groups. All three festivals thus implemented the decentralization policy on a different scale. In France the phrase *théâtre populaire* covers a wide range of definitions and lends itself to polymorphous interpretations. Firmin Gémier's 'collective theatre' addressed the lower classes (Caune 1999: 74); Jacques Copeau's ritualized theatre, which called for national regeneration, only reached a limited audience; Jean-Paul Sartre's activist theatre targeted the working classes. Vilar, who systematically referred to Shakespeare when theorizing popular theatre, embraced the meaning it had back in the Renaissance as a synonym of 'universal theatre' (1953: 1–2) or just 'theatre' (1975: 188). His theatre for all people meant to engage with large and socially mixed audiences everywhere in France:

> The word [popular] may please or displease; be understood this or that way ... It means I have the duty to provide for all people, from the storekeeper in Suresnes to the high-ranking magistrate, from the manual labourer in Puteaux to the stockbroker, from

the postman in a rural area to the academic, a great pleasure of which they should never have been deprived.

(1975: 178)

In comparison, Gémier's discourse proved much more socially selective:

When I put on a Shakespeare play, I say to the Shakespeareans: 'I do not put on Shakespeare's plays for you, as you know them so well. Stay at home! Read Shakespeare by the fireplace! Do not come here. I play Shakespeare for taxi drivers, cloakroom attendants and my cook'.

(2008: 210–11)

Both *Le Printemps* and *Shake-Nice!* adopted the Vilarian perspective. The 'cultural solidarity' policy enforced in the Hérault district is based on three main principles: developing the theatre as a service to the population in Hérault; bringing art and the theatre to under-served territories; providing all people with a diversified cultural offer (Archives: 2102W/100). *Shake-Nice!* developed partnerships with the local Emmaus Community and the Malongo coffee factory.[7] The Avignon Festival has pursued Vilar's enterprise by making theatre accessible to the inmates of the local prison (March 2020). All three festivals also emphasize generational diversity. Their policy goes much beyond offering reduced-price tickets to students and the unemployed. Vilar favoured the participation of young spectators in his festival. The *Ceméa*, a national movement for the development of education methods based on cultural action founded in 1937, was and still is very active in Avignon. *Le Printemps des collégiens*, a Shakespeare school festival whose name echoes *Le Printemps des comédiens* in which it is embedded, launched its first edition in 2016. Brook also implemented a parallel school festival in Nice and its conurbations: *Shake Free Style*. These innovative educational projects aim to give the students an opportunity to discover Shakespeare through an experience of individual and social empowerment, as well as to rejuvenate today's festival audiences and build tomorrow's. To get a better chance of achieving social diversity, the Avignon and the Montpellier festivals provide large venues that can accommodate wide audiences: the Honour Court of the Popes' Palace in Avignon can fit two thousand spectators, whereas the *Amphithéâtre d'O* and the *Théâtre Jean-Claude Carrière* in Montpellier have seating capacities of respectively 1,800 and 1,200. Transcending geographical, socio-economic and generational divisions to address all people, the Avignon, the Montpellier and the Nice festivals thus define themselves as inclusive, on the model of Shakespeare's theatre. For Brook, quoting Vilar: 'The Art of the theatre takes on full significance when it succeeds in bringing people together'.[8]

Vilar contended that Shakespeare's texts are at the crossroads of popular and elite cultural traditions and may therefore be appropriated by all types of audiences through performance and contemporary translations. Following his successful production of *Richard II*, Vilar wrote that 'people from the lower classes who go to the theatre always understand Shakespeare, even though it is such or such a history play based on fourteenth-century English history' (Wehle 1981: 100). Statistics corroborate his statement.[9] The tremendous success of Thomas Jolly's eighteen-hour production of the three parts of *Henry VI* for the 2014 edition of the Avignon Festival in particular, twenty years after Stuart Seide's triumphant marathon production of the same trilogy in Montpellier and Avignon, provide further evidence that Vilar was right. To enable spectators to access demanding repertoires, democratic festivals challenge their curiosity. Vilar's administrator, Paul Puaux, claimed: 'Avignon should be like a construction site where everyone can see theatre in the making' (1983: 68). Such festivals also create opportunities for the sharing of experience and debate with the artists. For Vilar, 'Avignon is the quest for a place for reflection, for debate and ... hope' (Puaux 1983: 67). Shakespeare is thus envisaged not as a final objective but as a facilitator to access, beyond his plays, the complex art of the theatre. Through Shakespeare, festivals of art theatre for all enforce a specific pact of performance with festival-goers, which involves a reevaluation of space and time, as well as the nature of their commitment.

In Avignon, Vilar reinvented the relationship between stage and audience, to encourage a pact of performance inspired by Ancient Greek and Elizabethan theatres – that is, based on direct address to large audiences in open-air venues – so as to magnify the sense of togetherness in a society sorely afflicted by the war. Vilar's project questioned the architectural and aesthetic codes of the Italian playhouse which divide instead of bringing together. Firmin Gémier, the founder of the Shakespeare Society in France in 1916 and of the *Théâtre National Populaire* in 1920, had already argued that after the First World War had gathered all social classes in the trenches, performing in Italian playhouses, in which the vertical distribution of the audience mirrors and reinforces the social hierarchy, was no longer relevant (2008: 67). In the same way, the imaginary fourth wall dividing stage from audience had to be broken. For obvious economic reasons in postwar years, Vilar had to turn to a place that was not initially designed as a theatre, although it was highly theatrical – but in the bad sense of the term, as he immediately became aware of. Too pregnant with history, the medieval Honour Court posed a challenge to performance, opposing monument to movement and permanence to transience. The playwright who helped him negotiate with the bare stone was Shakespeare, 'the best friend of the Popes' Palace' (Faivre d'Arcier 2007: 21–2) and 'the factotum of the Honour Court' (Thibaudat 1985). The open-air courtyard surrounded by walls is reminiscent of the inclusive shape of the Shakespearean 'wooden O' – a resemblance that was deliberately emphasized from 1982 to 2002 with the audience surrounding the stage on three sides and two galleries being erected and furnished with wooden benches. The 'wooden O' is also echoed in Montpellier's *Domaine d'O* and its synecdochally named venues *Théâtre d'O* and *Amphithéâtre d'O*, as well as in the circular seventeenth-century *Grand Bassin* and the circus rings and tents scattered across the park which recall both the arenas of the Elizabethan playhouses and the popular tradition behind the festival.

Festivals also involve a reevaluation of time: time grafted upon time when the Avignon Festival contaminates the city, turning it into a huge theatre for three weeks; 'time out of time' (Falassi 1987) when the *Printemps*, confined to the ovoid-shaped *Domaine d'O*, forms a sort of bubble within the city. The festival-goer's experience extends before and after the shows, through conference talks, debates and exhibitions that accompany them in their discovery of demanding texts in performance. The specific morphology of festivals thus entails a reevaluation of the spectator's role through their physical, intellectual and emotional commitment.

In Avignon and Montpellier, most performances take place in the open, unsheltered from bad weather, so that the spectators' commitment is physical, making them stand in complete solidarity with the artists, just as in Shakespeare's time. The following humorous comment on a night performance of an adaptation of *Richard III* by Dan Jemmett for the *Printemps*, in the 2012 golden book of the companies,[10] epitomizes a not-uncommon situation in either festival: 'Thank you for your reception, your kind + helpful technicians and above all for the thunder, lightning and rain – special effects that were well beyond our budget.' In his famous prologue to *Henry V*, Shakespeare gives the terms of a pact of performance based on the spectator's imagination and his capacity to decode and reencode the sign system produced on stage. Drawing on the model of the committed spectator of Elizabethan public playhouses who actively cooperated in the show, Vilar and his heirs in Avignon, Montpellier and Nice rely on a 'participating spectator' (Vilar 1991: 93) whose powerful imagination goes together with his capacity for critical analysis. The O that designates the different places of performance in Montpellier metaphorically signals an empty space, a hole that needs to be filled in by the festival-goer. In a similar way, Roland Barthes wrote about the Honour Court of the Popes' Palace in Avignon: 'The place required that the spectator be treated not as an immature child whose food you should pre-chew, but as an adult who is given the show to make' (1993: 395). The successive directors of all three festivals believed that the driving force behind the spectators' commitment was their curiosity, their capacity for wonder, their faculty to question themselves, push the boundaries of what they knew so as to explore new territories, confront their opinions with those of the festival-goers around them – in short, run the risk of being unsettled, destabilized, decentred. The Avignon, the Montpellier and the Nice festivals constantly evidence Barthes' statement that 'popular theatre trusts in man' (1993: 431). Shakespeare's ethical presence guarantees the humanist tradition at the root of these festivals.

The ritual programming of Shakespearean productions in southern France festivals goes much beyond a homage paid to a monument of classic literature. A tutelar figure, a source of inspiration and a measure of their evolution, Shakespeare informs them structurally, aesthetically and ethically. Anything but museums, the Avignon, the Montpellier and the Nice festivals aim, or aimed, on different scales, to be open laboratories that show theatre in the making and generate new modes of spectating, while simultaneously celebrating the festive, joyful nature of theatre as a medium. In keeping with the Elizabethan tradition of a theatre for all people he encapsulates, they view Shakespeare as an inclusive author, who fosters dialogue with other dramatic corpora, a 'founder of discursivity' for '[he] ha[s] created a possibility for something else than [his] discourse, yet something belonging to what [he] founded' (Foucault 1991: 114).

Vilar's attempt to implement a theatre for all has often been called a utopia (Puaux 1983; Loyer 1997). Yet his 'theatre for all … whose artistic concerns must first be civic and social, while aiming at quality' (qtd in Loyer 1997: 98) rather seems to qualify as a heterotopia, that is, an 'enacted utopia', taking place here and now in 'the mode of the festival', a 'counter-site' opening up critical, discursive perspectives (Foucault ([1984] 1986: 24, 26). If, for Foucault, theatre is heterotopic by nature, the Avignon, Montpellier and Nice democratic festivals provide specific 'locations in which cultural and political meanings can be produced spatially' (Tompkins 2014: 1). Originating in national and local cultural policies, they define themselves as laboratories for aesthetic and socio-political alternatives. Endowed with transformative potential, they implement a political theatre that resonates with the actual world and establishes a relationship with audiences that may continue when they leave a venue. Thus engaged politically and aesthetically, southern France festivals are consistent with Tompkins' definition of heterotopic theatre that 'offers a model for (re)fashioning the present and the future' (2014: 6–7).

Notes

1 Web radio PCM, https://soundcloud.com/printemps-des-comediens (accessed 2 December 2020).
2 Radio news, *France Inter*, 8 April 2020, 7.30 am: https://www.franceinter.fr/emissions/le-journal-de-7h30?p=4 (accessed 2 December 2020). All translations from the French are mine.
3 Olivier Py, director of the Avignon Festival, on *France Culture* radio, 26 October 2020, from 1'13": https://www.franceculture.fr/emissions/la-grande-table-idees/la-grande-table-idees-2nde-partie-emission-du-lundi-26-octobre-2020 (accessed 2 December 2020).
4 The Avignon Festival and the OFF festival generate estimated economic spinoffs of one hundred million euros for the city and its immediate surroundings (Bibiloni 2020).

5 See the official definition of citizenship established by the French legal and administrative information department directly attached to the Prime Minister's office on their website: https://www.vie-publique.fr/fiches/23857-quelles-sont-les-valeurs-attachees-la-citoyennete (accessed 15 March 2021).
6 Portions of this section are reused or adapted from previously published material (March 2015).
7 In 2015, the first edition of the festival initiated a partnership with the local Emmaus Community. In 2015, the TNN team went to meet the members of the community to speak about *Tempête!* (Tempest!), the latest production of Irina Brook's company. In 2016, the Emmaus Community came to the TNN to attend two shows in the festival: *Shake*, adapted from *Twelfth Night* by Dan Jemmett, and *Cupidon est malade* (Cupid is sick), a rewriting of *A Midsummer Night's Dream* directed by Jean Bellorini. In the same way, the TNN also regularly decentralized theatre performances at the Malongo coffee factory where, for instance, they performed *Tempête!* in 2017.
8 TNN programme for the 2014/5 season, p. 1.
9 *Richard II*, *Macbeth* and *A Midsummer Night's Dream* were performed 186 times between 1947 and 1959 and attracted 363,946 spectators.
10 The non-inventoried archives of *Le Printemps des comédiens* include companies' and spectators' golden books, in which artists and audiences are invited to leave a record of their experience of the festival. The uniqueness and value of this device, which participates in building the memory of *Le Printemps*, cannot be better illustrated than by the following anecdote: in 2020, a theatre enthusiast living in Lyon found in a secondhand bookshop the companies' 2000–1 golden book, which had been stolen years before; she bought it and returned it to the festival where it belonged. This golden book contains a beautiful photograph of Ariane Mnouchkine and the signature of Jean-Claude Carrière, a well-known writer, translator and screenwriter, and the President of the festival Association from its early years, who passed away on 8 February 2021.

References

Archives départementales de l'Hérault [Archives of the Montpellier District], Montpellier, 2102W/100.

Barthes, Roland (1993), *Œuvres complètes* [Complete Works], ed. Éric Marty, vol. 1, Paris: Le Seuil.

Bibiloni, Olga (2020), 'Coronavirus: quel horizon pour le monde de la culture?' [Coronavirus: What Future in Store for Culture?], *La Provence*, 22 November.
Caune, Jean (1999), *La Culture en action. De Vilar à Lang: le sens perdu* [Culture in Action. From Vilar to Lang: The Lost Meaning], Grenoble: Presses Universitaires de Grenoble.
Engle, Ron, Felicia Hardinson Londré and Daniel J. Watermeier, eds (1995), *Shakespeare Companies and Festivals: An International Guide*, Westport, Connecticut and London: Greenwood Publishing Group.
Faivre d'Arcier, Bernard (2007), *Avignon, vue du pont* [Avignon: A View from the Bridge], Arles: Actes Sud.
Falassi, Alessandro (1987), *Time out of Time: Essays on the Festival*, Albuquerque: University of New Mexico Press.
Foucault, Michel ([1984] 1986), 'Of Other Spaces', trans. J. Miskowiec, *Diacritics* 16: 22–7.
Foucault, Michel (1991), *The Foucault Reader*, ed. and trans. Paul Rabinow, London: Penguin.
Gémier, Firmin (2008), *Firmin Gémier, le démocrate du théâtre. Anthologie des textes de Firmin Gémier* [Firmin Gémier's Democratic Theatre. An Anthology of Firmin Gémier's Texts], ed. Nathalie Coutelet, Montpellier: L'Entretemps.
Guignebert, Jean (1953), 'La Tragédie de Richard II' [The Tragedy of Richard II], *Libération*, 9 November.
Helgerson, Richard (1992), *Forms of Nationhood: The Elizabethan Writing of England*, Chicago, IL: University of Chicago Press.
Johansson, Marjana (2020), 'City Festivals and Festival Cities', in Ric Knowles (ed.), *The Cambridge Companion to International Theatre Festivals*, 54–69, Cambridge: Cambridge University Press.
Kennedy, Dennis (2003), 'Shakespeare and the Cold War', in Angel-Luis Pujante and Ton Hoenselaars (eds), *Four Hundred Years of Shakespeare in Europe*, 163–79, Newark, DE: University of Delaware Press.
Kennedy, Dennis (2009), *The Spectator and the Spectacle: Audiences in Modernity and Postmodernity*, Cambridge: Cambridge University Press.
Kott, Jan (1964), *Shakespeare Our Contemporary*, trans. Bolesław Taborski, Garden City, NY: Doubleday.
Loyer, Emmanuelle (1997), *Le Théâtre citoyen de Jean Vilar: une utopie d'après-guerre* [Jean Vilar's Civic Theatre: A Postwar Utopia], Paris: Presses Universitaires de France.
March, Florence (2010), '*Richard II* in the Honour Court of the Papal Palace: Forgetting Shakespeare in Order to Find Him?', *Shakespeare*

en devenir – The Journal of Shakespearean Afterlives. Available online: http://shakespeare.edel.univ-poitiers.fr/index.php?id=469 (accessed 2 December 2020).

March, Florence (2015), 'Shakespearean Celebrations in South France Festivals', *Shakespeare Jahrbuch* 151: 85–100.

March, Florence (2018), 'Translating Shakespeare into Postwar French Culture: The Origins of the Avignon Festival (1947)', *Shakespeare Studies* 46: 59–69.

March, Florence (2020), '*Macbeth Philosophe* [*Macbeth the Philosopher*], 19 July 2019', *Cahiers Élisabéthains* 103: 75–8.

March, Florence, and Janice Valls-Russell (2016), 'Shaking up Shakespeare in Europe – Two New Festivals', *Cahiers Élisabéthains* 90: 155–70.

Puaux, Paul (1983), *Avignon en Festivals ou les utopies nécessaires* [Festivalizing Avignon or Necessary Utopias], Paris: Hachette.

Roy, Claude (1987), *Jean Vilar*, Paris: Calmann-Lévy.

Shakespeare, William (2009), *King Richard III*, ed. James R. Siemon, London: Bloomsbury/Arden.

Shakespeare, William (2011), *The Tempest*, ed. Virginia Mason Vaughan and Alden T. Vaughan, London: Bloomsbury/Arden.

Thibaudat, Jean-Pierre (1985), 'Festivals: vent maudit sur *Macbeth*' [Festivals: The Cursed Wind that Blew on *Macbeth*], *Libération*, 8 July.

Tompkins, Joanne (2014), *Theatre's Heterotopias: Performance and the Cultural Politics of Space*, New York: Palgrave Macmillan.

Vilar, Jean (1953), *Théâtre populaire* [A Theatre for All People] 1 (May–June).

Vilar, Jean (1971), *Chronique romanesque* [A Fictional Chronicle], Paris: Grasset.

Vilar, Jean (1975), *Le Théâtre, service public* [Theatre as a State Service], Paris: Gallimard nrf.

Vilar, Jean (1991), *Jean Vilar par lui-même* [Jean Vilar by Himself], Avignon: Maison Jean Vilar.

Wehle, Philippa (1974), 'Model for the Open Stage: A Study of Jean Vilar's Theatre for the People', PhD diss., Columbia University.

Wehle, Philippa (1981), *Le Théâtre populaire selon Jean Vilar* [Model for the open stage: a study of Jean Vilar's Theatre for the People], trans. Denis Gontard, Avignon: Alain Barthélémy and Actes Sud.

3

Shakespeare at the Almagro festivals: Reinventing the plays in Spain

Isabel Guerrero

On 7 September 1984, a storm was staged in the Church of Saint Augustine in the Castilian village of Almagro (Spain) in the seventh season of the Festival de Teatro Clásico de Almagro.[1] The festival focused on Spanish Golden Age drama; nevertheless, this storm was not part of any of those sophisticated stage effects either in Calderón de la Barca's late plays or in any of the hundreds of plays by Lope de Vega, but the one opening William Shakespeare's *The Tempest*. The seventeenth-century church provided the scenery to stage the play with only six actors, who used masks to perform the different characters. Directed by Edgar Saba with the Spanish company La Pajarita de Papel, this production was the first Shakespeare production in the history of the Almagro Festival.

Located 400 kilometres south of Madrid, in the high plains of La Mancha, the baroque old town of Almagro, with its Plaza Mayor, churches, palaces and convents from the sixteenth and seventeenth centuries, provide the perfect backdrop for the official festival, founded in 1978. The festival adopted as its main venue the *Corral de Comedias* built in 1628, rediscovered and restored in the 1950s (García de León Álvarez 2000). Since its inception, the festival has been devoted to the preservation and celebration of Spanish classical theatre, an aim that has remained central to its annual celebration in July. The first performance of a Shakespeare play was only possible after the festival widened its scope to include international playwrights and companies in 1983. Since then, companies from South America and Europe, but also from Asia, have travelled frequently to Almagro with Golden Age productions and plays by their own local authors.[2] In 2011, the festival incorporated the Almagro Off, a contest alongside the official festival run by the same organization. In this festival-within-the-festival, ten productions compete for an award and three extra performances in the official programme. The aim of the contest is to promote sixteenth- and seventeenth-century drama among early-career theatre directors. Thus, the two Almagro festivals are defined by their time focus, which means that only plays composed during the period corresponding to the Spanish Golden Age are eligible for performance.[3] This turns Shakespeare into the perfect candidate to share the stage with Golden Age playwrights.

The period-specific focus of the Almagro festivals immediately establishes an association with a very precise moment in theatre history, a moment that the festivals constantly evoke and invite their audiences and artists to reimagine together. This connection with the past is not based on claims of authenticity of performance. Over the years, there have been no example of so-called original practice nor any attempt to recreate Renaissance venues as in the case, for instance, of Shakespeare's Globe in London. Instead, the Almagro festivals revisit the past by using authentic seventeenth-century spaces which work as sites of authority for performance. Apart from the *Corral*, other non-theatrical spaces from the early modern period are used as festival venues (e.g. the Universidad Renacentista, the Hospital de San Juan or the Patio de Fúcares), but it is due to the presence and the uniqueness of the *Corral de Comedias* that the celebration of the festivals in a town on the margins of the country's cultural hubs – namely Madrid and Barcelona – has been possible.

The *Corral* can be described as a 'haunted house' (Carlson 2001: 131). That is, due to its historical origin, the venue activates the connection between the productions and the past of the Spanish Golden Age. In addition, the time focus brings such a connection to the fore, whether the productions are performed in the *Corral*, in historical non-theatrical spaces or in more contemporary venues.

Apart from providing a picturesque setting appealing to tourists, the Spanish baroque townscape stands as a site of authority not merely to stage the past, but to remember it from the present and find some sort of continuity between sixteenth- and seventeenth-century drama and the contemporary stage. This remembrance takes place amidst a temporal community of theatre practitioners and audiences, who invade the venues at 10.45 pm, the starting time for most of the performances in order to avoid the heat of the Castilian summer. After the last shows, which finish as late as 2.00 am, audiences gather in the bars of the town to discuss what they saw until the wee hours. The purpose of the festivals, therefore, is not to recreate theatrical forms from the early modern period, but to shed light on how plays from those times can still be meaningful to a contemporary audience.

The festivals, thus, encourage the constant negotiation between contemporary and sixteenth- and seventeenth-century theatre. At the official festival, such negotiation favours text-based approaches in the mise en scène that foreground the connection of the plays with their historical past. This connection comes, most often, via the playwright, which means that the festival usually features productions in which the source play is a stable referent and, as a result, the productions can be easily identified as Shakespeare's *Hamlet* or Lope de Vega's *The Dog in the Manger*, for instance. Thanks to its global scope, the festival also enables the comparison of early modern drama from different parts of the world. In the case of Golden Age drama, keeping the source play as a referent gives rise to productions with a rather limited range of approaches: the recontextualization of the plays is rare, the productions often rely on period costume and they use empty stages or settings that foreground their historical context. Conversely, experimentation with Shakespeare's plays is more frequent. In recent seasons, productions such as *Tempestad* (2012, dir. Sergio Peris-Mencheta), *La Tempestad* (2015, dir. Marta Pazos) and *Hamlet* (2016, dir. Miguel del Arco) have shown how the festival can function as a showcase for new takes on the plays, as happens in other European festivals, like the Avignon and Edinburgh International Festivals.[4] The Almagro Off takes a more experimental approach, giving rise to even more risqué adaptations of Shakespeare (e.g. *Claudio, tío de Hamlet* [Claudio, Hamlet's uncle], 2012, dir. Antonio Castro; *Hambret*, 2014, dir. Jessica Walker). Regardless of the differences in performance, the combination of Shakespeare and Golden Age plays in the Almagro festivals offers audiences the unique opportunity to compare two dramatic traditions from the same historical period with a distinct evolution in contemporary theatre practice.

This chapter is divided into two parts. The first section provides an overview of the Almagro festivals as sites for the negotiation of the theatrical and cultural ideas in Spain, examining the role of Shakespeare as one of the most often performed authors. The second part focuses on some of the most experimental Shakespeare productions in recent seasons, compares them to the trends in staging Golden Age drama and analyses how Shakespeare productions stand as representatives of early modern theatre and of contemporary performance in Almagro.

Shakespeare and the Spanish stage at the Almagro festivals

To understand the late adoption of global companies and authors – including Shakespeare – at the Almagro festivals, it is necessary to briefly examine the festival's history. Special attention is paid to the early years of the official festival, created when the first conference on classical theatre, devoted to the study of Golden Age drama, was held in Almagro. The town was chosen because of its rich early modern architecture and, above all, because of the existence of the *Corral*. The conference programme included several lectures alongside the performance of three Spanish Golden Age plays in the *Corral*.[5] Due to the success of the performances, the plays became the main attraction the following year. The event took the name of Almagro Festival and set the celebration and preservation of Spanish Golden Age drama as its main aim.

The official Almagro Festival has provided a space particularly suitable for the negotiation of theatrical and cultural ideas in Spain. The beginning of the festival in 1978 coincided with the vote of the Spanish constitution.[6] In contrast to the postwar cultural regeneration in countries such as France and the UK, which prompted the Avignon and Edinburgh International Festivals, Spain had to wait until the end of Franco's regime and the beginning of democracy to experience a similar process. The end of the dictatorship brought with it the abolition of censorship and the reinvigoration of Spanish culture.[7] In this context, the purpose of the Almagro Festival was to revive Spanish Golden Age drama. Its plays had almost disappeared from the Spanish stages between the 1960s and the 1980s, and were still associated with the dictatorship, as they had been used to support the ideology of the regime in the 1940s.[8] The challenge of the festival, thus, was to bring back Spanish Golden Age drama, consolidate a dramatic tradition that had been absent for a good part of the twentieth century, and make the plays relevant in times of political and cultural change.

The preservation of Spanish Golden Age drama in the first seasons meant that the festival did not feature any works of foreign companies and playwrights. While productions of Shakespeare's plays have been present since the first season in other European festivals, they did not appear in Almagro until the 1980s. When Shakespeare was first performed, in 1984, the productions in the programme signalled the need to overcome some of the cultural restrictions of the dictatorship. Apart from *The Tempest* by La Pajarita de Papel, there were two other Shakespeare productions that season: *A Midsummer Night's Dream,* by the company Teatro Estable La Cazuela, performed in Valencian, one of the languages of Spain that had been banned in the early years of the dictatorship; and *Pericles*, by the British company Cheek by Jowl, on their first visit to Spain. These two productions illustrate the evolution of Spanish theatre under the new democratic government, with the 'teatro de las nacionalidades' (theatre of nationalities; Ruiz Ramón 1988: 103–14) – theatre in the regional languages of Spain often used to support the separatist movements of those areas – and the increasing numbers of foreign companies on the Spanish stages.[9] Once the festival opened its doors to global authors and companies, it was only a matter of time until Shakespeare made the top-chart of playwrights at the festival, alongside indigenous names such as Lope de Vega and Calderón.

Over the years, the English playwright has secured his position as one of the most often performed authors in Almagro. By 2016, the 400th anniversary of Shakespeare's death, there had been 132 Shakespeare productions. With such high numbers, Shakespeare's presence has not gone unnoticed. In 2013, the newspaper *ARN* featured an article about the Almagro Festival entitled 'La sombra de Shakespeare es alargada' ('Shakespeare's shadow has extended';

García 2013). The article comments on the large number of Shakespeare productions in that year's programme (eleven in total) and describes the playwright as a giant against which Spanish authors cannot fight. The number of Shakespeare productions has remained high in the twenty-first century, whereas his presence was more intermittent in the 1980s and 1990s. The rise of Shakespeare productions over the last two decades has led to festival seasons in which they have outnumbered the plays by individual national authors (Guerrero 2017: 31–4).

In its short existence, the Almagro Off has usually offered an even more imbalanced programme regarding Shakespeare and national authors. New theatre directors often choose Shakespeare at the Almagro Off over Golden Age playwrights. In 2012, for instance, half of the productions in the contest were of plays by Shakespeare as opposed to three by Lope de Vega, only one by Calderón and one adaptation of the prose works by María de Zayas, one of the female authors of the Spanish Golden Age. In the 2014 and 2015 contests, Shakespeare also remained the playwright with a higher percentage of productions.[10] This predilection for Shakespeare and, above all, for his most popular plays, might be related to the need of new theatre directors to raise their market value within the competitive sphere of theatrical economy, as the plays allow them to experiment and, at the same time, establish their reputation.

Shakespeare's presence at the Almagro festivals has been, if not overtly problematic, at least somewhat threatening to the central aim of preserving and celebrating Golden Age drama. The abundance of Shakespeare productions on the Almagro stages reflects the general theatre landscape in Spain since the 1990s (Gregor 2010: 1–2). However, the festival directors take care to avoid Shakespeare completely taking over the programme. The number of plays by national authors put together always exceeds those by Shakespeare, maintaining the celebration of Golden Age Spanish drama at the core of the event. The festivals also ensure that national authors are the focus on anniversary occasions. The coincidence of Shakespeare's and Cervantes' 400th death anniversaries in 2016, for instance, provided the perfect opportunity to commemorate both authors while privileging the national author: eight Shakespeare productions were included in the official programme, while those based on Cervantes' plays and prose works doubled this figure.

Since 2019, the new festival director, Ignacio García, has been working hard to design a more balanced programme with fewer foreign playwrights and, thus, less Shakespeare, and a wider variety of Golden Age plays and playwrights. His first season as a director only included four Shakespeare productions. On the other hand, foreign drama has been completely suppressed from the Almagro Off. The contest rules changed in 2019 and, instead of accepting productions based on dramatic texts from anywhere in the world that met the time focus of the festival, only those from Hispanic origin are now eligible. The directorial decisions to reduce foreign drama at the official festival and the moratorium on non-Spanish plays at the Almagro Off were taken to promote and preserve the national repertoire, and turn Almagro into the world's capital of Golden Age drama. Despite the drop in Shakespeare productions at the official festival and its complete ban from the stages of the Almagro Off, the analysis of the performance of Shakespeare and Golden Age plays in previous seasons sheds some light on the different trends that these two theatre traditions have faced in the twenty-first century, as the next section shows.

Shakespeare in performance: challenging the limits of experimentation

Productions of Shakespeare's plays at the official Almagro Festival negotiate the link between theatre history and contemporary performance, as the festival simultaneously encourages the staging of early modern plays, and the introduction of contemporary elements and new theatre styles. In the summer of 2016, for instance, audiences were offered an array of approaches to early modern texts and had to navigate their way between different modes of production. Ophelia went mad and sang reggaeton on a stage built inside one of the seventeenth-century venues, the Universidad Renacentista. This *Hamlet*, directed by one of the most acclaimed directors of present-day Spanish theatre, Miguel del Arco, was co-produced by the National Company of Classical Theatre (CNTC).[11] The co-production of this *Hamlet* was a rare exception for the CNTC, devoted to the performance and dissemination of Golden Age drama, and remains the only Shakespeare play with which the company has been involved to date. The whole production revolved around a bed, centre stage: at the beginning of the play, Hamlet and Ophelia were shown talking as they were lying on it, emphasizing the intimacy of the couple; later, the bed was occupied by Claudius and Gertrude, confirming Hamlet's accusations of lust against his mother. The bed became Ophelia's tomb in the burial scene and appeared once again as an actual bed where Hamlet spent his time trapped in his own thoughts. This piece of furniture located the action (e.g. in Hamlet's or Gertrude's chamber, the graveyard) and added an extra nuance of depression to Hamlet's personality, as his melancholy seemed to keep him in bed. The production altered the order of the scenes, shortened some and lengthened others, and brought onto the stage actions that are usually told, not shown, in other productions. Such was the case of Ophelia's drowning. The actress jumped into the arms of her fellow actors and screamed in order to suggest Ophelia's fall into the stream. Meanwhile, Hamlet, who was sleeping in his bed downstage, awoke violently the moment she fell. The spectators could not tell whether this was what really happened or only one of Hamlet's nightmares – or both. The scene did the trick, as the director wanted the audience to have the feeling of being inside Hamlet's mind.

Only a few metres away from this *Hamlet*, in the Hospital de San Juan, the young company of the CNTC performed *The Lady from Getafe*, by Lope de Vega. The production used contemporary attire, a multi-level stage and projections to situate the action in the twenty-first century, an approach that is not very common in productions of Golden Age plays. Early modern songs became rap and part of the action was set in a petrol station, instead of a traditional inn. A few days before, the main company of the CNTC had performed *The Mayor of Zalamea* by Calderón on the same stage. In contrast to the updating of *Hamlet* and *The Lady from Getafe*, this production brought the attention back to the seventeenth century. Period costumes, brown and grey colours, and a high upstage wall with some fences on the sides were the only scenography used to evoke Spain's national past.

Festivals are binge theatre, which means that some spectators in the 2016 season had the chance to attend these three productions and find some common points between them: all were classical plays produced or co-produced by the CNTC, staged in historical spaces and part of the Almagro Festival of Classical Theatre. However, while *Hamlet* and *The Lady from Getafe* took a similar approach to classical texts (recontextualizing the action in order to make it contemporary to the audience), *The Mayor of Zalamea* followed a different direction: it recreated and evoked the past through modern resources. Although some degree of experimentation and updating is sometimes introduced in the staging of Golden Age plays, the approach to *The Mayor of Zalamea* has remained the predominant one not only at the Almagro official festival, but in the whole country. The immediate association of Golden Age plays with the national past, the lack of a solid performance tradition due to their absence from the Spanish stages between the 1960s and 1980s, as well as some of their characteristics such as the topics (many of them deal with honour and religion) or language (they are written in rhymed verse), explain this trend.

Even when they are not contextualized in the Golden Age, recent productions in Spain in general and Almagro in particular avoid contemporary settings, as was the case in *The Dog in the Manger* (2017), *The Phantom Lady* (2017) and *The Knight of Olmedo* (2014), all by the CNTC and performed at the Almagro Festival. The first two clung to a sense of the historical by placing the action in nineteenth-century Madrid, and *The Knight of Olmedo* used peasant and countryside imagery to suggest a pervasive pastness, locating the action in a forgotten and rural Spain that could as much refer to the sixteenth century as to the early twentieth century. When it comes to Golden Age plays, approaches such as the one in *The Lady from Getafe* are the exception rather than the rule. Instead of making Golden Age classics our contemporaries by recontextualizing the action in the present, the festival finds intrinsic value in locating the plays in their own theatrical moment.

Shakespeare productions, on the other hand, frequently attempt to reinvent the plays with added reflections on theatricality and the recontextualization of the action in the present. *Tempestad* (2012), directed by Sergio Peris-Mencheta, and *La Tempestad* (2015), by Marta Pazos, offered two updated visions of Shakespeare's *The Tempest*. Magic, power and, above all, theatrical effects dominated the stage in Peris-Mencheta's *Tempestad*.[12] Shakespeare's play was presented as a play-within-a-play and the production started with a group of male actors rehearsing the play, with the one performing Prospero as the theatre director. Miranda was played by a male actor, recalling Renaissance theatre practice, and actors doubled and tripled characters, as a cast of seven actors gave life to twenty characters. Character transformations were not hidden but shown onstage. In contrast to the doubling and even tripling of roles, Ariel was performed by three actors simultaneously, which enhanced the magic powers of the character. Other theatrical effects included the shipwreck, performed with the actors' movement, umbrellas and water being poured over their heads. The production also exploited the technological resources of contemporary theatre to locate the action in the present. For instance, part of Prospero's magic was conveyed using onstage cameras that recorded the action of different characters and projected the image upstage. Thanks to the cameras, Prospero was able to control everything that happened on the island. The production combined traditional theatrical effects (the doubling of characters, mimicry, metonymy, etc.) with contemporary resources, such as the use of onstage cameras, to convey the magic world of *The Tempest* in the present.

Pazos' *La Tempestad* had many elements in common with the Peris-Mencheta production. *La Tempestad* was also framed as a play-within-the-play, with Prospero orchestrating the action. He took the lead to comment on some scenes, ordered actors to stop thinking and just deliver the text and even interviewed Ferdinand to assess whether he was a suitable husband for his daughter, Miranda. The opening shipwreck was performed by the actors dancing onstage while another actor played 'Stormy Weather' the song by Harold Arlen and Ted Koehler popularized by Ethel Waters in the 1930s, on the piano.[13] The production included several references to popular culture, too. For instance, on his first entrance, Ariel appeared disguised as the Little Mermaid, the Disney princess of the same name; later, a delivery guy entered with pizzas that were used for the banquet in 3.2. The metatheatrical play and the pop culture elements indicated that the time of the action coincided with the time of the spectator, as was the case in Peris-Mencheta's *Tempestad*.

As William Worthen points out, 'Shakespearean drama not only occupies the sphere of the "classic," but has also frequently provided the site for innovation in the style, substance, and practice of modern performance' (2003: 2). Shakespeare productions at the official Almagro Festival, like del Arco's *Hamlet* or the two examples of *The Tempest*, exemplify this double status: on the one hand, the curation of the festival, restricted to sixteenth- and seventeenth-century plays, highlights their categorization as 'classics'; on the other, the approach to the plays favours experimentation.

While theatre directors at the Almagro Festival and in Spain generally see Shakespeare's plays as suitable material for experimentation, they regard Golden Age plays only exceptionally as having this potential. Nevertheless, many of the innovative Shakespeare productions at the official Almagro Festival are relatively conservative in their adherence to the source texts. It is rare for the festival to feature radical adaptations that freely rewrite Shakespeare's texts. As Margaret Jane Kidnie suggests, 'although the work has no material reality in a text (or anywhere else), it functions in practice as though it did' (2009: 64). That is, although there is not an actual stable reference against which one can compare adaptations of *Hamlet*, there is a series of aspects that set the idea of *Hamlet*, allowing spectators to identify a production as an example of such play. The adherence to the source texts, thus, restricts the type of experimental approaches for the productions that are showcased at the Almagro Festival. Approaches challenging that referent, such as Romeo Castellucci's *Giulio Cesare* (based on *Julius Caesar*) or Angelica Liddell's *El año de Ricardo* (*Richard's Year*) inspired by *Richard III*, for instance, and other radical productions that are typical of international festivals like the Avignon Festival, would be out of place in Almagro. Instead, the festival favours a more controlled type of experimentation: one that locates the action in the present, uses the typical resources of contemporary theatre and experiments with those resources without pushing too far the boundaries defined by the reference to the source plays.[14]

The selection of productions at the Almagro Off is less concerned with such boundaries. The contest encourages new theatre directors to innovate in the staging of classical plays and, therefore, features some productions that have attempted to go a step further in the reinvention of Shakespeare's plays, offering auterist readings of the plays that contribute to establishing the artistic reputation of theatre directors in the early stages of their careers. Such was the case of *Hambret* (2014), a work-in-progress exploring violence and human relations through Shakespeare's *Hamlet* and instances of physical theatre.[15] The production dismembered Shakespeare's text, with acts and scenes performed in no apparent logical order, and a succession of scenes with the actors running, screaming and bumping into each other. The third edition of the contest in 2012 featured two pieces that were freely based on Shakespeare – *Exhumación* (Exhumation, dir. Carlos BE) and *Claudio, tío de Hamlet* (Claudius, Hamlet's Uncle, dir. Antonio Castro Guijosa) – whose mechanics of adaptation can also be compared to those of *Hambret*. *Exhumación* is a new script based on *Hamlet* in which two historians and a philologist living in Denmark decide to explore the real facts surrounding the story of the original Hamlet, those narrated in the Scandinavian folk-tale by Saxo Grammaticus. The play is all about exhuming *Hamlet* in the sense of finding the source of Shakespeare's story. Also based on *Hamlet*, *Claudio, tío de Hamlet* places the focus on Claudius, telling the story from his perspective and convincing the audience of his reasons for killing his brother. These three productions were not only inspired by Shakespeare's play; they completely altered the play's structure and used the source texts as a springboard for the creation of a completely new script.

Hambret and the two productions based on new scripts claim their autonomy from *Hamlet*, questioning the stability of Shakespeare's play as a referent. The three productions introduce quotations from and references to the play text, but they do not reproduce the parameters (above all in terms of plot and structure) usually associated with the idea of *Hamlet*. In fact, the productions are not adaptations of *Hamlet* but, rather, examples of theatre practice derived from Shakespeare's play. In doing so, the connection between the productions and Shakespeare as an author is loosened. This dissolution diminishes the effectiveness of the productions in the context of the Almagro Off, as they can no longer stand as representative of the historical period to which the festival is devoted. Significantly, neither of these productions won the contest and, therefore, they were not performed on the main stage of the Almagro Festival, an opportunity reserved for the winner of the Almagro Off. This means that, despite the Almagro Off's promotion of experimentation, certain types of productions seem to have limited chances to win the contest precisely because of the tendency of the official festival to avoid radical approaches.

The three winning Shakespeare productions in the history of the Almagro Off show how the festival favours types of theatrical creativity that are less problematic in the transmission of their referent. *Giulio Cesare* (2012, dir. Andrea Baracco), *Mendoza* (2014, dir. Juan Carrillo) and *Romeo and Juliet for 2* (2015), devised by the Idea Theatre Group, were all adaptations of Shakespeare's plays in which the source text (*Julius Caesar*, *Macbeth* and *Romeo and Juliet* respectively) was at all times identifiable in terms of their plot and structure, although they were performed in translation (in Italian, Spanish and Greek respectively). The innovations were introduced through two distinct approaches: *Giulio Cesare* and *Romeo and Juliet for 2* reflected on meaning-making in the theatre, exploiting meta-theatrical techniques,[16] while *Mendoza* presented a Mexican take on *Macbeth*, seeing the play through a Mexican lens and finding local equivalents for the character, the imagery, the language and some key moments in the action. These productions used similar strategies to those in the official festival, thus facilitating their transfer to the main stage of the Almagro Festival after they won the award.

On and Off at Almagro

The regular presence of Shakespeare productions on the Almagro stages reflects the theatrical landscape in Spain (with Shakespeare as one of the most popular playwrights), has catalysed some of the changes in the country after the dictatorship and exemplifies the efforts to keep a balance between national and international playwrights in order to preserve Golden Age drama. The time focus on the sixteenth and seventeenth centuries has favoured productions on the official programme that keep the source play as a reference, independently of whether they are Golden Age or Shakespeare's plays. The festival has also showcased the two main trends of Shakespeare in performance in Spain: on the one hand, those productions that keep the original source as a reference, as is the case of those in the official programme and the winning productions at the Almagro Off; on the other, the more radical productions that participate in the contest. Like other international festivals such as the Avignon Festival or the Edinburgh International Festival, the Almagro festivals stand as sites for innovation in theatrical performance, although their artistic policy tends to set limits to experimentation. The Almagro festivals share with those in the European Shakespeare Festivals Network their attention to the early modern period; however, while these festivals gather together different visions of plays by a single playwright, the Almagro

Festival and the Almagro Off are two of the few events in the world that enable the explicit comparison of different theatre traditions from the sixteenth and seventeenth centuries, bringing to the same city the plays of the Golden Age and William Shakespeare, thus giving rise to a theatrical continuum in which early modern theatre is not only preserved, but also reinvented on the Spanish stage.

Notes

1. The translation of the name of the festival is Almagro Festival of Classical Theatre.
2. Productions in languages other than Spanish include surtitles to facilitate the stage-auditorium communication.
3. The Spanish Golden Age is conventionally considered to begin in 1492, the year of Christopher Columbus' arrival in America and the expulsion of Muslims from the Iberian Peninsula, and to end either with the publication in 1659 of the first grammar of Spanish, *Gramática castellana* by Antonio de Nebrija, or with the death of Calderón de la Barca in 1681.
4. For a reflection on this in relation to the Avignon Festival, see March (2010, 2012). Guerrero (2020) focuses on the Edinburgh International Festival and its conception as a platform for international artists in connection to Shakespeare in performance.
5. The productions were *Medora*, by Lope de Rueda, *El despertar a quien duerme* (Waking up Those Who Sleep), by Lope de Vega, and *La estrella de Sevilla* (The Star from Seville), by Andrés de Claramonte.
6. Spain was not directly involved in the Second World War, but suffered its own civil war (1936–9) and lived under Franco's dictatorship until 1975.
7. The advent of democracy meant the evolution from the *teatro official* (official theatre), at the service of the dictatorship, to the conception of theatre as a public service, with the creation of the Centro Dramático Nacional (National Dramatic Centre) in 1985.
8. See Peláez Martín (1997: 25); García Lorenzo and Muñoz Carbantes (1997: 64); García Santo-Tomás (2000: 376); Bergamín (2017: 16).
9. Spain was not completely isolated from international theatrical life during the dictatorship. However, the presence of foreign companies increased significantly after 1975 (Berenguer and Pérez 1998: 36). The Almagro Festival was an active agent in the internationalization of the Spanish stages.

10 Four out of ten productions were based on Shakespeare plays in 2014 and 2015.
11 In Spanish, Compañía Nacional de Teatro Clásico.
12 For more on this production, see Guerrero (2014).
13 Derek Jarman's screen adaptation of the play featured Elisabeth Welch singing the same song.
14 *Songs of Lear* (2016), by the Polish company Song of the Goat, is one of the few exceptions. The production featured a series of dramatic poems sung by the actors in Polish. The actors stood still for most of the performance and the songs did not follow the plot of the play, which made it very difficult for audiences to follow the altered storyline unless they understood Polish. However, this production captured the essence and general feeling of Shakespeare's *King Lear*, as the reviews suggested, which means that the source play was still an emotional referent, even if its plot and structure were apparently abandoned.
15 For a description of the production, see Guerrero (2015).
16 Ric Knowles has observed that the use of meta-theatrical techniques allows transcending cultural specificities and proves particularly suitable for productions staged in international festival contexts (Knowles 2004: 188). This accounts for the abundance of productions relying on meta-theatre in Almagro.

References

Berenguer, Ángel, and Manuel Pérez (1998), *Tendencias del Teatro español durante la transición política (1975–1982)* [Trends of Spanish Theatre in the Political Transition (1975–1982)], Madrid: Biblioteca Nueva.

Bergamín, Beatrice (2017), 'Festival Internacional de Teatro Clásico de Almagro. 40 años. 1978–2017' [Almagro International Festival of Classical Theatre. 40 Years. 1978–2017], in *40 Ediciones. Festival de Teatro Clásico de Almagro* [40 Editions. Almagro International Festival of Classical Theatre], 8–27, Almagro: Fundación Festival Internacional de Teatro Clásico de Almagro.

Carlson, Marvin (2001), *The Haunted Stage: The Theatre as Memory Machine*, Ann Arbor, MI: University of Michigan Press.

García Lorenzo, Luciano, and Manuel Muñoz Carabantes (1997), 'Festival de Almagro: veinte años de teatro clásico' [Almagro Festival: Twenty Years of Classical Theatre], in *Festival Internacional de Teatro Clásico de Almagro. 20 años: 1978–1997* [Almagro International

Festival of Classical Theatre. 20 Years: 1978–1997], 63–96, Toledo: Caja de Castilla la Mancha.

García Santo-Tomás, Enrique (2000), *La Creación del Fénix: recepción, crítica y formación canónica del teatro de Lope de Vega* [The Fénix's Creation: Reception, Criticism and Canon in Lope de Vega's Theatre], Madrid: Gredos.

García, Juan I. (2013), 'Festival de Almagro: La sombra de Shakespeare es alargada' [Almagro Festival: Shakespeare Shadow is Extended], *ARN* 10 July 2013. Available online: http://www.arndigital.com/articulo.php?idarticulo=6607 (accessed 20 August 2013).

González, José Manuel (1999), 'Shakespeare in Almagro', in Tetsuo Anzai et al. (eds), *Shakespeare in Japan*, 244–60, Lewiston, NY: Edwin Mellen Press.

Gregor, Keith (2010), *Shakespeare in the Spanish Theatre: 1772 to the Present*, London: Continuum.

Guerrero, Isabel (2014), '*Tempestad* [Performance Review]', *SEDERI* 24: 220–4.

Guerrero, Isabel (2015), 'Shakespeare in Almagro 2014: *Hambret* [Performance Review]', *SEDERI* 25: 219–23.

Guerrero, Isabel (2017), 'Shakespeare in La Mancha: Performing Shakespeare at the Almagro Corral', *SEDERI* 27: 27–46.

Guerrero, Isabel (2020), '"My native English now I must forgo": Global Shakespeare at the Edinburgh International Festival', *Cahiers Élisabéthains* 103: 57–74.

Kidnie, Margaret Jane (2009), *Shakespeare and the Problem of Adaptation*, London and New York: Routledge.

Knowles, Ric (2004), *Reading the Material Theatre*, Cambridge: Cambridge University Press.

March, Florence (2010), 'Richard II in the Honour Court of the Papal Palace: Forgetting Shakespeare in Order to Find Him?', *Shakespeare en devenir – The Journal of Shakespearean Afterlives*. Available online: http://shakespeare.edel.univ-poitiers.fr/index.php?id=469 (accessed 14 July 2020).

March, Florence (2012), *Shakespeare au Festival d'Avignon: configurations textuelles et scéniques, 2004–2011* [Shakespeare at the Avignon Festival. Text and Stage Configurations, 2004–2011], Montpellier: L'Entretemps Éditions.

Peláez Martín, Andrés (1997), 'El Corral de Comedias de Almagro: un espacio y un patrimonio dramático recuperados' [The *Corral de Comedias* in Almagro: A Recovered Space and Heritage], in *Festival Internacional de Teatro Clásico de Almagro. 20 años: 1978–1997* [Almagro International Festival of Classical Theatre. 20 years: 1978–1997], 19–36, Toledo: Caja de Castilla la Mancha.

Ruiz Ramón, Francisco (1988), 'Del teatro español de la transición a la transición del teatro (1975–1985)' [From Spanish Theatre during the Transition to the Transition of Theatre (1975–1985)], in Samuel Amell and Salvador García Castañeda (eds), *La cultura española en el posfranquismo: diez años de cine, cultura y literatura en España, 1975–1985* [Spanish Culture after Franco: Ten Years of Cinema, Culture and Literature in Spain], 103–14, Madrid: Playor.

Worthen, William B. (2003), *Shakespeare and the Force of Modern Performance*, Cambridge: Cambridge University Press.

4

Shakespeare at Four Castles: Summer Shakespeare Festival in Prague, Brno, Ostrava (Czech Republic) and Bratislava (Slovakia)

Filip Krajník and Eva Kyselová

In the summer of 1990, Prague Castle, one of the city's dominant landmarks and the historical seat of Bohemian and Holy Roman Kings and, later on, of Czechoslovak presidents, temporarily assumed a rather unusual role. After forty years of being a symbol of communist power, the Castle became an open-air stage for actor and director Jan Kačer's production of Shakespeare's *A Midsummer Night's Dream*. The idea to turn the Prague Castle into a cultural venue came from the then newly elected Czechoslovak president Václav Havel, himself a respected dramatist, who decided to open the place to ordinary people once again and invest it with a new, democratic ethos. *A Midsummer Night's Dream*, a play in which fantasy turns into reality, proved to be a very fortunate choice, in many respects mirroring the atmosphere in the country which had just undergone a change in its political regime. The newspaper headline for one of the early commentaries on the production,

'We Play for People!' ('pl' [Pavla Landová] 1990), indicates the enthusiastic acceptance of the enterprise. Little did Havel or the audiences back then know that Shakespearean actors would return to the Castle just a few years later to establish a tradition of regular summer Shakespeare festivities in Prague. This tradition would later spread to venues in other Czech and Slovak towns and, at the time of writing, has now lasted for three decades. During this time, the Summer Shakespeare Festival – as the enterprise was later officially called – managed to establish itself as the most important single Shakespearean event in both the Czech Republic and Slovakia, attended by tens of thousands of guests, many of whom are not even frequent theatregoers during the main theatre season (Autumn–Spring). From a modest event, which in the early 1990s presented Shakespeare for the first time in forty years in a democratic environment, the festival has expanded and grown to become currently the oldest and biggest open-air theatre festival in Europe devoted to Shakespeare's works.

Although the Summer Shakespeare Festival is in many ways a unique and autonomous project in the context of Czech and Slovak theatre traditions, it is not entirely without a precedent. To understand fully its cultural resonances, it is necessary to look back at the modern history of what are nowadays called the Czech Republic and Slovakia and realize that Shakespeare, and Shakespearean festivities, have a strong tradition in the region and a special status for both the nations. Indeed, Shakespeare has been a prominent presence at critical times in the nations' modern histories. The following account of those histories may help explain why Shakespeare was so readily accepted as a symbol of change in 1990, and why two relatively small countries with a combined population of fifteen million people are home to the oldest existing open-air festival devoted to Shakespeare in continental Europe.

Shakespeare in the Czech lands: festivities before the festival

For Czechs, as for many other European peoples, Shakespeare holds the status of a national author of a kind, and the history of productions of Shakespeare's works in the Czech lands closely follows the trajectory of Czech cultural (and, by extension, social and political) history. Even in Shakespeare's lifetime, English travelling actors began touring continental Europe, giving performances in Prague (probably in 1595, certainly in 1602), throughout Bohemia (1607), in the Silesian town of Krnov (Jägerndorf, 1610) and in Bratislava (Pressburg, today's Slovakia, 1618), and many times afterward (Limon 1985: 109–11; Drábek 2017a: 11). The first productions of Shakespeare in the Czech language date back to the late eighteenth century, when Shakespeare had been rediscovered in his homeland (see Dobson 1992) and his cult started spreading to other national cultures. When the first provisional Czech theatre house was erected in what is now Wenceslas Square in Prague, Czech versions (based on then popular German adaptations) of plays such as *Macbeth*, *Hamlet* and *King Lear* played an important part in the theatre's repertoire, boasting the ability of the Czech language to present a great European classic. While the motives of the early Bohemian patriots to stage Shakespeare in Czech were not just national and political, but chiefly social and economic (see Drábek 2012: 75–102), the English playwright proved to be a powerful ally in their efforts.

By the mid-nineteenth century, especially following the 'Spring of Nations' events in 1848/9, Shakespeare had become a wholesale symbol of cultural emancipation of Czechs and a proxy for expressing their political positions. To commemorate the tercentenary of Shakespeare's birth, a new complete translation of Shakespeare's dramatic works into Czech was commissioned (published between 1855 and 1872, being the first of its kind in a Slavonic language) and in 1864, opulent Shakespearean festivities organized by preeminent Czech artists and theatre practitioners of the time were held in Prague. The festival culminated in a procession of characters from Shakespeare's plays and concluded with the oration of Shakespeare's Perdita, who allegorically stood for the 'lost Czech culture' which needed to be rediscovered. As Drábek maintains, the event was 'both popular and profoundly political', marking 'a moment of great expectations for the Czech nation' (2017a: 17). With perhaps even stronger political overtones, Jaroslav Kvapil, the then artistic director of the Czech National Theatre's drama ensemble, staged a cycle of fifteen Shakespearean plays on the occasion of the 300th anniversary of Shakespeare's death in 1916. As Ivona Mišterová points out, what might have looked like a chiefly theatrical achievement was also 'a presentation of the Czech national self-awareness and identity' and a demonstration of 'the Czech pro-Allied sympathies' in the period of the First World War (2015: 80–1). While fifty-two years earlier, a Shakespeare festival had helped Czechs to express their desires for cultural emancipation within the Austro-Hungarian Empire, through a similar event at the beginning of the twentieth century, they demanded political autonomy.

When the independent Czechoslovak state was established in 1918, Czech (and, with some delay, Slovak) theatres entered into a creative dialogue with other European theatre cultures, including productive connections with 'Austrian art nouveau, German expressionism, Russian constructivism, French cubism and surrealism, and many other art styles' (Koubská 2017: 21). Shakespeare remained a staple of the theatres' repertoires. Between 1921 and 1927, Kvapil returned to his endeavour of the previous decade and staged a cycle of eleven plays in the Vinohrady Theatre, the then second most important theatre in Prague. Having been heavily influenced both by impressionism and stage realism, Kvapil was not a director who would attempt radical adaptations or marked updates of the texts. In contrast, early twentieth-century directors such as Karel Hugo Hilar, whose work represents the so-called second phase of modern Czech directing (see Císař 2006: 36–51), had no scruples about adapting, updating or rewriting Shakespeare's plays. Hilar's productions (for instance of *Romeo and Juliet* in 1924 and *Hamlet* in 1926) conformed to the modern reading of Shakespeare by a twentieth-century audience, who had witnessed the transformation of the society and its values and had undergone the traumatic experience of the First World War. The aim was no longer to present the audience with the Renaissance author in his historical contexts and outmoded poetics, but as a contemporary reflecting on the state of individuals in uncertain times.

Following the occupation of Czechoslovakia's border regions (the so-called Sudetenland) in 1938 by Nazi Germany and the rest of the territory of Bohemia and Moravia in 1939, Czechs once more lost their cultural and political independence. (Slovakia gained a fictitious independence, effectively becoming a pro-Nazi puppet state.) While theatres in the 'Protectorate of Bohemia and Moravia' could function until September 1944, even staging Shakespeare's plays, their operation was strictly bounded by German censorship and, especially in the later stages of the war, productions of

English plays were rare. In the context of the war atrocities, it is interesting to point out the theatre activities in the Jewish ghetto of Terezín (Theresienstad) in North Bohemia, where Germans built a 'model camp' for the (mainly Czech) Jewish community.[1] Paradoxically, Jews in Terezín were allowed to perform music and stage plays that were otherwise forbidden in the rest of Germany; their theatre endeavours including productions of Shakespeare's *Measure for Measure* and *Richard III* (Tuma 1976: 17; Koubská 2017: 24). In spite of the suggestive idea of these performances being an act of resistance (both *Measure for Measure* and *Richard III* are plays about tyranny and injustice), Mirko Tůma, one of the surviving prisoners who organized the theatre in the ghetto, maintains that 'the equation between artistic activities in Terezín (particularly in theatre and music) and rebellion or rather calculated rebellion, has been in most instances a myth. The theatre and music were quintessentially *l'art pour l'art*, with *l'art*, however, transcending itself and acquiring a dimension of sheer survival' (Tuma 1976: 17).

The issue of Shakespeare under Communism between the late 1940s and late 1980s and the playwright's importance for Czech and Slovak cultures has been thoroughly discussed and is too complex to cover here, even in the form of a brief outline.[2] Yet, the importance of Shakespeare in this period is a key factor for understanding the reception of his works after the revolution in 1989. After the communist coup in 1948, Shakespeare became both a showcase for the new regime (as he was, to an extent, during the rather paradoxical celebrations of the 390th anniversary of Shakespeare's birth in 1954, when Czech theatres opened nineteen productions of eight Shakespeare plays; see Černý 2007: 415) and a space of freedom which allowed artists to abandon 'the tendentious, ideological and ideologically corrupted discourses of our political realities' (Drábek 2017b). As Drábek asserted in an unpublished keynote lecture, 'Shakespeare has been used in Czech theatre for political purposes but also for exactly the opposite: his plays were also staged *because* they were *apolitical*' (2017b). On the one hand, Shakespeare was an ally of Czech and Slovak nations in the same fashion as he had been at the times of previous cultural, political and moral crises. Indeed, risky enterprises such as the staging of Pavel Kohout's *Play Makbeth*[3] by Vlasta Chramostová's[4] illegal Living Room Theatre in 1978 (the production inspired Tom Stoppard's well-known *Cahoot's Macbeth* of 1979) made Shakespeare one of the symbols of Czechs' and Slovaks' yearning for political freedom. Yet on the other hand, we must not forget that it was predominantly Shakespeare's art that made him the most popular – and most commercially successful – author staged in Czechoslovak theatres, and a retrospective reading of political motives into the majority of Shakespearean productions of the time could be seen as part of 'the post-1989 re-definitions of the Czech and Slovak cultural identities' (Drábek 2017b).

Shakespeare in Czech and Slovak castles: festival in the Era of Freedom

With the fall of the regime, Czechoslovak theatres went through a transitional period during which their purpose and social roles needed to be thoroughly redefined. While in the times of cultural and political restrictions, theatres might have served as a political substitute and an island of freedom for the audiences, in the young democracy, these functions were no longer needed or even desired. Although Shakespeare remained a staple in theatres' repertoire (in fact, it might be argued that his works significantly contributed to the consolidation of the role of the theatre in the newly gained freedom), the audiences' expectations of his productions had changed: Shakespeare was expected to be a classic, but accessible and entertaining rather than ostentatiously political. The last of the requirements was reflected in the temporary increase in the number of productions of Shakespeare's comedies in Czechoslovak theatres in the 1990s at the expense of his tragedies.

Despite the nation's aversion (based on the experience of communism) to the politicization of culture, it was nevertheless a political gesture that initiated the tradition of annual summer Shakespeare festivities in Czechoslovakia (and, later on, in the Czech Republic and Slovakia). It was not only Havel's desire to open up the former seat of communist presidents to a wider audience – it was also the *locus* itself that lent the event a highly evocative air. The setting of Kačer's production of *A Midsummer Night's Dream* (and, subsequently, all the major productions of the Czech part of the festival) was the yard of the old Supreme Burgrave House in the Castle's complex, a marvellous thirteenth-century Gothic building (renovated in the sixteenth century in a Renaissance style) that has played an important role in the country's history. Although probably unbeknownst to the production's organizers at the time, this choice proved to be crucial for the future character and expansion of the festival. Ever since 1990, the Summer Shakespeare Festival (as the tradition was officially called in 1994) has been organized in historical open-space settings that bring the productions of Shakespeare closer to the original conditions of the English Renaissance (including the whimsical weather which occasionally interrupts the production), while at the same time underscoring Shakespeare's status as an adopted Czech national poet by placing him in an urban environment with a historical significance for the country.[5] The number of premieres and revivals has increased every year: in the 1990s, the festival offered no more than three core productions per season; currently, the number of core plays is about ten every year, with occasional incoming guest productions (see below). This expansion relied on the addition of new playing spaces, including a second regular venue in Prague (the open yard of the historical Liechtenstein Palace), as well as the Špilberk Castle in Brno, Moravia (in 2000), Bratislava Castle in Bratislava, the capital of Slovakia (in 2001) and the Silesian-Ostrava Castle in Ostrava, Silesia (in 2008). Like the Prague Castle, all of the venues are important historical sites for their respective nations, being either former royal palaces or military posts (the Špilberk Castle even served as a prison in the Austro-Hungarian period). On the other hand, these venues serve chiefly as playing spaces which, although sometimes effectively integrated into the production's scenic design, are not a key element in the plays' interpretation (there is no particular difference between the castles' significance for serious history plays or light-hearted comedies). Making these sites homes for the greatest European classic was – and still is – mainly a symbolical manifesto of the central role that culture has played in both nations' past and present and their espousal of Western culture, to which both nations after the fall of the communist regime naturally inclined. Moreover, it could be argued that staging the festival in the administrative centres of former Czechoslovakia still unites the country even after its split in 1993 on a cultural level, with Shakespeare allowing for a vivid exchange between Czechs and Slovaks and their theatre cultures.

Indeed, the collaboration between Czech and Slovak theatre practitioners at the Summer Shakespeare Festival, which started in its 1999 season in Prague with the incoming production of *The Merry Wives of Windsor* by the Slovak National Theatre (dir. Emil Horváth), has given the event a unique cross-border quality – something that is not typical of either current Czech or Slovak theatre practice. Aside from Slovak directors directing Czech productions or vice versa, it is not uncommon that the core festival productions have both a Czech and Slovak cast and are, therefore, acted bilingually. While such a way of staging drama is generally not common on either side of the border (apart from a handful of rather specific theatre experiments) and has become one of the unique features of the festival, it may also be seen as a reference to a strong partnership between Czech and Slovak theatre professionals, especially in the early stages of the professional Slovak theatre at the beginning of the twentieth century. While both theatre traditions (and, indeed, the Czech and Slovak languages) have their own specific features, in the case of bilingual productions, it is their commonalities rather than differences that transpire. As such, Shakespeare provides a common space for both Czech and Slovak theatregoers, reminding them of both the nations' shared history and (having spent most of the twentieth century in one state and one socio-cultural context) common characteristics.

It is important to stress that the Summer Shakespeare Festival is not a festival in the sense of a meeting place of diverse theatre groups presenting their productions – rather, it is a special summer repertoire, compiled and coordinated by the organizing theatre agencies (SCHOK Agency in Prague and Brno, PaS de Theatre in Ostrava and JAY Production in Bratislava), which approach the directors and actors from various theatres (often local to the organizing towns), selected ad hoc for the event. It is an unwritten rule that actors playing prominent roles in the core productions are very well known either for their theatre career or from film and television. The festival's starry cast tends to be the main attraction for the incoming audience, oftentimes more than the name of the director.

Every year, one or two premieres are produced while the rest of the core repertoire consists of revivals from the previous three or so seasons. (The latest season, in 2020, was an exception and did not offer a new premiere, as it was long uncertain whether the festival would take place at all due to the pandemic situation in the country.) After a certain number of performances, the production usually moves to another town so that the audiences can enjoy the same overall repertoire in each of the venues (with the exception of Bratislava, whose dramaturgy only partly overlaps with the Czech portion of the festival). Besides these, there have been special guest productions: in the past, these were coming from various Czech and Slovak theatres, performing in their mother tongue (for instance, the aforementioned *Merry Wives of Windsor* by the Slovak National Theatre in Prague in 1999). More recently, guest productions have been performed in foreign languages, lending the festival an international aura and inviting foreigners who either live in the town or are there as tourists to attend the event (for instance, the Polish production of *Richard III* by Teatr Ludowy in 2008 in Ostrava, the English productions of *Much Ado About Nothing* and *A Midsummer Night's Dream* by the British Shakespeare Company in 2009 in Prague or the English production of *Richard III* by the Prague Shakespeare Company in the jubilatory 2016 season in Prague).

In addition to its four main venues, the festival has sporadically taken place in several smaller towns in both the Czech Republic and Slovakia, although these have not become the festival's permanent homes. Prague remains its chief venue: while the Brno, Ostrava and Bratislava portions of the festival take about twenty days altogether in July and August, the programme in Prague (where the season's new productions usually open) begins in late June and closes in early September.

Given the exceptional character of the festival within the Czech and Slovak cultural context and the fact that it takes place outside the main theatre season, the audiences for the event are not necessarily the usual Czech and Slovak theatregoers. While, especially in the past, the festival had a reputation of being a tourist attraction of a kind, Drábek disagrees with this assessment, calling the event 'a true *national*, popular theatre festivity' (Drábek 2012: 283; trans. F. K. and E. K., italics original). The term 'popular' – which may overlap with the word 'commercial' – is significant. In order to appease the audiences who otherwise do not frequent mainstream theatre houses, the dramaturgy of the festival chiefly focuses on the well-known plays, which are, in some form, familiar to an average Czech or Slovak audience. Since the 1990s, the festival only staged about twenty of Shakespeare's plays: the most staged piece is *Romeo and Juliet*, which has accompanied the festival from its beginnings,[6] followed by *Hamlet* and *Macbeth*. From the comedies, *A Midsummer Night's Dream*, *Twelfth Night* and *As You Like It* are the most popular. On the other hand, only two histories have appeared at the festival so far: *Henry IV* (in one part, directed by Lucie Bělohradská for the 2010 season) and *Richard III* (directed by Martin Huba, having premiered in 2012). The tendency to rely on certain plays can be observed in the frequent 'rotation' on the festival bill: in 2015, a Slovak-Czech production of *Twelfth Night*, directed by Enikö Eszényi, premiered in Bratislava, while only a year later, a new production of the play by Jana Kališová opened in Prague; similarly, Janka Ryšánek Schmiedtová's production of *Hamlet* premiered in Ostrava in 2016, while in 2017, another production, this time by Michal Vajdička, opened in Prague, making it one of two different *Hamlet*s staged by the festival that season. The same happened with *Richard III*, which premiered in Bratislava in Marián Pecko's production in 2011 and the following year in Prague, directed by Martin Huba.

From tradition to experiment: innovation, translation, celebration

In the three decades of its existence, the Summer Shakespeare Festival has seen not only a profound shift in terms of the quantitative growth of its repertoire and related geographical expansion – factors that both testify to the immense popularity of this endeavour – it has also undergone a change in terms of its artistic quality. Indeed, the event has increasingly become a space for theatrical experiments which have both created and attracted more demanding audiences, who do not merely seek easy entertainment (which, as mentioned above, was not only a prevailing tendency of the festival in the 1990s, but also, to an extent, of Czech and Slovak theatres in general). The work of translator and literary scholar Martin Hilský has been crucial to the evolution of the festival and we conclude this section with an account of Hilský's distinctive contribution, especially as it related to the anniversary events of 2016.

We begin, though, with an earlier landmark (and one in which Hilský was also involved): Slovak actor and director Martin Huba's

2002 staging of *King Lear*. Although the production itself was rather conventional, 'telling the familiar story' so to speak, rather than being an attempt at a radical, fresh (re-)interpretation of the play, it was a key event in the festival's history for several reasons. Firstly, it was the first premiere of a tragedy since actor and director Boris Rösner's 1998 production of *Macbeth* at the Prague Castle, which ultimately helped to solidify the Summer Shakespeare Festival as a serious and ambitious cultural event rather than merely lighthearted summer entertainment. (A year after *Lear*, in 2003, this trend continued with the premiere of *Hamlet*, the very first time the play had been staged at the festival.) Secondly, and as importantly, Huba decided to cast the 65-year-old Jan Tříska, a living legend of Czech film and theatre, in the title role as King Lear. Tříska's previous major Shakespearean role was Romeo in the 1963 staging of *Romeo and Juliet* by Otomar Krejča at the Prague National Theatre (which in its four-year life-span reached 110 performances). After signing the Charter 77 proclamation,[7] however, Tříska emigrated to the United States and disappeared from the Czech stage for a quarter of a century. The role of King Lear was thus Tříska's big comeback to Czech theatre and subsequently earned him that year's Alfréd Radok Award for the best actor.[8] It could be argued that the casting of a dissident-actor at least partly referred to Václav Havel's original idea to overcome the totalitarian past of the Prague Castle during the era of communism and fill the place with a new, democratic ethos.

Thirdly, Huba's production of *Lear* was important for textual reasons. The director commissioned a new modern translation of the play-text from Prague Professor of English Literature Martin Hilský (a pre-eminent translator whose earlier translations were regularly staged at the festival from the mid-1990s; see below),[9] further underscoring the importance and special character of the production. By this point, Hilský's name and work were well known enough to audiences to form an attraction in themselves.

As has been mentioned, Huba's production of *King Lear* itself was predominantly conventional. Huba and Slovak set designer Jozef Ciller effectively employed the castle wall, which formed the border of the stage, leaving the platform itself almost bare, with the exception of a huge heap of sand on the left side, which served multiple technical purposes throughout the play and, at the same time, aptly symbolized the instability of Lear's kingdom, of the relationships at his court and, ultimately, of his own mind. Most of the attention was thus centred on the actors themselves, chiefly on Tříska, whose wild physical gestures, swift and expressive work with emotions and, above all, mastery of voice (before his emigration, Tříska was a popular dubbing actor as well) dominated the production from the very beginning. In the iconic storm scene in Act 3, Tříska stripped completely naked beside Jiří Langmajer playing Edgar (who a year later returned to the festival as Hamlet and, in 2012, as King Richard III in Huba's staging of the play), not hesitating to express the King's physical suffering by exposing his own aged body – something still unprecedented on Czech or Slovak stages in the early 2000s.

Tříska's Lear immediately gained iconic status at the festival and, when five years later, he and Huba returned to the festival as Caliban and Prospero in Jakub Korčák's production of *The Tempest*, it was Tříska in the smaller role of Caliban that appeared on the cover of the 2007 printed programme of the festival, showing that his name and face were the main attractions for that year's audiences.

FIGURE 4.1 *Jan Tříska as Caliban and Martin Huba as Prospero in* The Tempest *(2009). Photograph by Viktor Kronbauer. By permission of AGENTURA SCHOK.*

Huba's staging of *King Lear* in 2002 turned the festival into a critically acclaimed event. As theatre critic Vladimír Mikulka commented on the production: 'Every year, the Summer Shakespeare Festival offers its audiences a decent theatrical menu. This year's *King Lear*, however, significantly surpasses the ordinary boundaries of an easy summer theatre' (Mikulka 2002: B5; trans. F. K. and E. K.). The organizers made use of this success with confidence, taking further brave steps. They started approaching younger, more irreverent directors, able to combine both a popular appeal with a more active and topical communication with audience members. From the early 2010s, the organizers ceased to produce Shakespeare merely as a showcase for lavishly traditional set designs and for Hilský's text-centred translations; this opened the dramatist up to pop-cultural references, as well as contemporary topics and social issues. Perhaps the most interesting entry into the Summer Shakespeare Festival in this respect has been the contribution of the directing duo SKUTR (comprising Lukáš Trpišovský and Martin Kukučka). Its two members hold an irreplaceable position in Czech theatre. Their direction embraces an eclectic array of forms, including circus, opera and ballet, and always emphasize artistic imagination without boundaries. Their first production at the event, the 2013 staging of *A Midsummer Night's Dream*, prefigured the advent of the new form of the Summer Shakespeare Festival, which would respond more fully to contemporary developments in Czech theatre. SKUTR came up with the vision of shifting the play towards an amusing spectacle full of humour, joy and situation comedy, but which also raised real questions relating to the partnership between a man and a woman, the masculine and feminine views of the world and marriage stereotypes. The production's subtitle, 'A Crazy Wedding Comedy about the Eternal Wandering in the Forest of Relationships', opened the door to the actors' unrestrained exhibition, exaggerated passion and eroticism, emphasizing the instinctive and sexual undertones of the play, which had been suppressed in the previous decades rather than being the basis for the work's interpretation. The directors decided to cast actors of the younger middle generation, David Prachař and Vanda Hybnerová, in the roles of Theseus and Hippolyta (and Oberon and Titania). The two coped brilliantly with Shakespeare's verse and their theatrical flexibility and broad register allowed them to create sensuous and passionate characters, who could also cynically distance themselves from their love relationships.

In addition to these, SKUTR decided to cast actors who had gained prominence in various forms of alternative theatre culture (such as stand-up comedy and political satire), or film and television, and whose personalities and ideological backgrounds created new modern variations of the archetypal characters of Bottom and Quince (played by Marek Daniel and Josef Polášek). Unlike in other productions of the play, the audiences were shown Puck as a being on the border between a human and a mythological creature, whose elusive character was difficult to fathom (in contrast with the other characters in the play, whose delineation was complex but easily identifiable). Slovak actor and performer Csongor Kassai created his Puck by means of stylized motions, smoothly shifting between drama and dancing.

The production met with tremendous success and, although heavily employing experimental devices, it managed to gain the favour of a broad popular audience, which is the reason why it remained in the festival's repertoire until 2019. SKUTR tried to repeat the success with a production of *Romeo and Juliet* in 2015 but it did not accomplish the desired aim and closed in the 2018 season. In 2020, the duo were about to return to the festival yet again with their new take on *The Tempest*. As mentioned above, however, the premiere did not take place due to the pandemic situation in the country in spring and summer 2020.

In strong contrast to the complexities of 2020, the year 2016 now appears cheerfully uncomplicated. It was entirely indicative of the key position of the festival in Czech and Slovak theatre cultures that the main celebrations of the 400th anniversary of Shakespeare's death took place on the Summer Shakespeare Festival's stages. Apart from the premieres of *Twelfth Night* (dir. Jana Kališová) and *Hamlet* (dir. Janka Ryšánek Schmiedtová), seven revivals and a special guest production of *Richard III* in English, the festival for this occasion included a special thematic programme entitled *Pocta Shakespearovi* (Homage to Shakespeare), comprising a selection of popular scenes from several Shakespeare plays (such as *The Merchant of Venice, Romeo and Juliet, The Taming of the Shrew, The Merry Wives of Windsor* and others), accompanied by the recitation of Shakespeare sonnets and music by baroque composer Alessandro Scarlatti. In this 'best of' selection from Shakespeare, Jan Tříska reprised (albeit in a much more modest way) his role of King Lear, combined with that of Prospero and, through the sonnets that he pronounced on the stage, even of Shakespeare himself. The actors and musicians were not, however, the centre of attention this time – this privilege belonged to the aforementioned Martin Hilský, the translator and author of the event, who was also the programme's host and who, by means of 'coaching' the actors before the audience's eyes, provided the theatregoers with contextual information and guidance.

This was not the first time Martin Hilský had dominated the festival's stage. Towards the end of the twentieth and in the early twenty-first centuries, Hilský became the leading translator of Shakespeare into Czech and, with numerous radio and television programmes, interviews and public lectures, a leading figure in the popularization of Shakespeare in the country (for which he was named an honorary holder of the Order of the British Empire in 2001). It is not surprising that his name has been closely connected with the Summer Shakespeare Festival since 1995, when his translation of *The Taming of the Shrew* (dir. Milan Schejbal) was staged at the Prague Castle. In the subsequent years, Hilský became the main translator to be staged at the event (with some of the translations even being commissioned by the organizers), being also one of the most recognizable faces of the event. On several occasions, Hilský compiled special themed evenings in the same vein as *Homage to Shakespeare*, namely *Blázni, milenci a básníci* (Madmen, Lovers, and Poets) in 2004, a collage of the best love scenes from Shakespeare, and *Shakespearovi šašci* (Shakespeare's Fools) in 2005, a themed evening about Shakespeare's fools, jesters and clowns. In both cases, Hilský took the role of the evening's host and his popularity among the audiences could easily be compared to that of the actors'.

It is debatable whether it was Hilský's popularity and the sound of his translations that helped to establish the festival among the general audience or whether it was the festival that helped to establish Hilský's current reputation as the most prominent Czech Shakespeare scholar. The truth remains that although Hilský finished his translation of Shakespeare's complete works with a monumental one-volume edition of collected Shakespeare in Czech in 2011,[10] even a decade later, he still holds the position of virtually the only Czech translator of Shakespeare staged at the festival and, in terms of popularity, his translations of Shakespeare among Czech audiences have little competition.

***

In its thirty years of existence, the Summer Shakespeare Festival has established itself as the most important single Shakespearean event in both the Czech Republic and Slovakia, attended even by guests who are not regular theatregoers or lovers of Shakespeare in the traditional sense. From a modest event, which in the early 1990s presented Shakespeare for the first time in forty years in a democratic environment, the festival has expanded and grown to become currently the oldest and biggest open-air theatre festival in Europe devoted to Shakespeare's works.[11] With this popularity, a shift towards commercialization of Shakespeare at the event is discernible; this is not, however, necessarily a point of criticism, as before being a (trans)national classic, Shakespeare was mainly part of the cultural industry, where he naturally still belongs.

Some of the recent productions at the event, such as SKUTR's *A Midsummer Night's Dream*, show that the Summer Shakespeare Festival has been constantly developing and has become a legitimate contribution to the tradition of Shakespearean productions in the Czech Republic and Slovakia, responding to the latest trends in theatre practice and collaborating with distinguished directors and actors (such as Michal Vajdička's 2017 production of *Hamlet* with actors from the Dejvice Theatre, one of today's most prominent Prague theatre ensembles). It is not easy to anticipate the festival's further development, as culture and arts, just as all the spheres of life, have been recently affected by the coronavirus epidemic. The festival will have to cope with the impaired economic situation and the question is how this factor will affect the event's artistic growth. It is, however, necessary to stress that, in the thirty years of its existence, the Summer Shakespeare Festival has undergone a significant evolution, from easy summer entertainment without significant artistic aspirations into an enterprise that strives to follow recent trends in theatre production and attracts younger generations of directors and theatre professionals, who are not afraid to experiment with Shakespeare's plays. There is a hope that there will be more productions that will surpass the confines of the festival and become relevant parts of the broader Czech and Slovak theatre context and its critical discourse, and that the

Summer Shakespeare Festival will continue its tradition of creative adaptability in the post-Covid world.

Notes

1. The Terezín ghetto was a kind a 'Potemkin village' which was supposed to show how humanely Germans treated their enemies. One of the most monstrous examples of this propaganda was the documentary *Der Führer schenkt de Juden eine Stadt* (The Fuhrer Gives a City to the Jews, 1944), which presented Terezín as a paradisal place where the Jews work peacefully for the Reich, having enough food and entertainment. Shortly after the film was finished, most of its involuntary actors were transported to death camps to die in gas chambers.
2. On the topic of Shakespeare in (particularly Eastern) Europe, including communist Czechoslovakia, in the twentieth century, see, for instance, Wild (2015), Sheen and Karremann (2016) or Stříbrný (2000).
3. For more on Kohout's adaptation and its immediate context, see Worthen (2007).
4. Vlasta Chramostová (1926–2019) worked in theatres in Brno and Olomouc; since 1950 she played in the Czechoslovak Army Theatre (today's Vinohrady Theatre). Between 1970 and 1972, she was a member of the permanent ensemble in the Divadlo za branou (Theatre beyond the Gate, Prague), upon the closing of which she could not perform publicly for political reasons. Chramostová was one of the first persons to sign the Charter 77 proclamation. Besides her theatre career, she also gained prominence in film. She could return to public acting only after the fall of the communist regime in 1989.
5. While Prague was the capital of Czechoslovakia between 1918 and 1992, it is markedly more historically important for Czechs than Slovaks, who were not part of the so-called Lands of the Bohemian (Czech) Crown.
6. Staged for the first time in 1994, dir. Tomáš Töpfer, with the most recent premiere in 2015, dir. Lukáš Trpišovský and Martin Kukučka.
7. Charter 77 was a civic initiative in socialist Czechoslovakia founded in 1977 that criticized the country's communist government for violating human rights that it promised to implement in the country's constitution. Signing the Charter 77 proclamation (which was distributed illegally) almost automatically meant dismissal from work

and other forms of harassment from the government, including forced emigration in some cases.

8 Named after the distinguished Czech stage director, the Alfréd Radok Award was presented between 1995 and 2013 for achievements in Czech theatre in several categories. The winners were voted for by theatre critics.

9 Prof. Martin Hilský (b. 1943) is the most prominent member of the latest generation of Shakespearean translators into Czech, his translations appearing on various Czech stages since 1983 (see Drábek 2012: 263–302). Counting all the productions of Shakespeare since the fall of the communist regime in Czechoslovakia in 1989 up until 2012, David Drozd maintains that about a half of all the Czech stagings of Shakespeare in the period had been performed in Hilský's translation (see Drozd 2012: 178–9).

10 Martin Hilský has become the second person to single-handedly translate Shakespeare's entire *oeuvre* into Czech, the first being the amateur translator František Nevrla in the early 1960s (see Drábek 2005: 119).

11 According to the 8 September 2019 news release, the 2019 season, between 25 June and 6 September, staged 153 performances for 99,782 theatregoers in Prague, Brno, Ostrava and Bratislava (see Letní shakespearovské slavnosti 2019).

References

Černý, Jindřich (2007), *Osudy českého divadla po druhé světové válce: Divadlo a společnost 1945–1955* [Fortunes of the Czech Theatre after WWII: Theatre and Society 1945–1955], Prague: Academia.

Císař, Jan (2006), *Přehled dějin českého divadla* [A Survey of the History of the Czech Theatre], Prague: Akademie múzických umění.

Dobson, Michael (1992), *The Making of the National Poet: Shakespeare, Adaptation and Authorship, 1660–1769*, Oxford: Oxford University Press.

Drábek, Pavel (2005), 'František Nevrla's Translation of *Hamlet*', *Brno Studies in English* 31: 119–27.

Drábek, Pavel (2012), *České pokusy o Shakespeara* [Czech Attempts at Shakespeare], Brno: Větrné mlýny.

Drábek, Pavel (2017a), 'Shakespeare in the Czech Lands', in *Shakespeare in Prague: Imagining the Bard in the Heart of Europe*, Exhibition catalogue, Columbus Museum of Art, The Ohio State University's College of Arts and Sciences Arts Initiative, Arts and Theatre Institute,

Prague, Czech Republic. Available online: https://www.uiw.edu/chass/_docs/theatre/shakespeare-in-prague-catalogue.pdf (accessed 28 November 2019).

Drábek, Pavel (2017b), '"Spirit, fine spirit, Ile free thee": Shakespeare's Spaces of Freedom on the Czech Stage', unpublished keynote lecture at the *Shakespeare in Prague* conference, Ohio State University, 3–4 March 2017.

Drozd, David (2012), 'William Shakespeare: Dílo. Překlad Martin Hilský. Vklady, výklady (a úklady) shakespearovského překladu' [The Works of William Shakespeare translated by Martin Hilský: Contributions, Interpretations (and Intrigues) of Shakespearean Translation], *Theatralia* 15 (1): 179–89.

Koubská, Vlasta (2017), 'The Search for the Play, Fate, and Dream in Shakespeare's Scenographic Space: Zelenka, Tröster, and Muzika', in *Shakespeare in Prague: Imagining the Bard in the Heart of Europe*, Exhibition catalogue, Columbus Museum of Art, The Ohio State University's College of Arts and Sciences Arts Initiative, Arts and Theatre Institute, Prague, Czech Republic, National Museum, Prague, Czech Republic. Available online: https://www.uiw.edu/chass/_docs/theatre/shakespeare-in-prague-catalogue.pdf (accessed 28 November 2019).

Letní shakespearovské slavnosti [Summer Shakespeare Festival] (2019), 'Tisková zpráva, 8. září 2019', Press Release, 8 September. Available online: https://www.shakespeare.cz/2019/cz/-tz-uctyhodnych-dvacet-let-podporuje-skupina-ppf-letni-shakespearovske-slavnosti-ty-maji-za-sebou-dalsi-vydarenou-sezonu-/290/ (accessed 28 November 2019).

Limon, Jerzy (1985), *Gentlemen of a Company: English Players in Central and Eastern Europe 1590–1660*, Cambridge: Cambridge University Press.

Mikulka, Vladimír (2002), 'Triumfální divadelní návrat Jana Třísky' [Jan Tříska's Triumphant Theatrical Comeback], *Mladá fronta Dnes* 13.155: B/5.

Mišterová, Ivona (2015), 'Inter Arma Non Silent Musae: Shakespeare as a Symbol of the Czech Pro-Allied Attitude during the Great War', *Brno Studies in English* 41 (2): 73–89.

'pl' [Pavla Landová] (1990), 'Hraje se pro lidi!' [We Play for People!], *Tvar* 1.23: 3.

Sheen, Erica, and Isabel Karremann, eds (2016), *Shakespeare in Cold War Europe: Conflict, Commemoration, Celebration*, London: Palgrave Macmillan.

Stříbrný, Zdeněk (2000), *Shakespeare and Eastern Europe*, Oxford: Oxford University Press.

Tuma, Mirko (1976), 'Memories of Theresienstadt', *Performing Arts Journal* 1 (2): 12–18.

Virtual Study of the Theatre Institute [of Prague, Czech Republic] (n.d.). Available online: https://vis.idu.cz/?lang=en (accessed 28 November 2019).

Wild, Jana B., ed. (2015), *Zrkadlá (pre) doby: Shakespeare v divadle Strednej Európy* [Mirrors of/for the Times: Shakespeare in Central European Theatre], Bratislava: Vysoká škola múzických umení.

Worthen, Hana (2007), 'Within and Beyond: Pavel Kohout's *Play Makbeth* and its Audiences', *Gramma: Journal of Theory and Criticism* 15: 111–32.

5

Globolatry in Germany: The Shakespeare Festival at Neuss – a dramaturg's perspective

Vanessa Schormann

Prologue

William Shakespeare would surely be amazed to see the scale of his popularity in Germany today. Already at the turn of the nineteenth century, the German writer and translator August Wilhelm von Schlegel declared that William Shakespeare was '*ganz unser*' (entirely ours). In 1864, on Shakespeare's 300th birthday, the German Shakespeare Society was founded, now one of the world's oldest Shakespeare Associations. And in 1904 one of the first and now longest-standing statues of Shakespeare on the European continent was erected in Weimar. German was the first language into which Shakespeare's plays were translated and today his life and works are taught in German schools and universities. Shakespeare is the most often played author in German theatres and every year there are more Shakespeare productions staged in Germany than in the UK (see Dickson 2015). Therefore, it should be no surprise that one of the most successful international Shakespeare festivals takes place in Neuss, Germany, in a replica of the Globe Theatre.

Looking at the long and fruitful relationship between Shakespeare and German culture, this chapter will focus on the history and development of the International Shakespeare Festival at the Globe Theatre in Neuss. As the festival's Dramaturg and Director of Globe Neuss Education I will not only introduce the Globe replica as an ideal theatre location for a Shakespeare festival but discuss the challenges associated with this particular theatre as well as the advantages it offers for audience and actors alike. I will argue that the festival's international and diversified programme not only creates a special experience but manifests a celebration of Shakespeare and his work that is unique in Europe and has its roots in Shakespeare's time when companies left England to bring his plays to the continent.

Globetrotting

The German fascination with Shakespeare began within his own lifetime. In the late sixteenth century, when theatres in England were closed due to the plague, the companies left London and crossed the English Channel to show the plays by Shakespeare and other English playwrights all across Europe. These plays were staged at fencing schools, town markets, inn-yards and churchyards as well as royal courts. Depending on the location and different audiences, the performance style and the scripts were adjusted and adapted.

In Germany, the so-called 'English Comedians' regularly visited Dresden, Nürnberg, Frankfurt and Kassel, cities in which they often enjoyed aristocratic patronage. In Kassel and Gdansk – the latter now in Poland (and with its own eminent Shakespeare festival) but in the seventeenth century an independent German-speaking cosmopolitan port city – they even built a theatre for the travelling players, resembling the Elizabethan playhouses in form and function (see Limon 1985 and Williams 1990). In the nineteenth century, the German dramaturg and director Ludwig Tieck erected a Shakespearean stage for the first production of *A Midsummer Night's Dream* in German which he directed in Potsdam in 1843. The first full replica of the Globe Theatre was built in London in 1912 and inspired the building of replicas in the USA from 1934 onwards (Schormann 2002: 31). As a young man, the American actor Sam

Wanamaker played in one of the Globe replicas in Cleveland, and this experience inspired him to reconstruct Shakespeare's Globe near its original site when he came to London in the 1940s. The planning was time consuming and it was not until 1988 that the laying of the foundation stone took place. By that time, replicas of the Globe had already been built in Tokyo, Japan and Rheda-Wiedenbrück, Germany.

German Globes

In London in the mid-1980s nobody knew whether Wanamaker's dream to reconstruct Shakespeare's Globe would come true; but at the same time, a small replica of the Globe opened in Rheda-Wiedenbrück, a little town in the west of Germany. In 1987, the German actor and director Reinhard Schiele planned to build a mobile stage for his touring theatre company Schloßtheater Overhagen. Being inspired by the plans for Shakespeare's Globe in London, his aim was not to build a replica of Shakespeare's original Globe Theatre, but to design a touring stage in a twelve-sided building that resembled elements of an Elizabethan theatre and could be erected and dismantled on any market place or fairground. However, due to fire regulations, he was forced to develop a structure of heavy steel and wood which made it impossible to use it as a touring stage. The Globe in Neuss resembles the idea of an Elizabethan playhouse and can be seen as a modern interpretation of Shakespeare's Globe Theatre, built with today's technology and material. It revives an important tradition of the European theatre in form and function (Schormann 2002: 129).

This modern Globe replica was built in about ten weeks and opened with a production of *A Midsummer Night's Dream* on 11 June 1988 as part of the National Garden Festival in Rheda-Wiedenbrück. The cultural event ran all summer and involved several guest companies. One of them was the Bremer Shakespeare Company, one of the best-known Shakespeare companies in Germany, founded in 1984. After the closure of the Garden Festival the city of Rheda-Wiedenbrück had no interest in keeping the theatre and offered it for sale. The cities of Kassel, Frankfurt, Nürnberg, Bochum and Bremen all showed an interest, but it was eventually the city of Neuss, one of the oldest cities in Germany, situated on the Rhine not far from Düsseldorf, that bought the theatre.

It was during the negotiations for a guest performance of the Bremer Shakespeare Company for the Neusser Bauverein's 100th anniversary in Neuss that one of the company's founding members, Norbert Kentrup, a native of Neuss, mentioned that the Globe in Rheda-Wiedenbrück was up for sale.[1] For the actor Kentrup this little Globe Theatre, unique in Europe at the time, was a revelation.[2] In 1991 town officials, architects and engineers from Neuss went to look at it and the city council decided to buy it. In Shakespeare's time the first purpose-built theatre, called the Theatre, was dismantled and its timbers carried across the River Thames to be reused for the erection of a new theatre called the Globe. Likewise, the Globe in Rheda-Wiedenbrück was taken apart and its pieces were 'carried' to Neuss to be re-erected there. For its location, the old river bed of the Rhine was chosen, a place in the middle of greenery, next to the horse racecourse in Neuss (see Maurer and Schanko 1998).

The city of Neuss is a thriving business location with a population of about 160,000. It is situated at the crossing of both historic and modern trade routes. After the Romans had established a huge military camp south of the old city, a civil settlement was founded at the site of latter-day Neuss. It developed into a flourishing centre of trade, a position that Neuss has managed to maintain until today. Set in the unique landscape of the Lower Rhine region, it is close to the North Rhine-Westphalian capital of Düsseldorf as well as to Köln and the cities of the Ruhr metropolis.[3]

Neuss is not primarily known as a tourist city despite the fact that there are several cultural institutions. Most famous are the Langen Art Foundation and Insel Hombroich at the outskirts of the city. In town there are touristic sites like the Sels Museum or historic buildings like the impressive Basilica of Saint Quirinus, the Obertor – both dating from the thirteenth century – or the Zeughaus, a seventeenth-century monastery, reused by Napoleon as an armoury before it became a concert hall today. Although they are all within walking distance to the Globe, audiences who come to Neuss to visit the Shakespeare Festival seldom stay to get to know these attractions. Rather, they enjoy the short distance to the cities of Düsseldorf or Köln for a visit there. On the other hand, people who come to stay in Neuss on a business trip or to attend a conference do not necessarily visit the festival. And there are many citizens in Neuss who do not even know about this treasure in their own town.

The Globe in Neuss is neither exactly a cultural heritage site nor does it function primarily as a tourist attraction. As a replica it is a modern idea of Shakespeare's Globe, with no intention of being architecturally or historically correct.[4] The same applies to the other Globe replicas in Germany which were built hereafter. The Globe replica in Schwäbisch Hall was built in 1999 and is officially described as 'a multi-storey, rain-proof and temperature-controlled open-air with a wide range of entertainment possibilities, which can seat a total of 370 spectators'.[5] It is mainly used for its own Shakespeare productions during the town's annual Theatre Festival in June. The former Rhein Opera Globe (ROM) built in Düsseldorf in 2006 as an interim theatre during the closure of the opera-house, is now situated in Rietberg, called Cultura Sparkassen Theater, and is used for concerts, various touring theatre productions and conferences. The Globe in Rust was originally built as a theatre in Switzerland. Since it was sold to the Europa Park Rust, it functions as a tourist attraction in the English Corner of the fun park (Schormann 2002: 141ff.). None of them offers a festival with international interpretations of Shakespeare's plays and so far none of them has been interested in an exchange or theatrical cooperation with the festival in Neuss.[6] What all have in common is the attractive 'one room' concept offering a unique intimacy between audience and artists.

The Globe Neuss

Reusing the material of the Globe in Rheda-Wiedenbrück, the Globe in Neuss is a twelve-sided building built in steel and wood. It measures 21 metres in diameter and would fit into the yard of the reconstructed Globe in London which measures about 30 metres in diameter. The Globe in Neuss is about 11 metres high and, just like the original Globe, the replica has three galleries for the audience. Theatregoers sit on cushioned seats in the first four rows in front of an apron stage and another four rows in the first gallery opposite the stage. The remaining audience is seated on wooden benches. A central entrance door is used on the main floor (stalls) and two external staircases lead up to the seats and benches in the galleries. As the stage does not project very far into the auditorium the audience does not really surround it on three sides, but the intimacy is comparable to the London Globe as actors on stage and the nearly 500 audience members share one room and are not separated by any proscenium arch or curtain.

No one in the audience sits more than 10 metres from the stage, there are no pillars on stage nor is there a roof above the stage. The second and third galleries in the auditorium extend above the stage offering a gallery space that can be used by the actors for certain scenes, though at the risk of restricted view for parts of the audience. Mobile staircases allow the actors to descend from the middle gallery onto the stage. A temporary gangway in front of the stage also allows actors to enter and exit the stage from the auditorium. Originally, the theatre was planned with a roof that could be opened in order to give the playhouse an open-air atmosphere. In Neuss this system is no longer in operation. The theatre today is covered with a white canvas that allows the daylight to shine through. Companies have the option to shut the light out with a black canvas that can be fitted underneath the roof canvas.

The empty stage is about a metre high and measures 100 square metres. There are four trap doors on stage which allow access from below. The stage extends to the back of the theatre and can be fully used by companies, bearing in mind that action at the back will be beyond the range of vision for part of the audience. Performing companies usually separate the back of the stage with fabrics and use the space behind as a backstage area, for example for costume changes. The greenroom, as well as two artist's wardrobes, toilets and showers are situated behind the stage galleries on the first and second floor. As the theatre has no heating or air conditioning system, air and daylight can only be let in by opening the black and white wooden shutters in the first and second galleries. These shutters are a distinctive feature of the theatre's exterior.

Shakespeare Festival at the Globe Neuss

The Shakespeare Festival at the Globe in Neuss is organized by the Neuss cultural office, which each summer rents the Globe Theatre from the city as a venue for the festival.[7] The Globe in Neuss opened on the weekend of 13 September 1991 with Shakespeare's *Der Widerspenstigen Zähmung* (*The Taming of the Shrew*) and *Antonius und Cleopatra* (*Antony and Cleopatra*) both played by the Bremer Shakespeare Company, who also presented *Der Sturm* (*The Tempest*) and *Die Lustigen Weiber von Windsor* (*The Merry Wives of Windsor*) on the following weekend. These four performances were already announced as 'The First Shakespeare Festival'. The success of these events convinced the city authorities to continue and they appointed Dr Rainer Wiertz, Officer for Cultural Affairs of the city of Neuss, to be the festival's artistic director. In 1992, the festival had already expanded to run for two weeks at the end of June. Apart from the Bremer Shakespeare Company, other companies from Germany were invited, as well as the Rheinische Landestheater which is the municipal theatre in Neuss but also functions as a touring theatre for the area.[8] An international touch was added by inviting the Medieval Players from London, the Roma-Theatre Pralipe from Macedonia and the Keli Company from India, who presented their celebrated *Kathakali-Lear*.

Over the years, the festival has not only extended in duration – since 1996 it has run for four weeks every year in June and July – but focused even more on international companies presenting their Shakespeare productions in their own language and style. By the third Shakespeare Festival in 1993, a tradition developed of inviting young actors from German and English drama schools to show a Shakespeare production, as well as inviting well-known musicians to give concerts of classical or modern music inspired by Shakespeare's plays. Another tradition began in 1994 when Patrick Spottiswoode, Director of Education at the Globe in London, came for the first time to present his now legendary lecture on *Shakespeare and the Globe*.

The close connection between the Globes in Neuss and London began when Sam Wanamaker accepted the invitation of Rudolph Küppers, one of the architects responsible for the re-erection of the Globe in Neuss, to attend its opening in 1991. Wanamaker's impression of the Globe replica is not recorded, but he was certainly fascinated by the Bremer Shakespeare Company's acting style as he invited them to play their production of *Die Lustigen Weiber von Windsor* (*The Merry Wives of Windsor*) on a temporary stage on the building site of the Globe in London in the spring of 1993. Due to this chance meeting, the first company to play in the reconstructed Globe in London was a German company. The happy relationship with the Globe as the 'bigger but younger brother' in London was intensified through the Globe Touring Ensemble, founded by the London Globe's artistic director Dominic Dromgoole. He revived the tradition of a Shakespearean travelling company and founded an ensemble which tours its productions after performing them at the London Globe.[9] Since 2008 they have been bringing their productions to Neuss. All travelling companies visiting the Shakespeare Festival in Neuss carry on a tradition that was already practiced in Shakespeare's time. But it is the 'Globe to Globe' partnership that is unique, as so far no other Globe replica worldwide runs an annual international Shakespeare Festival and is also visited by the Globe Touring Ensemble from London.

The Festival's programme, companies and productions

The annual programme is planned by Dr Rainer Wiertz, the festival's artistic director, and discussed with me as his dramaturg. Choices are made by travelling to various international and national theatre festivals, watching productions by theatres and companies who enrol to take part at the festival in Neuss, as well as by the exchange of information with a worldwide and national network of theatre practitioners.

Each year the Shakespeare Festival offers about forty different theatrical or musical events during its four-week run in June and July. There are usually about thirteen to sixteen different companies which present between twelve and fifteen productions. For most companies, it is a great privilege to be invited as it often helps them to promote their shows for further performances while on tour. Generally, the theatre has a 93 per cent occupancy. Each year about 14,500 visitors come to Neuss from all over Germany and its bordering countries, with a majority of people from North-Rhine-Westphalia, to enjoy one or more of the thirty to thirty-six performances of the national and international globetrotting companies. Whether comedies, tragedies, histories or his late plays (romances), all genres of Shakespeare's plays are welcome at the festival in Neuss. Throughout the last thirty years, some plays have been presented more often than others. *A Midsummer Night's Dream* is the most popular among the comedies and has been presented about twenty-five times in thirty years, followed by twenty-three different productions of *Twelfth Night*. The comedies *Much Ado about Nothing*, *As You Like It*, *The Taming of the Shrew*, *The Comedy of Errors* and *The Merchant of Venice* have been performed more than ten times since 1991, as have Shakespeare's late plays *The Tempest* and *The Winter's Tale*. Among the tragedies, *Romeo and Juliet* has been presented more often than any other, followed by *Macbeth* and *Hamlet*. Each has been played about twenty times in different interpretations, while *King Lear* and *Othello* have been played more than ten times so far. Although there are usually fewer productions of Shakespeare's histories on offer, *Richard III* has been shown in more than eight national and international variations so far. Even *Henry V* and *Henry VIII* have been played more than three times each in the past years. Edward Hall's production of *Henry V* with his company Propeller in 1997 prompted the longest applause in the festival's history: it lasted nearly fifteen minutes.

Apart from Shakespeare's plays, the festival's programme regularly offers plays by Shakespeare's contemporaries Ben Jonson, Thomas Middleton, John Fletcher or Christopher Marlowe. Adaptations of Shakespeare's plays or dramas which deal with themes of Shakespeare's time, for example Friedrich Schiller's *Maria Stuart* (*Mary Stuart*) are also welcome, as are contemporary plays like Mike Bartlett's *Charles III*, written in Shakespearean pentameter. The festival's theatrical programme is also often supplemented by classical or pop concerts, readings, lectures and other arts like puppet theatre. Internationally well-known musicians come to sing or play music inspired by Shakespeare's plays. Henry Purcell's semi-operas, like *The Fairy Queen* or *King Arthur*, have already been presented in fascinating productions. Famous actors, for example the well-known German actress Senta Berger, have been invited to read Shakespeare's sonnets or poetry and are often accompanied by musicians who even sometimes play on period instruments. A special highlight was the jazz version of Shakespeare's sonnets composed and performed by the pianist and singer Caroll van Welden from Belgium in 2013.

More than eighty different companies have performed nearly all of Shakespeare's plays on the Globe stage in Neuss since the opening of the Shakespeare Festival in 1991. Until now about twenty different companies from Germany, seventeen companies from London and six more from other cities in Britain, ten companies from France and seven from Italy have been invited to the festival. Other companies that give the festival further international character come from Sweden, the Netherlands, Switzerland, Austria, Spain, Portugal, Israel, Hungary, Latvia, Poland, Georgia, Russia, as well as from the USA, Argentina, Brazil, Africa, South Korea, China and Japan.

Since the founding of the European Shakespeare Festivals Network (ESFN) in 2010, Shakespeare Festivals in Armenia, Bohemia (now, the Czech Republic), Denmark, England, Germany, Hungary, Romania, France, Macedonia, Serbia and Poland regularly exchange information on companies and productions and sometimes even cooperate in financing the travelling expenses of companies that are invited to the European Shakespeare Festivals.[10] The benefits of being in a close exchange with one another and regularly visiting the other festivals are stated by Rainer Wiertz (2020):

> I learned much about the other festivals, and specially about the big differences between each of them; differences in financing (from no subsidies to enormous state money), in ticket fees (from as little as the equivalent of €5 to more than €60), in program preferences (from community work and audience oriented traditional performances to the hippest avant garde productions). The exchange with the colleagues is always a gain of knowledge, and the visit to their festival highly fascinating. Much more interesting than the European funding, at least for us in Neuss.

The Shakespeare Festival in Neuss is a self-financed organization which largely gets by without subsidies, living off the sale of tickets, the income from the bar and shop, as well as the generous donations from the 'Friends of the Globe' and the main sponsor, the Sparkasse Neuss. As Wiertz comments: 'They all contribute significantly to the fact that our Shakespeare Festival can be held with selected German and International productions for the joy and benefit of the numerous and paying audience.'[11]

In seeking productions for the festival in Neuss we have to bear in mind that most Shakespeare productions produced for a traditional proscenium arch stage – with their large stage designs and sets as well as superstructures and technical equipment – do not fit the Globe stage. We therefore look for companies that combine a high quality of acting with unusual interpretations offered in a simple setting. Therefore, most of the invited companies are small, independent and unsubsidized. They often do not have their own theatre and are dependent on touring their productions. Not only do they have to attract a wide audience but they have to be responsive to a variety of stage conditions. This flexibility helps when coming to the festival in Neuss as the Globe stage is limited in space and offers special challenges like playing to three sides and heights in the auditorium. Companies who use or incorporate modern versions of the 'original practices' of Shakespeare's time sometimes find it easier to adapt their acting style to the Globe stage. As Wiertz notes:

> With the programme's selection we want to show that folk theatre and quality are not mutually exclusive, but can even form a constituency for a fresh and refreshing form of theatre. Whether traditional or avant-garde, it must always be close to the audience, the stage should not be closed off from the audience and the audience should not only witness an event, but be involved and emotionally part of it.
>
> (2010: 300)

As in Shakespeare's time, when just about everyone in London society went to the theatre, the festival's broad audience encompasses a wide range of ages and classes and therefore we aim to offer productions for all tastes and expectations. Among the audience members are the ones who want to enjoy a nice evening in an unusual setting. Some come to watch a German Shakespeare production shown on a 'Shakespearean stage', others claim to know their Shakespeare and want to see a new production in the original language, and then there are the ones who want to see a special production that is exotic or experimental.

Most popular are the English-speaking companies with their productions. Just as in Shakespeare's time, the audience come 'to hear a play', which means they want to familiarize themselves with the spoken text of Shakespeare in the original. Not only teachers and school classes come to see the play that is to be read in class put into practice, but the theatre freaks, members of the educated classes, native speakers and newcomers to Shakespeare alike come to seize the opportunity to deal with the original. Whether Edward Hall's Propeller Company, Stephen Jameson's Alma Mater, the Handlebards or the Globe Touring Company from the Globe in London, they all enjoy great popularity and guarantee a sold-out house every year. From the USA, companies like Aquilla Theatre Company from New York, the Shenandoah Shakespeare Company (now the American Shakespeare Center based in the Blackfriars Theatre in Staunton, Virginia) or the legendary Q-Brothers from Chicago, who rap Shakespeare, also have a huge fan base among the festival's visitors. While planning the programme we also have audiences in mind who are curious to listen to foreign and exotic languages as well as watching companies that combine their cultural heritage with the story and themes of Shakespeare's plays. Unforgettable are the visits of the Roy-e-Sabs Theatre, Kabul (Afghanistan), the Kote Marjanishvili State Drama Theatre, Tiflis (Georgia) and the Maladype Theatre from Budapest (Hungary).

Nearly every country in the world has its own Shakespeare tradition, but it is the mixing or incorporating of their own cultural stories, customs and traditions into Shakespeare's plays that makes their interpretations incomparable and deeply touching. Neuss audiences are frequently exposed to non-Anglophone and non-European theatre-making by companies who come from the far corners of the Earth, such as Ryutopia Noh Theatre Shakespeare Company, Niigata (Japan), Tang-Shu Wing Theatre Studio, Hong Kong (China), Yohangza Theatre Company (South Korea), Cia Completa Mente Solta, Rio de Janeiro (Brazil) and Over the Edge (Zimbabwe). All these companies impress and inspire with their special aesthetics as well as their individual characteristic interpretations and acting styles and enrich the festival with an international flair.

The main attraction of watching a German Shakespeare production at the festival goes hand in hand with the companies' advantage of using a modern German translation that turns a 400-year-old text into everyday language with all the risqué and ambiguous allusions Shakespeare used in his time. Apart from the fact that the translation helps a German audience to understand the story and themes of the play, the experience of listening to the text is much closer to the one at the time when Shakespeare presented his plays.

Among the most popular German companies is the Bremer Shakespeare Company, who opened the festival in 1991 and since then has been presenting one or two productions annually. They know how to inspire the audience with their Shakespeare productions that are performed with a combination of poetic intensity and knockabout physicality that probably characterized theatre in Shakespeare's time. With simple sets and costumes, as well as Elizabethan playing devices like cross-dressing and the direct addressing of the audience, they demonstrate the vivid power of Elizabethan theatre. The festival's audience loves the company's unique style, which is characterized by its small cast, lots of gender switches and quick costume changes. They understand their performance as a joint event celebrated with the audience and actors alike. The ensemble relies on the audience's imagination, on their delight in thinking about and sympathizing with what they see or hear.[12] Other German companies, such as the Neues Globe Theater, Globe Ensemble Berlin, Shakespeare Company Berlin and the Poetenpack, follow this approach in a variety of ways and therefore enrich the festival's programme with lively productions often presented in a certain recognizable aesthetic and often enriched with specially produced live played music.

The Neuss experience

Although only a small replica of the original Globe, the Globe Neuss nevertheless still focuses on the same devices Shakespeare had in mind when writing his plays: the close relationship between actors and audiences. Patrick Spottiswoode, founding Director of Globe Education London who annually performs his celebrated lecture on Shakespeare's Globe at the festival, states:

> I relish the intimacy of the space and the intellectual curiosity of the audience in Neuss. Every day a different language and every day a different performance style but the audiences keep coming. It is a hidden gem. It is certainly a difficult space to play – even for a one person show. There is only a small rectangle on stage the size of a table tennis table from which you can be seen by everyone in the theatre. But the intimacy is extraordinary: the entire Globe Neuss would fit within the yard of the Bankside Globe.
>
> (2020)

Rainer Wiertz confirms: 'It is the intimacy, the semi-circular arrangement of the rows of seats around the stage which the spectator seizes at the right moment as an opportunity to be enchanted by the energy that rises from the joint action between the stage and the audience like in a pressure cooker' (2010).

As the Neuss Globe Theatre consists only of stage and auditorium, facilities like the foyer with bar, shop, catering area and toilets are situated in a building opposite the Globe, a former horse-racing betting hall from the 1950s, which outside festival time is used as a venue for cultural events, dance parties and concerts. Every year a design team decorates the hall with fabric and furniture to give it a cozy theatrical atmosphere. Colours of red and gold dominate and many Shakespearean figurines, flowers, candles and painted quotes from Shakespeare's texts enhance the special interior design of this pop-up foyer. Outside the hall, around the Globe Theatre, this beautifully designed atmosphere expands into a 'Shakes-beer-garden' with benches and tables decorated with candles and flowers for the audience and artists to happily carouse deep into the night. At the indoor bar as well as in a small kiosk outside, drinks and snacks are sold before and after the shows, as well as during the intervals. Most popular are the handmade and pre-packed picnic baskets for two, which can be pre-ordered. Well-loved scones with clotted cream and jam are sold before the matinee shows at weekends. In a separate area, in front of the former horse boxes, audience members can bring and have their own picnic, a tradition that is also gladly followed.

Audience members often arrive two hours prior to the performance, to attend and enjoy the daily introductions to the play, the company and its production which are offered by me as the festival's dramaturg. The explanations and background knowledge of the individual approaches of each company facilitate access to their interpretations and help theatergoers understand different cultural approaches that might be unfamiliar. Incorporated in the introduction is a short interview with me and a director or actor of the performing company offering further insights and the opportunity to get to know the artist and thus already create a proximity that is usually not known in conventional theatres. The same applies to the popular 'Theatre Talks' and 'Meet and Greet' sessions offered after some performances.

These free events for the audience belong to the intensive Education programme, which since 2005 has been planned and organized by me as Director of Globe Neuss Education with my team.[13] During the four weeks of the festival we offer daily workshops for pupils and students, teacher's courses, study days, guided tours and lectures. Each season one show is offered just for schools at reduced ticket prices and ever since 2017 every festival season has had a special day for children. Children from the age of six to twelve spend a whole day at the Globe visiting workshops with foreign actors, Shakespeare storytelling sessions, guided tours around the theatre as well as workshops on tailoring costumes out of paper or building small Globe models. All this educational work takes place on the festival's site, in and around the Globe and therefore helps to arouse a curiosity among the next generation of spectators, not only for the festival but for Shakespeare and his timeless plays.

Epilogue

Assuming that Shakespeare wrote roughly half of his plays for the Globe Theatre, it is not surprising that a replica of this theatre today is an ideal venue for his plays at a festival. It is no coincidence that this has come to fruition in Germany, a country that has a reception history of Shakespeare's works stretching back to the playwright's own time and which has shown a sustained interest in the original performance space and its replication long before it was realized in the UK.

At the Shakespeare Festival in Neuss it is not only the skill of the actors, their language, gestures and expressions, the costumes, the music or the effective lighting which takes centre stage. It is the wide range of the programming around Shakespeare's work, the mixture of German and international companies and their varying interpretations of Shakespeare's plays, often presented with simple sets in different styles and languages, that makes the festival outstanding and attractive for a broad audience.

With more than thirty productions annually, the multifaceted festival programme shows the different ways in which Shakespeare's works can be realized. Watching the German and international productions shown at the festival throughout the last thirty years the spectator not only gets a fascinating overview of the worldwide theatre-productive engagement with Shakespeare's work, but can see that even the most peculiar translation, the most remote processing, in the most radical reduction where there are only indelible traces of his work, can offer exciting new insights. Played in a room that follows the simple devices of the stage and auditorium which Shakespeare had in mind when writing his plays enhances the experience of listening to the plays, their themes and stories. It even helps to discover a dramaturgy that is often lost in Shakespeare productions elsewhere.

Whatever the individual spectator's intention is to revisit the festival in Neuss each summer, year after year, whether it is a company's specific style and aesthetic or the opportunity to listen to Shakespeare in his original or another foreign language, what all audience members have in common is that they want to enjoy a special evening, sharing their experience of celebrating Shakespeare in a unique theatre space and its unusual surroundings with likeminded people. As I have argued, the Globe in Neuss is neither a tourist attraction nor an historical heritage site, but it is the Globe's challenging simplicity as well as the festival's relaxed, intimate and uncomplicated atmosphere before, during and after the shows which create a real pleasure for all senses, a fascinating Shakespeare experience that has now been celebrated in Neuss for thirty years and will hopefully be enjoyed for many more to come. Globe and Shakespeare – a consummation for which many have devoutly wished, and one that has been brought to thrilling and festive life in Germany.

Notes

1 Since its foundation in 1891 the building association has been shaping the residential and building culture in Neuss in close cooperation with the city, https://www.neusserbauverein.de/ (accessed 20 March 2021).
2 For Kentrup it was the theatre Peter Brook talks about in his book *The Empty Space* (1968) or Robert Weimann describes in *Shakespeare and the Popular Tradition in the Theatre* (1967). See Norbert Kentrup (2018).

3 Neuss: City Profile, https://www.neuss.de/english/city-profile/neuss-location (accessed 20 March 2021).
4 The same applies to the other three German Globes and the ones being planned in Berlin and Coburg.
5 Freilichtspiele Schwäbisch Hall: Das Neue Globe, https://www.freilichtspiele-hall.de/neues-globe/das-theater.html (accessed 20 March 2021). The former Globe here, opened in 2000 (see Schormann 2002: 148ff.). It was dismantled in 2016 and brought to Berlin to be re-erected there; see https://globe.berlin/ (accessed 20 March 2021).
6 This also applies to the Globe replica in Rome, Italy, which also runs a Shakespeare Festival (see Chapter 7 of this volume).
7 Officially, the Globe can be rented for any cultural event, but apart from the Shakespeare Festival there are only occasional events like concerts, musical shows or wedding ceremonies.
8 For many years, the Rheinische Landestheater used the Globe Theatre for one of their productions, usually shown outside the festival's season but also once during the festival. Until today, the Rheinische Landestheater still presents at least one of its productions as a guest performance during the festival.
9 In addition to the Globe Touring Ensemble, actors from the Globe in London produced *Hamlet*: they went on a two-year tour to every country in the world from 2014 to 2016 and called it 'Globe to Globe Hamlet'; see Dromgoole (2017); also http://globetoglobe.shakespearesglobe.com/ (accessed 20 March 2021).
10 A joint application for funding was approved by the European Commission for the first time in 2010. For more information on the European Shakespeare Festivals Network, see http://esfn.eu/ (accessed 20 March 2021).
11 Wiertz (2010: 299). Translation by the author of this chapter.
12 For further information about the company, see https://www.shakespeare-company.com/ (accessed 20 March 2021).
13 For more information, see https://www.shakespeare-festival.de/de/education/ (accessed 20 March 2021).

References

Dickson, Andrew (2015), *Worlds Elsewhere: Journeys Around Shakespeare's Globe*, London: Penguin.
Dromgoole, Dominic (2017), *Hamlet: Globe to Globe*, Edinburgh: Canongate Books.
Kentrup, Norbert (2018), *Der süße Geschmack von Freiheit* [The Sweet Taste of Freedom], Bremen: Kellner Verlag.

Limon, Jerzy (1985), *Gentlemen of a Company: English Players in Central and Eastern Europe, 1590–1660*, Cambridge: Cambridge University Press.

Maurer, Burkard, and Ulrike Schanko, eds (1998), *Globe Theater Neuss*, Neuss: Stadt Neuss, Der Bürgermeister in Zusammenarbeit mit dem Rheinischen Landestheater.

Schormann, Vanessa (2002), *Shakespeares Globe. Repliken, Rekonstructionen und Bespielbarkeit* [Shakespeare's Globe. Replicas, Reconstructions and Playability], Heidelberg: Winter Verlag.

Spottiswoode, Patrick (2020), in conversation with Vanessa Schormann, 19 November 2020.

Wiertz, Rainer (2010), 'Gelegenheit und Augenblick. 20 Jahre Shakespeare-Festival in Neuss' [Opportunity and the Moment. 20 Years of the Shakespeare Festival in Neuss], in Thomas Ludewig and Jens Metzdorf, eds, *Novaesium 2010. Neusser Jahrbuch für Kunst, Kultur und Geschichte* [Novaesium 2010. Neuss Yearbook for Art, Culture and History], Neuss: Clemens-Sels-Museum und Stadtarchiv Neuss.

Wiertz, Rainer (2020), in conversation with Vanessa Schormann, 11 November.

Williams, Simon (1990), *Shakespeare on the German Stage: 1586–1914*, Cambridge: Cambridge University Press.

6

A world's stage for many players: The International Shakespeare Festival – Craiova (Romania)

Nicoleta Cinpoeş

In a spectacle of epic proportions, *Ubu Rex with Scenes from Macbeth* swept its audiences off their feet, first in Craiova and then in Edinburgh and Braunschweig, with its high-energy, mesmerizing and iconoclastic mash-up of Jarry and Shakespeare, who made perfect bedfellows in Silviu Purcărete's auteur-ial hands. The production dissected meticulously the relationship between power and the masses it subordinated: swaddled in white onesies, like giant toddlers, Ma and Pa Ubu threw tantrum after tantrum and stepped over every single body in their way to climb to the top. With malice and egos inflating as fast as their fat costumes, they disposed of their minions with the same easiness they discarded one accessory or outfit after another, eventually saturating the white chromatics of their world with red.

The picture this production painted was too close for comfort, both for audiences in Craiova when it opened in 1990 and when it toured to the Edinburgh Festival and Braunschweig's Theaterformen, in 1991. For Romanians, it 'bore painful similarities with Romanian reality' less than a year after the 1989 Revolution

(Ichim 1991). For international audiences, the 'two plays about bloody tyrants ... shown to be absurd photographic negatives of each other' in this production freshly out of the Eastern Bloc 'gave a horrid frisson of topicality' as it opened in Edinburgh just as 'the August coup against Gorbachev' made world news (Taylor 1997). The production's lingering final image, of 'the Ceaușescu-like Ubus', '[u]pright in their satin-lined coffins', Taylor recalls, 'fix[ed] the audience with a fatuous, knowing smirk, as if to say "Don't worry, we'll be back"' (1997).

And back they were, in ways 1991 could only partially envisage. Romania's return to neo-communism and Craiova's National Theatre's return to Edinburgh bringing another 'not ... pretty' (Taylor 1997) Shakespeare Purcărete-style in 1992, make the backdrop to my pursuit here. Its main story is about the outcomes and long-term impact of Craiova's National's festivalling experience abroad. Edinburgh and the success of Purcărete's Shakespeare productions with the Craiova National Theatre brought home the managing director Emil Boroghină's dream of creating a festival, entirely dedicated to Shakespeare, as he has said on numerous occasions (Cinpoeș 2003). Fuelled by Boroghină's 'vision and boundless courage' (Shevtsova 2012: 352) as actor, director and, at the time, manager of the National, this dream began to gain substance slowly but surely with the inauguration of the Craiova Shakespeare Festival in 1994. Marking Shakespeare's 430th birthday year proved fortuitous: the festival has been growing since in status, outreach, reputation and sheer size, both in theatrical and in civic terms. Looking back at its activity over the past twenty-five years, this chapter will chart the directions the festival has been taking in its development and examine the impact it has achieved locally, nationally and internationally, which, I argue, have been intrinsic to the transformation of Craiova from a city festival into a festival city.

My approach is cued by Johansson's argument that festival and city stand in a 'mutually co-constitutive' relation (Johansson 2020: 69). While acknowledging this interdependence, my chapter also examines how it was established in relation to other Shakespeare (in) festivals discussed in this volume *and* explores its changing dynamics. The festival model in Craiova stands in clear opposition to those in festival cities such as Edinburgh and Avignon. It also contrasts with the model found at Shakespeare festivals such as Gdańsk or Verona, both of which trade on a spatial connection (whether real or fictional) with Shakespeare.[1] Furthermore, Craiova does not have either a tradition of festivalling or a site-specific (touristic) incentive or a multicultural community or a Shakespeare footprint/connection that would naturally lend the city what Temple Hauptfleisch (2007) terms 'festivalizing' qualities.

Charting the festival's emergence and key stages of development, I explore the shifts in terms of aims, organization, programme, participation, audiences that have turned the festival from a celebration of Shakespeare's work taking place in an industrial and university city of a former Eastern Bloc country into a large-scale international biennial event, a founder of and key player in the European Shakespeare Festivals Network (ESFN) in 2010, and a destination on the Shakespeare tourism circuit. My unpacking of the Craiova festival sees it as a 'vehicle for performance-based cultural expression, regeneration, and social inclusion' (Johansson 2020: 55) that has reconfigured, beneficially and at times somewhat disruptively, its urban home, the Romanian theatrical landscape *and* international Shakespeare production.

New Europe, old structures and the festival syndrome

For half of the continent, the reconstruction of new Europe, literal and cultural, began in the aftermath of the Second World War and theatre festivals played a key role in this rebuilding programme.[2] For the other half, which fell, as history lots were drawn, into the Soviet gulag, it took another forty-five years to join *that* new Europe. The fall of the Berlin Wall – the physical (and symbolic) border that marked this split – in November 1989, and the subsequent collapse of one communist regime after another in the Eastern Bloc, re-opened Europe and re-established cross-national contacts severed for almost half a century. For Romania, a country ghettoed within its national borders and subjected to strict surveillance, the overthrow of Ceaușescu's rule in December of the same year opened the door to the West – and the rest of the world. As the euphoria of movement across national borders matched that of unprecedented freedoms within its borders, the country embarked on its journey of recovery and self-discovery.

As with the new Europe project after the the Second World War, theatre and festivals in Romania took up a healing role. What proved a more daunting part was rebuilding a culture imprisoned and 'debilitated by [forty-five] years of deprivation [and] corruption' (Eyre 1990) and fear, a period in which theatre and festivals, alongside every institution and cultural activity, had been gradually requisitioned by the regime and tasked with singing its tune. With theatres nationalized and culture centralized under full state control since 1961 (when the wholesale nationalization was completed at immeasurable cost to life), cultural production was employed to systematically rewrite history and everyday reality by regurgitating Party propaganda. A new level of national-scale indoctrination began after the Ceaușescus' presidential tour of China, North Korea, Mongolia and North Vietnam. The ensuing Mini-Cultural Revolution of Maoist inspiration (enshrined, by decree, in the July 1971 Theses of the Communist Party) redefined culture's sole mission as the construction of the new man in the socialist humanist vein, dispelling any remaining illusion, as advertised to the West, that this regime represented communism with a human face. The approach was good old socialist realism revamped in a national(istic) style. It enabled the Ceaușescus' personality cult and in the process commandeered all public means – print, press, theatre, television, radio – and community participation. Festivities and festivals became enforced regime praising exercises, customized for every age group, reaching megalomaniac proportions in the annual *Cântarea României* (Songs of Praise to Romania) and a regular calendar of similar celebrations.

With venues, budgets, repertoires and discourse redeployed to glorifying the Party and its leaders, theatre retreated to underground spaces and sharpened its dissident language. The louder and more ostentatious the socialist realist performance outside, the subtler and more dissident the theatre inside. In a reality that was rewritten, contemporary voices gagged or exiled and spectators turned into 'mute audiences', Shakespeare's plays provided a lifeline and a language for survival, one even the censors could not ban for being anti-regime. This was the heritage that theatre in Romania had to reckon with post-1989.

While theatre-makers and audiences were equally 'eager to release [theatre] from censorship, double-speak and intricate means of resistance' (Cinpoeş 2010: 191), their enthusiasm was curbed. All forty-two theatres were owned by a bankrupt state and 'thrice bound – to a building, a company [in residence] and a[n annual] repertory' (191). Insufficient subsidies, cavernous buildings expensive to maintain, artists treated as civil servants and audiences hard to tempt back when other forms of entertainment and commercial pap were easily available – these were the common denominators for theatres in the slowly expanding capitalist marketplace in Romania.

With the economics staked against culture, it was up to 'each theatre's husbandry of its respective artistic and managerial potential' (Cinpoeş 2010: 191–2) to navigate the new context. The Romanian Theatre Association (UNITER), founded in 1990, emerged precisely from theatre's need of a compass at the national level.[3] The borders and theatre doors opened to directors returning from exile certainly encouraged mobility and collaboration, but effecting these entailed opening up from within. This ranged from opening the repertory to previously banned authors and titles, to revising the contractual terms to short-term collaboration and exchange, and rethinking subsidization so that local and private sponsors could become invested in cultural production. By starting small, with a collaboration, a workshop or a seminar, then building up to an anniversary event or a one-off festival, theatres could channel the general enthusiasm, test the waters of the new reality and begin to find a new theatrical language. Some of these initiatives focused on previously marginalized areas (such as Romanian Theatre on the Radio, in 1990), or responded to new interests (such as the International Theatre Festival of American Drama, in Braşov, 1993). They opened up to new practitioners and practices (for example, the 'Open Door Week' which presented to the wider public the graduation projects of the Bucharest Academy of Theatre and Film students). Others engaged with pressing topics, such as the 'Theatre and National Identity', organized by Concepts UK and 'Power and the Theatre', organized by UNITER, as a direct response to Decree 442 (1994) which 'put theatres' patrimony, budgets and sponsorship' *and* the appointment of managing directors 'directly under the control of the Ministry of Culture' (Cinpoeş 2010: 197). This was the context that the National Theatre in Craiova was negotiating as it prepared to organize a 'Shakespeare Festival' in 1994.

From festivity to 'cultural event'

According to Hauptfleisch, 'festivals are not only where the work is; it is where the artistic output of the actor, director, choreographer, etc. is *eventified*' (2007: 39). Having started as an 'everyday *life event*' on the stage of the Craiova National Theatre, *Ubu Rex with Scenes from Macbeth* (the first Shakespeare adaptation this theatre staged in new Romania) was eventified, in quick succession, at festivals in Romania (where it scooped the National Theatre Festival's award for best production and UNITER's best director of the season) and across the world (Edinburgh, Braunschweig, Parma, Tokyo, Jerusalem). Its success and the company it kept in the international arena gave the theatre's managing director Emil Boroghină the courage of his old conviction that 'as actors test their metal by doing Shakespeare, so do theatres' (Festival Programme 1994: 6) and a form for his dream of making Craiova an eventifying locus for Shakespeare's work. The repeat success with *Titus Andronicus* directed by Silviu Purcărete in 1992 and Boroghină's galvanizing personality at the helm of Craiova National Theatre led to extending this dream, beyond the commitment to stage a Shakespeare play every two years. By 1994, Boroghină established the William Shakespeare Foundation, a registered charity whose mission, unpolitical by (its own) definition, was 'to organise the Shakespeare Festival' and 'to stimulate the study of Shakespeare's work in Romania and beyond' (Statutes 1994 Article 1). Running within the Craiova National, the Foundation pledged to organize conferences and symposia, facilitate the publication of theatre criticism through a programme of translating world Shakespeare critical studies into Romanian and supporting the publication of work generated by its own events in order to bridge the gap in Shakespeare criticism available to Romanian readers. Its ambitious cultural goals also included, from the start, creating a Shakespeare library and a museum archive, alongside incentivizing (indigenous and international) creatives to work on Shakespeare premieres at Craiova, and sharing global Shakespeare knowledge (by bringing together theatre historians, literary and theatre critics, and theatre practitioners). Additionally, it aimed to organize research visits to the UK and European centres with traditions in Shakespeare studies, and to fundraise for 'bursaries to widen the horizon of research on Shakespeare performed' (Statutes 1994 Article 2: 1–8).

The first Craiova Shakespeare Festival took place in the autumn of 1994. Its modest offerings – six productions, two book launches and several workshops over five days – were transformational; their impact, long-lasting. The festival opened with Cheek by Jowl's *As You Like It* and continued with four Romanian productions from Bucharest theatres (Ion Creangă Theatre's *Tempest*, Bulandra Theatre's *Winter's Tale*, the Odeon's *Richard III*, the National's *Romeo and Juliet*). The sixth production was the homegrown *Titus Andronicus*. Both Cheek by Jowl's production and Elsom's book incentivized the exploration of contemporary Shakespeare making. The stripped-down aesthetics of the former (especially on the first night, when the company performed without their set and costumes which were stuck at some border crossing on the way to Romania) invited attention on acting and words, both of which had been buried in the metaphoric realism that kept censors at bay for decades in Romania. The latter challenged Romanian stage practice head-on to investigate Shakespeare's role in the 'now'.

The two organizers, Craiova's National and the William Shakespeare Foundation, secured an impressive patronage, ranging from the Romanian Ministry of Culture, the British Council, the Romanian-British Cultural Programme NOROC, to regional (Dolj District Council, Dolj District Prefecture) and local (Craiova Guildhall) sponsors. Its consumers were not so much the local theatregoers but the wider artistic community in Romania and invited international guests. This was an event that celebrated diversity as much as it showcased it, 'a significant *Cultural Event*, framed and made meaningful by the presence of an audience and reviewers' tasked with 'respond[ing] to the celebrated event'. Planned as such, the Craiova Shakespeare Festival 'became a means of retaining the event in the cultural memory of the particular society in which it [wa]s taking place' (Hauptfleisch et al. 2007: 39).

The following two editions (in 1997 and 2000) continued to build on the festival's mission and commitment to make a cultural difference, in spite of financial challenges and bureaucracy, aggravated further by the political swing from one extreme to the other.[4] It took hard graft and sheer determination to defy the odds and the critics' pessimism: the festival delivered on the statutory promises of the Shakespeare Foundation, albeit every three (rather than two) years, and asserted its potential as cultural player nationally, regionally (in 1997) and internationally (in 2000).

The 1997 edition embodied success by collaboration and exchange in the programme it offered, the in-house production Craiova staged and the wider financial support it accrued. Between 23 and 30 April, Craiova hosted seven visiting stage productions[5] and its own *Hamlet*, and screened one television *As You Like It*, one big screen adaptation and two cinematic experiments.[6] Craiova's *Hamlet* brought together Gábor Tompa, a Cluj-based director, Bucharest actors Adrian Pintea (Hamlet), Oana Pellea (Gertrude) and Mihai Constantin (Claudius) and Craiova National's artistic and creative crew, a collaboration that earned it major accolades – the Best Production of the 1996/7 season, Best Actor (Adrian Pintea) and Best Supporting Actor (Mihai Constantin) awarded by the Romanian section of the International Association of Theatre Critics (IATC). Acquiring the necessary financial backing also entailed extending collaborative initiatives, so alongside its 1994 portfolio of patrons, the festival garnered further support: internationally, from the French Cultural Service and Alliance Française in Romania; regionally, from the Culture and Art Inspectorate of Dolj District; and locally, from the Craiova Municipal Council, and increasing private sponsorship.

By and large, this was an edition which showed that diversity, younger directorial voices and the collaborative model were the way out of the theatre crisis, both in terms of artistic development and economic sustainability, nationally and in the eastern region of Europe. All were symptomatic of Craiova Shakespeare Festival's progress from the euphoria of celebration and festivity following the 1989 Romanian Revolution, to becoming, in Hauptfleisch's terms, 'a *cultural event* which in its own way *eventifies* elements and issues of the particular society in which it is taking place' (2007: 39). As Craiova's *Hamlet* saw it (in 1997), the Danish Prince might have sacrificed himself to settle old accounts, but Horatio firmly left the past behind: taking with him the versatile box (his travel trunk, the production's miniature puppet theatre and later grave), Horatio reluctantly received the tokens for remembrance the cast rushed to salvage (a violin, Yorick's skull, the Ghost/Shakespeare's manuscript, Ophelia's dismembered doll, his own guitar) as the symbolic Iron Curtain (of the production's design) fell for the last time to the sound of Pink Floyd's 'The Wall'. Like Horatio, Romanian Shakespeare had fulfilled its duty to tell *that* story and was ready to embrace its freedom and the present (Cinpoeş 2010: 210–11), one that exercised democracy, celebrated diversity (generational, ethnic, geographical) and artistic exchange.

Political change – to neo-communism, which dragged Romania back to older policies – and the consequent budget uncertainty[7] threatened the very existence of the festival in 2000, with sceptical voices already seeing it as a thing of the past. Delayed until 15–22 June, the third edition offered a streamlined programme (five productions) which relied on the network and collaborations the festival had established nationally and in former Eastern Europe. The choice of plays spoke of the changing times – as in the case of Craiova's in-house production *Timon of Athens* directed by Cluj-based Mihai Măniuțiu and of Gdańsk's Wybrzeże Theatre's *Richard III* directed by Krzystof Nazar, both radical in grounding their approaches in contemporary reality. It also spoke of changing practices in Shakespeare-making at Craiova's NT, whose *Timon*, 'mounted fast, on a time-scale typical of western theatres', 'seriously demonstrated that Craiova's National could work with directors other than Purcărete or on loan from abroad' (Ichim 1999),[8] and beyond. Touring from the Zsámbék Summer Festival (Hungary), *A Midsummer Night's Dream* in Beatrice Bleonț's hands – as director, adapter and choreographer – was an innovative psychological and theatrical exploration, not least in terms of working with a mixed ensemble of actors (Romanian and Hungarian), having fashion designer Doina Levința in charge of costumes, and performing outdoors, in the theatre square, at midnight. Shakespeare's words and ideas gained affective corporeality in Răzvan Mazilu's one-person 'dance, music and poetry recital' (Festival Programme 2000) *Playing Shakespeare*, a production that – like Bleonț's – delighted audiences with its choreographic range and nuances (directed by Romanian ballet icon Ioan Tugearu), Janine Fashion Design costumes and Liana Tugearu's libretto which collaged Puccini, Mahler, Rossini and Shostakovich. Ștefan Iordănescu's *Macbeth* from the Târgu-Mureș National proposed a Macbeth made of flesh, blood and tangible suffering, in a modern dress production, dominated by red and black, and whose sound and (laser) lights conversed seductively and uncannily.

Shakespeare-making, and making sense of Shakespeare, were the focus of not only the book launches – theatre historian Ileana Berlogea's volume on Romanian director Liviu Ciulei and Shakespeare academic Emil Sîrbulescu's *The Elements of Drama* – but also of two other new initiatives: the workshops led by the Romanian branch of IATC and John Elsom, the Honorary President of the association, and the partnership Craiova established with the Gdańsk Shakespeare Festival. Both were collaborations that would shape the future work of the festival, and build its world cultural influence. Showcasing Shakespeare in all arts and reaching a wider public, both in its programme and how it was framed – by opening with an exhibition of Shakespeare-related books, photography and paintings, and concluding with a screening of *Shakespeare in Love* – the festival delivered on its outreach and educational aims. Having withstood the test of time, the Craiova Shakespeare Festival was there to stay, and the initiatives launched at the 2000 edition signalled future developmental directions, now that its exploratory years were well and truly behind.

From exploration to conceptual unity

Continuing to develop and diversify the programme the festival offered every three years and securing the necessary funding to run an increasing number of events – from stage productions, opera and concerts, book, costume and art exhibitions, book launches and even stamp series (!) – that reached larger audiences free of charge, or heavily subsidized tickets, remained the main visible activity over the three editions of the third millennium: 2003, 2006 and 2008. The time in between editions, however, was one of festival soul searching as the organizers engaged with questions at the heart of the festival's identity and sustainability. Having moved on from exclusively celebrating liberation and breaking diehard norms inherited from the previous regime (both reminiscent of festivals' carnival traits), to experimenting with new models and showcasing excellence, the festival did not settle on doing just more of the same. Its answer to impatient voices asking 'what next?' was to embark on probing its efficacy as a cultural tool that continued to 'validate a sense of community' and 'cement a city's sense of cultural status' – both roles, Georgia Seffir argues, that are intrinsic to contemporary festivals (2006: 15).

There was talk in the press of an imminent relocation to Bucharest, a move some favoured because of the benefits the capital would naturally provide in terms of infrastructure, subsidy, sustainability and outreach, while others identified the move as a threat to the festival's identity and very existence. The virtue of 'Craiova's theatrical and geographical position', George Banu pointed out, was precisely 'not being a "theatre in the capital"', one among many in a place with an intense cultural life (Festival Programme 2003). Its location outside Bucharest was crucial to earning the 'province' cultural capital by devolving arts funding away from the capital and encouraging more investment in theatres across the country. In doing so, it incentivized theatres in Romania[9] to secure a place for Shakespeare in their repertoires and re-cast his plays as productive terrain for experimentation – both decisions they may not have taken otherwise. There was also talk of moving away, at least occasionally, from the exclusive single-author focus, and 'alternate' a Shakespeare edition with 'one on contemporary theatre', as well as making the work of Marin Sorescu (the playwright whose name the Craiova National bears) a fixture in the festival's programme – a 'formula' George Banu saw as 'extremely attractive for the theatrical life of a city … and the artistic wellbeing of Craiova's National Theatre' (Festival Programme 2003). The colloquia, book launches, post-show talks and workshops for theatre students the festival programmed were as attractive and crucial, not only to the festival's wellbeing, but also to the health and future of staged Shakespeare and Romanian theatre more broadly, as theatre critic and director of the periodical *Scena* [The Stage] Alice Georgescu put it on numerous occasions.

Rosabeth Moss Kanter argues that

> communities need both magnets and glue. They must have magnets that attract a flow of external resources – new people or companies – to expand skills, broaden horizons, and hold up a comparative mirror against world standards. The flow might involve customers, outside investors, foreign companies, students, or business travelers. Communities also need social glue – a way to bring people together to define the common good, create joint plans, and identify strategies that benefit a wide range of people and organizations.

(2003: 127)

In the case of festivals, the 'glue' are the leaders whose festival spirit and experience brings people together to strategize and devise joint plans that effect social cohesion. For many theatre critics and festival consumers, the Craiova National was *'the magnet'* and Boroghină *'the glue'* that ensured the entity and continuity of the Shakespeare Festival as a cultural act no longer viewed as local but as national; as Victor Parhon put it: 'what country can wish for more than having a National Theatre Festival (Romania has the I. L. Caragiale National Festival) and a Shakespeare Festival?' (Festival Programme 2003). Conversely, Dumitru Solomon hoped that the festival would 'attract, in time, the creative forces from Europe' (Festival Programme 2003) and John Elsom saw the festival as the locus for practising Shakespeare as our *lingua franca*: 'we need [such] events ... to understand better what a shared Europe means' (Elsom qtd in Popa-Buluc 2000).

What the festival organizers achieved, between 2000 and 2008, defied newspaper speculations and exceeded even the most optimistic predictions. If in 1994, the line-up was six productions, by 2006 just one day in its calendar scheduled as many; while its first edition brought one visiting production (from the UK), by its fifth edition Craiova was a coveted destination for many international companies (in addition to Shakespeare's Globe from the UK, the edition featured productions from the Netherlands, Lithuania, Montenegro, Hungary, Israel and Russia). If in 1994, Bucharest theatres brought Shakespeare to Craiova, the tables turned in 2006 when the festival announced the opening of a festival season in the Romanian capital, a development enabled by formalizing the organizational partnership between the Shakespeare Foundation (in Craiova) and the Cultural Centre of Bucharest Municipality (ARCUB). This development strengthened the festival by pooling their respective networks and portfolios of sponsors, and impacted positively on its sustainability: while sharing the costs, they could offer some visiting companies twice the exposure and, in some cases, succeeded in bringing productions that Craiova found logistically impossible to schedule.[10] In 2006 Craiova became a stage for world players: the selection of Shakespeare productions it curated went global; so did its educational programmes when acquiring the patronage of the UNESCO Chair of the International Theatre Institute, which led to the training workshops for students at the Bucharest National University of Theatre and Film to open to students from around the world. Both justified Craiova's festival rebranding as an International Shakespeare Festival, and the momentum they built led to revising its occurrence to biennial and curating each edition thematically. UNITER recognized the 'exceptional quality' of the 2006 edition by conferring the festival its Excellence Award; Ian Shuttleworth's review concluded: 'Programmers of the Barbican's Bite strand of international theatre presentations, please take note' (2006).

Shakespeare has been part of Craiova's cultural footprint: the first encounter was in 1855, with a production of *Othello*, followed by a rich history of Shakespeare productions totalling thirty-three by the time the festival was born (Firescu and Gheorghiu 2000: 479–504). Craiova's theatre has always been a welcoming home for experiment whose success is intrinsically linked to groundbreaking directorial work, whether the work of Vlad Mugur (ousted from Bucharest and buried in the 'province' by the censors) whose *Hamlet* in 1958 was not only the first post-Stalinist production of the play, but a national event that 'irremediably broke with the two diehard norms in Romanian theatre practice: *ut musica poesis* and *ut pictura theatrum*' and paved the way for a Shakespeare that was contemporary with Meyerhold, Kantor, Pirandello and Brecht (Cinpoeș 2010: 120), or Silviu Purcărete's epic scale Shakespeare that took Craiova on the national and the international theatre circuit. Directorial auteurship remained Craiova's USP which the festival consolidated during the 2000s, with programmes that in 2003, 2006 and 2008 combined, showcased the work of top directors from around the world (including Declan Donnellan, Yoshihiro Kurita, Oskaras Koršunovas, Dejan Mijac, Janusz Kica, Eimuntas Nekrošius, Lev Dodin, Pavel Szotak and Omri Nitzan)[11] and an impressive line-up of homegrown names, from returned exiles (such as Liviu Ciulei and Vlad Mugur) to established names (Alexandru Tocilescu, Alexander Hausvater, Gelu Conceag) and new kids on the block (such as Felix Alexa, Beatrice Bleonț, Ion Sapdaru and László Bocsárdi), while also maintaining a close collaboration with Silviu Purcărete.[12] At the 2008 edition (entitled 'Great Performances, Great Directors, Great Theatres of Europe and the World'), the festival formalized its role as a directors' powerhouse by launching the Festival Prize which, to date, has always gone to directors with the exception of 2014, when it was awarded to Sir Stanley Wells.[13] Its increasingly influential critics' seminar earned the patronage of the International Association of Theatre Critics in the same year.

Having fulfilled its initial and 'immediate target of giving "Romanian theatre specialists and audiences the chance to see the work of great directors"' (Shevtsova 2012: 353), the festival's work during the 2000s consolidated its director-focus (which had impressed Boroghină at Braunschweig festival Teaterformen back in 1991) on a global scale, established its conceptual unity, biennial activity and relational priorities – in terms of artistic partnerships and exchanges, training beneficiaries and consumer communities – all of which repositioned the festival locally and globally, preparing it for the role of cultural influencer it would take up in the following decade.

Putting Craiova on the world Shakespeare tourist map

The decade began for the Craiova Festival with an exception to its customary exertions: an entire edition dedicated exclusively to one play. While Kronborg castle in Helsingør might legitimize such exclusivity, doing it in Craiova sounded more like wishful thinking, Boroghină intimated during our brief encounter as spectators at the Gdańsk Festival in 2009. His dream, 'close to obsession', was regarded as anything between farfetched ambition, a risky enterprise and the first 'audacity of its kind' (Festival Programme 2010: 6). Boroghină's assiduous pursuit of productions of the play and the festival organizers' assessment of the festival's final output of the thematic cycle 'Meetings and Dialogues' offered in 2010 the '*Hamlet* Constellation'. Having navigated the very tough selection procedure and a worse-than-usual set of festival hazards (travel mishaps, schedule clashes, environmental disasters, funding limitations), the seventeen productions bill opened on Shakespeare's birthday with OKT/Vilnius City Theatre's *Hamlet*. Directed by Oskaras Koršunovas, the production set the tone for the enquiry and dialogue the festival promised: beginning with the entire cast on stage as actors facing their individual reflections in the make-up table mirrors that stared back at us, it asked again and again 'Who's there?' (1.1.1), a question emerging from 'an acute need of self-analysis, in order to understand our environment and the decisions we make about living'.[14]

Diverse *Hamlet*s, new and old, took the stage and the screen. Robert Wilson returned with 'a lecture and the video of his making of *Hamlet* in 1996, in which he had performed all the parts' (Shevtsova 2012: 356), and so did Eimuntas Nekrošius and Meno Fortas' 1997 production that was dominated by sound, ice, fire, pain and the growing lucidity of its (Lithuanian rock-star) Prince.[15] From Poland came Wrocław Theatre's production directed by Monika Peçikiewicz (the only female director in the festival) in which the dynamics between Ophelia and Gertrude was strongly reminiscent of Lavinia and Tamora's in *Titus Andronicus* (a play she had previously directed), and Piotr Kondrat's one-man show in the scenic meadow of Port Cetate by the Danube after sunset. Three Asian *Hamlet*s were advertised: Street Theatre Troupe's, which ended with the return of Fortinbras as Hamlet resurrected in Lee Youn-Taek's direction; Ryutopia's Noh *Hamlet* – which ended up being screened because the Japanese company was stranded in Paris by the eruption of Eyjafjallajökull volcano; and the Shanghai Theatre Academy's production (directed by Richard Schechner) which turned the studio theatre at the Craiova National into a white box traverse stage for a *Hamlet* with a difference. The cast included professional actors, drama teachers and students, and a TV crew that filmed and projected the live action – a reference to surveillance not communist but reality TV show, which blurred the boundaries between 'to be' and 'to seem' further. The props and set were versatile: when lifted, the platform where Gertrude and Claudius were crowned opened a sand pit – no playbox for the young protagonists, but their early grave, while the mops which abounded in this production served as weapons, phallic symbols and hands-on cleaning instruments for blood which splattered on the white tarpaulin floor as it dripped from the ceiling into a conspicuous bucket. Doubling was as versatile, with Ophelia standing in for Marcellus and Polonius returning as the Priest – alongside the Ghost ghosting the production as the Head Player and First Gravedigger (Cinpoeş et al. 2010). Equally immersed in the 'now' was Thomas Ostermeier's *Hamlet* with the Schaubühne Theatre, Berlin. Characters entered and exited Elsinore, a giant trough of earth in this production, through a chain curtain hanging from the lighting rig, a set element that also served as a screen on which Hamlet's handheld camera videos were projected. Dirt and voyeurism were literally at the forefront of this *Hamlet*: it started with a burial (King Hamlet's? Shakespeare's? Previous

*Hamlet*s?)[16] forestage and kept it fresh both in Hamlet's memory and the audience's eyes – especially as we saw power-craving Claudius and Polonius digging out, barehandedly, the crown from the grave's earth.

Dialogue across time, spaces and media abounded: there were screen *Hamlet*s – Peter Brook's 1999 (with Adrian Lester) and Craiova's own 1997; music from Shakespeare's plays and Shakespeare's time (by Andy Rouse and Simply English) and Tchaikovsky's *Hamlet* and *Romeo and Juliet* (by the Craiova Philharmonic Orchestra), ghosts in the cupboard (the key stage design element in László Bocsárdi's *Hamlet* for the Odeon Theatre, Bucharest) and ghosts in the machine (whether the computer deck that erased Richard Burton's *Hamlet* or the many small screens that multiplied it in the Wooster Group's production).[17] The epitome of dialogue, for me, was *Hamlet Facing Hamlet*, an event that placed in live conversation two Danish Princes of the 1980s: Michael Pennington (RSC, 1980) and Ion Caramitru (Bulandra Theatre, 1985).

The year 2010 set up the festival's directions of development for the decade with two new collaborations. One was the 'Shakespeare in Performance Seminar', subsequently under the aegis of the European Shakespeare Research Association (ESRA). The other was a new Romanian *Shakespeare Complete Works* which, in Alice Georgescu's words, was both a need and a duty: 'as we have a good (International) Shakespeare Festival, shouldn't we have a (national) *Shakespeare Complete* to match up to it?' (2003). Together, the collaborations aimed to bridge the gap between page and stage practices in Romania, a rift that kept theatre practitioners and university-based academics in separate camps and which needed healing.[18] Together, they turned the festival into a world's stage for cultural exchange on Shakespeare Studies as a discipline and, crucially, they effected cultural change in Romanian Shakespeare making – both aims of the Shakespeare Foundation from its inception. Two volumes of the *Complete Works* were launched in 2010; a decade and thirteen volumes later, the project reached completion. The fresh playscripts were 'tripping on the tongue', 'clean' and un-bardolatrized,[19] and enabled new stage practices as they freed productions of the political clichés and subtext typical of Shakespeare behind the Iron Curtain. To boot, it galvanized indigenous expertise (in Romanian as opposed to published abroad) to fill the gap in Shakespeare criticism in Romania. Alongside being employed in surtitling non-Romanian productions at the festival,[20] the translations have been slowly becoming the-stage-Shakespeare in Romania: if in 2012, the Craiova's National's *A Tempest* was one of the two productions using them, the count – to date – is twenty-six productions of eighteen plays in sixteen theatres across Romania. Besides continuing the much-needed dialogue, these two initiatives I launched back in 2010 have grown from guest cameos within the festival to becoming cultural co-producers of Shakespeare: from Shakespeare criticism and a modernized *Shakespeare Complete* in print, to its latest event: *Viewing & Reviewing*, a fortnight of workshops in which the festival's stage productions in 2018 were collectively attended, debated and reviewed.[21]

The decade began with formalizing collaborations between Shakespeare Festivals in Europe by founding the European Shakespeare Festivals Network (ESFN), in which Craiova was a key player (alongside Bath, Gdańsk, Gyula and Neuss). A 'structure which facilitate[d] artistic national catching up with international Shakespeare and a dose of mutual regional exchange' to begin with, the ESFN has doubled its membership in a decade and acquired agency that has been 'instrumental in effecting change, with individual festivals thus gaining agential traction in areas beyond the artistic and the cultural, and into the civic, educational, and socio-economic domains' (Cinpoeș 2021: 75).

These accelerated the festival's move from being a 'world's stage' for Shakespeare productions to becoming a key 'player' in the production of Shakespeare – in Romania and globally. The festival's programmes in 2014, 2016 and 2018 confirm its curatorial prowess and attention to diversity, no mean feat in the unregulated neo-liberal market. The Craiova festival continued to be one of the keenest promotors of collaboration, whether between international creatives and Romanian theatres, or Romanian creatives and world theatres. This practice has put the festival firmly on the world map and made it a destination on the Shakespeare tourist circuit, while at the national level, it has led to changes in the Romanian theatre landscape and its operational structures.

But it is not only the festival that has changed from being a consumer of Shakespeare to being a producer (and promotor and disseminator and archive!), too. Participants in the festival – whether creatives, audiences or organizations that make up the local infrastructure – have become 'prosumers' and 'produsers', hybridizing their positions of consumers, producers and end-users (Minier and Pennacchia 2019: 15). Parrabbola and Teatrulescu's

FIGURE 6.1 *Fairies taking over Craiova in* A Midsummer Night's Dream *(2018). By permission of the Archive of the International Shakespeare Festival, Craiova, Romania.*

A Midsummer Night's in 2018 offered the perfect example of this hybridization. Directed by Philip Parr, this promenade production cast Craiova (the community *and* the city) as its main protagonists. All eighty volunteers were accepted in the final cast of 'children, acting students, office employers, housewives, and retired people' (Cinpoeş, Guntner and Valls-Russell 2019: 95). Even the language and modes of delivery emerged in rehearsal: Oberon (an opera student) sang his lines; Theseus spoke Romanian and resorted to a translator to communicate with English-speaking Hippolyta and her entourage, 'giving the scene the diplomatic formality of an arranged wedding' (95). Each individual played a role (identifiable by name and spoken lines), even in the case of Puck cast as 'a "collective" of actors, similarly dressed but with individualized features and actions' (95). The production took everyone on a journey of discovery as actors and spectators went to 'areas of the city they ignored', passers-by found themselves in scenes from Shakespeare and residents experienced their homes as Athens and the woods outside it: *Dream* started in the carpark of Craiova University, moved into its sumptuous marble-floored entrance hall for the court scene, 'down a main street through a small, tree-shaded square where fairies perched in the foliage', onto 'a garden overlooked by appartement where people could watch the mechanicals' rehearsal below' (95). Participation and serendipity defined the production: 'on reaching a church, the performance literally walked into a wedding ... before finishing on a street lined with bridal shops, where a long table with drinks awaited the whole wedding party – performers, spectators, and passers-by'; by-standers gave directions, were keen to resolve Puck's mistake and adamant to prevent Pyramus' suicide; the mechanicals delivered *Pyramus and Thisbe* on 'a make-shift stage ... erected ... on the back of a lorry' in a square flanked by cafés and bistros, to an audience of followers and impromptu spectators who shushed, in irritation, 'Theseus, Hippolyta and the lovers who watched from a balcony' and their mocking comments (95–6).

Parrabbola's *Dream* is indicative of Craiova's transformation into a festival city endowed by the Shakespeare festival with the 'co-creative agency underpinning the tourist experience [that] opens up opportunities for keeping the "placeness" of the visited spaces alive' (Minier and Pennacchia 2019: 16) – both metaphorically and in immediate, civic terms. The regeneration projects in the past ten years have been impressive in scope and size, with the drive to offer the 'Shaxperience' negotiating differently development, heritage preservation, ecological and gentrification concerns.[22] Festivalization, in Craiova's case, has been dynamic in terms of spatial and economic reshaping. Aware of its socially and culturally interventionist role that effected Craiova's alterity when it changed the local into a global destination, thus making it same *and* different (O'Dair 2008; Stevens and Shin 2014), the festival has become increasingly 'careful that people's neighbourhoods do not turn into mere spectacle for the benefit of the audience's festival gaze' (Johansson 2020: 64). In a quarter of a century, the dynamics between festival and city has changed: 'the city is not simply a backdrop for the festival ... rather, the festival produces, as it is produced by, city space' (60).

Coda

Festivals, Ros Derrett argues, 'are seen to build social capital and in community development terms showcase the strengths of a community at play and demonstrate its capacity to cope with external stresses and disturbance as a result of social, political and environmental change' (2009: 109). Craiova Shakespeare Festival is certainly one such festival: back in 1994, it was the coping strategy of the Romanian community of theatre-makers and -goers starved of artistic expression, mobility and exchange over four decades of communism, and trapped between censorship and indoctrination. The experience and resilience amassed in navigating propitious – as well as less so – times and circumstances over twenty-five years of festival-making has equipped the local community and the wider communities it has established – national, European and global – with creative coping agency.

This could not have been more poignant during the past two years which tested the festival's metal. As the Covid-19 pandemic raged across the world, closed theatres and locked down country after country, Craiova had to shelve its ambitious 2020 edition and discard two years of careful preparations. At very short notice – between 12 March, when it announced its cancellation, and 23 April – it reinvented itself as the 'Shakespeare Festival – from home!' As 'the first Shakespeare Festival entirely online, Craiova 2020 scored several other firsts: its week-long programme comprised of non-simultaneous events (an unachievable dream previously) that alternated between scheduled live interventions and posted messages from around the globe as well as encores of handpicked productions' broadcast on Facebook and TVR3 (the national cultural channel) (Cinpoeş 2021: 77–8). This was 'a productive exercise in digging deep into [the festival's] rich and unique archive, and in testing the potential of Shakestivalling' online, though the high appeal of this format (*c*. 300,000 log-ins) needs to be considered in 'relation to the timing of the festival – early in the theatre lock-down, when little if anything was available for theatre-savvy audiences' (Cinpoeş 2021: 78).

It is Craiova Shakespeare Festival's track-record of self-discovery, a strong legacy of opening up opportunities, being at the cutting edge of theatre practice and committed to its role of thinking through challenging times that has listed it among the first places where Covid-safe theatre was on offer – albeit in distanced productions in the park initially. It is also what has enabled the latest project of its National Theatre: 'Hektomeron: 100 days/ 100 stories/ 100 directors from 100 countries' created and experienced digitally (https://hektomeron.com/, 2021) – one more confirmation that when times and theatre are a-changing, the Craiova Shakespeare Festival is one direction to turn to.

Notes

1 While Gdańsk boasts a Shakespeare footprint with its Shakespeare Theatre built on the site of the early modern fencing school which doubled as a theatre venue for travelling players during the early modern period (see Chapter 8 of this volume), Verona's connection is the site where Shakespeare sets the story of the 'star-crossed lovers' (see Chapter 7).
2 Three festivals were prominent: the Festival d'Avignon that opened in 1947 (see Chapter 2), 'the Edinburgh International Festival' (1947) and 'the Festivals of Athens and Epidaurus (officially founded in 1954)' (Fischer-Lichte 2020: 90).
3 UNITER, founded in 1990, played a seminal role in facilitating exchanges and collaborations, and organized key initiatives, such as 'Seeding a Network', which launched Romanian directors on the international market and brought touring productions to Romania after the December 1989 Revolution. Doing away with its initial monolithic structure (four departments: actors, directors, designers and critics) and bureaucratic apparatus by 1993, UNITER became a leaner and more versatile organization that could focus 'on projects and programmes that prioritised and rewarded individual creativity, talent and theatrical activity (over keeping mediocrity on the payroll)' (Cinpoeș 2010: 197). The annual theatre awards UNITER established in 1993 (for best production, director, actor, supporting actor, etc.) stimulated both artistic competence and competitiveness.
4 The 1996 elections saw the Romanian Democratic Convention (CDR) win against the Social Democratic Party of Romania (PDSR). The balance of power shifted dramatically in the 2000 elections. The CRD (reduced in size) was ousted from government by the PDSR. The presidential elections pitted against each other two figures from the communist past: Ion Iliescu, the candidate of the PDSR and former member of the old nomenklatura, and Corneliu Vadim Tudor, the leader of ultra-nationalist party Greater Romanian Party (PRM) and former 'court poet' to Nicolae Ceaușescu. Tactical votes against Vadim Tudor (PRM) ensured a victory for the PDSR candidate.
5 The line-up included: *Troilus and Cressida* (dir. Dejan Mijač, Dramatic Theatre, Yugoslavia), *Oh, Romeo …, Oh, Juliet* (dir. Antal Pál, Hungarian section of Ariel Theatre, Târgu-Mureș), *Much Ado About*

Nothing (dir. Alexandru Dabija, Youth Theatre, Piatra-Neamț), *Twelfth Night* (dir. Victor Iona Frunză, Hungarian State Theatre, Cluj), *Measure for Measure* (dir. Theodor Cristian Popescu, Târgu-Mureș National Theatre), *Hamlet* (dir. Janez Pipan, National Theatre, Slovenia), *Hamlet* (dir. Sandu Vasilache, Chișinău National Theatre, Moldova).

6   Alongside *Richard III* (dir. Richard Loncraine), there were two French film experiments: *Shakespeare, Kings in Tempests* (dir. Claude Mourieras, on a screenplay by George Banu and Jean-Michel Déprats) and *The Ghost Scene in Hamlet* (a montage by the Academy of Experimental Theatre, Paris).

7   Despite being negotiated and approved a year before, governmental subsidy and support had to be reapproved by the new Minister of Culture. This legal obligation affects the festival every four years, when elections often bring a change of regime.

8   Purcărete left Romania in 1996 to take up the directorship of Théâtre de l'Union – Centre dramatique national, in Limoges, France, where he also set up a drama academy.

9   Apart from Romanian ones, the country's network of theatres includes several Hungarian- and German-language theatres as well as one Yiddish.

10 The Bucharest season was not a full repeat of Craiova's programme. Running in parallel or after Craiova's, it usually offered a selection of the main schedule of productions. It was a welcome solution to calendar clashes (which would have entirely missed productions or at best delayed their visits by two years) and to complex technical requirements that none of Craiova's venues could accommodate.

11 The list also includes Peter Brook and Robert Wilson, two directors the festival has been keen to host albeit with non-Shakespeare productions they were touring: *The Grand Inquisitor* and *The Lady from the Sea*, respectively. The other two exceptions are Declan Donnellan's *'Tis Pity She's a Whore* (2016) and Robert Lepage's *Needles and Opium* (2018).

12 Purcărete's work in the festival includes: *Twelfth Night* in 2004 (for the Craiova NT), *Troilus and Cressida* in 2006 (for József Katona Theatre, Budapest), *Measure for Measure* in 2008 (for the Craiova NT), *A Tempest* in 2012 (for the Craiova NT) and *As You Like It* in 2014 (for the National Theatre of Budapest).

13 Its recipients were Declan Donnellan (2008), Silviu Purcărete (2010), Eimuntas Nekrošius (2012), Thomas Ostermeier (2016) and Krzysztof Warlikowski (2018).

14 See https://www.okt.lt/en/plays/hamlet/ (accessed 22 July 2021).

15 This was the first in Meno Fortas' *Shakespeare Trilogy* (alongside *Macbeth* and *Othello*) that only the Bucharest section of the festival managed to schedule in 2008.

16 On this production's approach to burying 'the father', see March (2003).
17 The Odeon and Wooster Group productions only featured in the Bucharest programme of the festival.
18 The ESRA seminar and bringing the translation project to Craiova were my initiatives and the focus of my work over the past ten years.
19 The last stage-focused translation (of a dozen or so plays) dated back to 1940. The 1960s *Complete Works* project was a party enterprise of varied translation quality, ideologically pitched by 'bespoke' introductions; the 1980s project improved on the quality considerably but remained essentially philological in its approach.
20 The practice, besides amending previous mishaps, sought to match the 'words' with the 'action' not only in terms of spoken quality but as a translation of the productions' contemporary takes on the plays.
21 This has led to the publication of eighteen collective reviews of nineteen productions, each co-ordinated by two to five individuals from the forty-one conveners of the workshops and informed by dialogue with theatre companies and wider public. See Cinpoeş and Valls-Russell (2019: 51–5) and individual reviews (Cinpoeş and Valls-Russell 2019: 75–122).
22 Walking around Craiova, one delights in the many green areas, parks, pedestrianized streets, piazzas, conservation areas and restored period buildings. The outcome of the city planning over the past ten years, this new landscape includes a higher number of hotels, restaurants, coffee shops not only in the old city but across it, too, and an airport on the outskirts. All are indices of exponential growth linked to the demand created partly by the cultural tourism generated by the Shakespeare Foundation and festival.

References

Cinpoeş, Nicoleta (2003), Personal interview with Emil Boroghină, Craiova, August.
Cinpoeş, Nicoleta (2010), *Shakespeare's* Hamlet *1778–2008: A Study in Translation, Performance and Cultural Appropriation*, New York and Lampeter, Wales: Edwin Mellen Press.
Cinpoeş, Nicoleta (2021), 'Shakestivalling in the New Europe', *Theatralia* 23 (1): 65–83.
Cinpoeş, Nicoleta, and Janice Valls-Russell, eds (2019), 'Prologue: Viewing and Reviewing 'Planet Shakespeare' (Craiova 23 April–6 May

2018) and individual reviews, *Cahiers Élisabéthains* 100 (1): 51–5, 75–122.
Cinpoeş, Nicoleta, Lawrence Guntner and Janice Valls-Russell (2019), '*A Midsummer Night's Dream*', *Cahiers Élisabéthains* 100 (1): 94–6. Available online: https://doi.org/10.1177/0184767819867410g (accessed 14 March 2021).
Cinpoeş, Nicoleta, Saffron Walkling, Aneta Mancewitz and April Chaplin (2010), Interview with Shanghai Theatre Academy's *Hamlet* cast and production team, 29 April.
Derrett, Ros (2009), 'How Festivals Nurture Resilience in Regional Communities', in Jane Ali-Knight et al. (eds), *International Perspectives of Festivals and Events: Paradigms of Analysis*, 107–24, Amsterdam and New York: Elsevier Academic Press.
Eyre, Richard (1990), 'Noises off in Elsinore: On the Subversive Romanian *Hamlet* of Ion Caramitru', *Guardian*, 13 September.
Firescu, Alexandru, and Constantin Gheorghiu (2000), *Istoria Teatrului Naţional din Craiova 1850–2000* [The History of the National Theatre of Craiova], Craiova: Editura AIUS.
Fisher-Lichte, Erika (2020), 'European Festivals', in Ric Knowles (ed.), *The Cambridge Companion to International Theatre Festivals*, 87–100, Cambridge: Cambridge University Press.
Georgescu, Alice (2003), 'Festivalul, pentru un oraş' [The Festival, for a City], *Dilema*, 10–16 October.
Hauptfleisch, Temple, Shulamith Lev-Aladgem, Jacqueline Martin, Willmar Sauter and Henri Schoenmakers, eds (2007), *Festivalising! Theatrical Events, Politics and Culture*, Amsterdam and New York: Rodopi.
Hektomeron, https://hektomeron.com/ (accessed 10 March 2021).
Ichim, Florica (1991), 'Spectacole ale lipsei de speranţă' [Spectacles of the Absence of Hope], *România liberă*, 5 February.
Ichim, Florica (1999), '*Timon din Atena*' [*Timon of Athens*], *România literară*, 7 January.
International Shakespeare Festival Programme, Craiova, 1994.
International Shakespeare Festival Programme, Craiova, 2000.
International Shakespeare Festival Programme, Craiova, 2003.
International Shakespeare Festival Programme, Craiova, 2010.
Johansson, Marjana (2020), 'City Festivals and Festival Cities', in Ric Knowles (ed.), *The Cambridge Companion to International Theatre Festivals*, 54–69, Cambridge: Cambridge University Press.
Kanter, Rosabeth Moss (2003), 'Thriving Locally in the Global Economy', *Harvard Business Review* 81 (8): 119–27.
Knowles, Ric, ed. (2020), *The Cambridge Companion to International Theatre Festivals*, Cambridge: Cambridge University Press.

March, Florence (2003), '"My death [...] is made the prologue to their play": killing the literary father in 21st century stage productions of *Hamlet*', in Sandra Pietrini (ed.), *Picturing Drama*, 249–57, Alessandria: Edizioni dell'Orso.

Minier, Márta, and Maddalena Pennacchia (2019), 'Place, Memory, Participation: Shakespeare and Tourism in Focus', in Marta Minier and Maddalena Pennacchia (eds), *Shakespeare and Tourism: Place, Memory, Participation*, 9–24, Napoli: Edizioni Scientifiche Italiane.

O'Dair, Sharon (2008), 'Virtually There: Shakespeare and Tourism in the Twenty-First Century', 5–23, *The Upstart Crow* 27: 5–23.

OKT Vilniaus Miesto Teatras Homepage. Available online: https://www.okt.lt/en/plays/hamlet/ (accessed 26 January 2021).

Popa-Buluc, Magdalena (2000), 'Shakespeare, amprenta genetică a culturii europene' [Shakespeare, the Genetic Code of European Culture], *Curentul*, 20 June.

Shevtsova, Maria (2012), 'Reasons for Joy and Reflection: Engaging with Shakespeare at the Craiova Festival', *New Theatre Quarterly* 28 (4): 352–62. Available online: https://doi.org/10.1017/S0266464X12000656 (accessed 30 January 2021).

Shuttleworth, Ian (2006), 'The Bard Reinterpreted', *Financial Times*, 3 May. Available online: https://www.ft.com/content/2d12fcae-dac7-11da-aa09-0000779e2340 (accessed 1 January 2021).

Statutul Fundaţiei Shakespeare, Craiova [The Statutes of the William Shakespeare Foundation, Craiova] 1994. Courtesy of the Archives of the National Theatre of Craiova.

Stevens, Quentin, and HaeRan Shin (2014), 'Urban Festivals and Local Social Space', *Planning Practice and Research* 29 (1): 1–20. Available online: https://doi.org/10.1080/02697459.2012.699923 (accessed 11 March 2021).

Taylor, Paul (1997), 'Not a Pretty Sight', *Independent*, 23 May. Available online: https://www.independent.co.uk/arts-entertainment/books/not-a-pretty-sight-1263097.html (accessed 27 January 2020).

7

Festivalizing Shakespeare in Italy: Verona and Rome

Lisanna Calvi and Maddalena Pennacchia

In present-day Italy, the only yearly recurring series of theatrical performances devoted to Shakespeare and held within a dedicated venue are Verona's Festival, which has been running since 1948, and the summer season of a Globe replica in Rome, the Silvano Toti Globe Theatre, founded in 2003. Both events happen in two places that Shakespeare himself often chose as a backdrop for his plays. As we will argue, the two events entertain a privileged, if different, dialogue with the cities that host them: while Verona's can be defined as a proper festival, Rome's falls within the category of festivalized theatrical events, that is, events that though not self-labelled as festivals present the characteristics of one.[1]

A long fidelity: Verona's Teatro Romano Shakespearean festival (1948–)[2]

Besides its noted 'fairness', Verona also boasts a more recent theatrical tradition linked to Shakespeare. Since 1948, it has been coming to life every summer at the open-air Teatro Romano during the Estate Teatrale Veronese, a programme devoted to drama, ballet and modern dance spectacles as well as jazz music.[3] The drama section's flagship is the annual 'Festival Shakespeariano'. Funded by the Verona city council, with the support of private local sponsors, the festival has run uninterrupted (save for 1953) and has presented almost the entire Shakespeare canon.[4] Although not directly commissioned by the festival, the productions are selected by the artistic director from among a series of new Italian proposals, which have not yet opened at their home theatres, and customarily have their opening nights in Verona before travelling to other Italian venues. Renowned Italian directors and actors have trodden the boards of the Teatro Romano over the years, but this space has also been a showcase for young Italian talents with a few concessions, especially in the 2000s, to the casting of TV actors and stand-up comedians. The festival has also presented internationally acclaimed productions that also had their Italian premieres in Verona, especially in the 1990s: Jérôme Savary's *Twelfth Night* (1991), Peter Brook's *The Tempest*, in the French adaptation of Jean-Claude Carrière (1991), Vanessa Redgrave's *Antony and Cleopatra* (1995), the Royal Shakespeare Company's *Romeo and Juliet* (directed by Michael Attenborough, 1998), Claus Peymann's Berliner Ensemble *Richard II* (2007), which Peter Stein also directed in 2017, and Propeller Theatre Company's all-male *The Taming of the Shrew* (2013), among others. Not only does this demonstrate the festival's vitality and desire to rank among the most important Shakespearean venues in Europe, but it also testifies to the peculiarity of its conceptual frame that aims at fusing the city's worldwide artistic renown and its Shakespearean literary and tourist reputation that relies on a number of popular festive initiatives as well as on the 'Letters to Juliet' phenomenon.[5] Pitching itself against the appropriation of Juliet as the city's *pre*-Shakespearean heroine, the Romano Festival was in fact born from and supports a different kind of cultural discourse.

In 1948, Verona was slowly emerging from the disasters of the Second World War and fascism, and the local authorities were determined to rebuild not only the city's economic and civic configuration but also its cultural identity. Emo Marconi – academic, theatre enthusiast, former partisan during the *Resistenza* and, at that time, Commissioner of the Arena Opera Festival – came up with the idea of hosting a Shakespearean performance at the Teatro Romano. Over the centuries, the site had been plundered of its marble and became literally buried under new buildings (Bolla 2016: 77). In time, various additions gradually eroded the boundaries of the ancient theatrical space, and it was not until the end of the nineteenth century that the remnants of the Roman edifice were rediscovered, thanks to Andrea Monga. A member of Verona's wealthy middle class, Monga had purchased over thirty buildings which stood in the area and, from 1834 onwards, started an excavation which allowed the former structures to emerge progressively (Ricci 1895; Franzoni 1988; Bolla 2016). The same space was later acquired by the city council (1904) and a new series of excavations as well as the restoration of the gallery above the cavea began, so that in 1926 actor Gustavo Salvini graced the site with a cycle of classic performances (including Sophocles' *Oedipus Rex*).[6] In the 1930s, the authorities' attention turned to other areas of the city, namely Juliet's (supposed) house and tomb. Their refurbishment followed a specific urban project, conceived by Antonio Avena, local historian and director of the Civic Museums. The project meant to create a Lefebvrian 'representational space' in which imagination takes over reality and appropriates a physical venue 'making symbolic use of its objects' (Lefebvre [1974] 1991: 39). Shakespeare's name was hardly ever mentioned in this scenario that aimed to construct a civic icon – the Veronese Juliet – of (fascist) female commitment, partially akin to but also strikingly different from the Shakespearean heroine.[7] Avena had also planned a new series of excavations at the Romano that would have transformed the area into a site of fascist civic commemoration. The plan included the construction of a crypt to contain five sarcophagi holding the remains of the Veronese black shirt martyrs.[8] The project, which never took off, pointed to the 'misuse' of the ancient performative space by converting it into a site of fascist ideological appropriation.

Another kind of appropriation was devised, in 1948, when the Shakespearean festival was launched with a production of *Romeo and Juliet*, Shakespeare's iconic Veronese play, which was at the time supposed to be staged, allegedly, every summer – much like the Oberammergau Passion Play. Directed by Veronese playwright and librettist Renato Simoni in collaboration with Giorgio Strehler, and using Salvatore Quasimodo's translation, the production opened on 26 July 1948. The lay celebration of the 'star-cross'd lovers'

(Prologue, 6) as emblems of the city's own history was rapidly subsumed, however, by a more significant purpose. Reclaiming a place that fascism had tried to overwrite in order to construct and celebrate its myths, entailed a wider scope than the mere exaltation of Romeo's and Juliet's 'piteous woes' (5.3.179). It gestured towards a sense of cultural and national rebirth from the obscurity of the dictatorship and the war, as well as towards a reaction against the fascist misappropriation of the 'true and faithful Juliet' (5.3.303) as an icon of heroic but tamed femininity. This was confirmed by the abandonment of the original plan, which imagined the festival as exclusively dedicated to *Romeo and Juliet*: in August 1949, the Romano hosted a production of *Julius Caesar* directed by Guido Salvini and Luigi Squarzina. Theirs was the play's first Italian staging after the 1935 production mounted at the Basilica of Maxentius in Rome, which downplayed the drama's concerns with tyrannical power, in favour of a grandiose staging (Sestito 1978: 128; Isenberg 2012: 92–6). Instead, the 1949 Romano production hinged on an idea of restoring the play's ambiguity. As Marisa Sestito remarked, 'Salvini's intuition was right in his approach to the various roles: everyone (perhaps with the sole exception of Caesar) moves indeed on a double level which reveals their rich many-sidedness' (1978: 136).[9] This was enhanced by the setting which, despite being an open-air venue, encouraged a rather intimate relationship between the audience and the stage, distantly reminiscent of Elizabethan conventions. The stage one sees today (20m x 13.5m) was built in 1976. St Siro and Libera's churchyard, which overhangs the steps, is occasionally used as a secondary acting space. The theatre can accommodate 1,724 people.

Far from the idea of 'theatrical utilizations of settings that in large measure *are* the things they represent' (Carlson 1989: 28), the Romano retains all the characteristics of a proper theatrical space. It stands in a separated and yet close-to-the-city area, adjacent to its river. On performance nights, the neighbouring streets are closed to traffic, granting (an almost surreal) silence and giving pride of place to the magic of the stage which is disturbed only by the nearby murmuring river. This was readily apparent in Franco Zeffirelli's 1964 *Romeo and Juliet*, with Anna Maria Guarnieri as Juliet and 21-year-old Giancarlo Giannini as Romeo.[10] The performance – in spite of the rain on the opening night – unfolded into 'an amazing and admirable communion with the city, which embraced the stage on all sides almost giving the impression that the soaring spires of the bell-towers on the other side of the river belonged to it, forming a large whole' (De Cesco 1979: 164). This continuity between the city and the stage was further enhanced by Zeffirelli's visual design, which included a set of walls akin to the medieval Castelvecchio, one of the city's landmarks, and the deployment of large groups of citizens in the first and fifth acts, possibly inspired by the scenographic frescoes of the Veronese fourteenth-century painter Altichiero.[11] The atmosphere of the city was reproduced through an expressly devised stage lighting which allowed the mise en scène to encompass the urban space by recreating its medieval aura, made of narrow streets and secluded corners, thus becoming a clear example that 'theatre *is a part* of the urban process, producing urban experience and thereby producing the city itself' (Harvie 2009: 7). It is a dialogue that has continued fruitfully, becoming one of the main characteristics of the festival.

Save for the occasional and very welcome presence of foreign, especially British, companies and productions, Shakespeare in Verona is first and foremost *Italian*. Famous Italian actors have tried their hand at Shakespeare on the Romano stage. If modern interpreters do not radically alter the playtexts, the choice of first-rate translations (from the ones by poets Salvatore Quasimodo, Eugenio Montale and Mario Luzi, to those of reputed scholars such as Agostino Lombardo, Masolino d'Amico, Alessandro Serpieri and Sergio Perosa) testifies to the will and desire to plunge the Shakespearean canon into a specifically Italian cultural pool – far and distinct from the sentimentalized Romeo and Juliet civic setups. This has been achieved not only through the (obvious) choice of having Shakespeare performed mainly in Italian, but also by giving space to Italian stage rewritings and adaptations engaging with Shakespeare 'as both icon and author' (Sanders 2006: 46). Such were Carmelo Bene's corrosive and ironic *Hamlet Suite* in 1994, Italian playwright Luigi Lunari's *Amleto ma non troppo* (*Hamlet but not too much*) in 1999, in which a walk-on is called to replace Laurence Olivier as Hamlet in a postmodern game of re-evaluation of a marginal role, and Jewish artist and writer Moni Ovadia's *Shylock: il mercante di Venezia in prova* (*Shylock: Rehearsing The Merchant of Venice*) in 2009. These rewritings use Shakespeare's plays as an occasion for theatre to reflect on itself and on the possibility – as Ovadia explained – to live on as the 'stronghold against imposture and hatred, as a fragile talisman of the most grandiose invention, that of identity' (qtd in Galetto 2009).

Alongside these productions, which may also recall and engage in a fruitful dialogue with the problematic construction of the early modern notion of subjectivity and identity, the Romano has also hosted 'disrespectful' appropriations of Shakespeare. In 2004, Lina Wertmüller directed her *Molto rumore (senza rispetto) per nulla* (Much Ado [with no respect] for Nothing), starring popular TV artist Loretta Goggi. The performance moved from the much-exploited dramaturgical device of a director (Goggi) trying to stage a Shakespearean play with 'full liberty in front of a sacred classical text in order to desecrate it' (Wertmüller 2004: 36). Rather than engaging in a sterile debate over issues of faithfulness and betrayal, her idea of 'disrespect' aimed at questioning the Italian theatrical tradition, which goes back to the nineteenth-century *grand'attori* and sees Shakespeare as the exclusive domain of highbrow directors and actors, as well as elite audiences – much in contrast with its early modern original spirit. Wertmüller transformed *Much Ado* into a deliberately disordered and supposedly culturally lower brow 1970s variety show, which provided 'an ironic metaphor of what we see every day', when 'everything gets mashed, confused, degraded, and vulgarized' (Wertmüller 2004: 36). It is a tendency Jonathan Miller had identified many years before when he wrote: 'Shakespeare is not honoured by constantly and conscientiously reproducing his intentions. Shakespeare is honoured in the complicated and plural ways in which he is attended to' (qtd in Holderness 1988: 200). A similar, although less critically aware, experiment was the 2011 *A Midsummer Night's Dream* whose cast, directed by Gioele Dix and Nicola Fano, was the stand-up comedians ensemble of the Italian TV show *Zelig*. Although at times grotesquely extravagant, the production confirmed the festival's flair for testing different cultural approaches – both high and low – to Shakespeare.

More recently, the festival has taken a new, twofold approach. On the one hand, it has emphasized the centrality of the word as in *Lost in Cyprus: sulle tracce di Otello* (*Lost in Cyprus: Looking for Othello*, 2014), translated by poet Patrizia Cavalli and directed by Giuseppe Battiston and Paolo Civati, or in the 2017 *Richard II*, directed by Peter Stein, using Alessandro Serpieri's translation and starring Maddalena Crippa as Richard. On the other hand, it has hosted visually centred performances that 'acknowledge contemporary concerns or issues' (Sanders 2006: 48). The current refugee and migrant crisis became the leitmotiv of Alex Rigoli's 2016 *Julius Caesar* (with Maria Grazia Mandruzzato as Caesar). Generally loud, this production's action frantically revolved around a larger-than-life puppet child lying on the stage – the embodiment of Alan Kurdi, the Syrian toddler whose dead body was washed up on a beach in Turkey earlier that year. The prop shockingly alluded to the ruthless dynamics of power, also symbolized by Mark Antony and the conspirators wearing oversized wolf heads and paws.

In her discussion of spatial and performative dynamics activated by the London Shakespeare's Globe, Joanne Tompkins points out that 'the tremendous weight of "history" associated with this venue can overpower performances' (2014: 107). Although on a lesser scale, this is also true of Verona's Teatro Romano and its festival, not only because the place is laden – as is the city itself – with the heritage of Roman antiquity, but especially because of the city's Shakespearean legacy. The latter could have led to the transformation of the Veronese festival into a 'passive receptacle of performances from the past' (Tompkins 2014: 108), or a strained re-enactment of a myth through the tiresome repetition of *Romeo and Juliet*. The Verona Festival has, instead, demonstrated the capacity of building on the city's Shakespearean repute but also looking beyond it and proving the existence of a world beyond the venue, a world 'without Verona walls' (3.3.17).

Shakespeare in Rome: the Silvano Toti Globe theatre summer season (2003–)[12]

If Verona's festival can be traced back to postwar political strategies of international 'spiritual recovery' (Kennedy 1998: 176), the Rome summer theatrical season devoted to Shakespeare is a third millennium phenomenon born of very different premises.

When strolling through Villa Borghese's gardens, one might be struck by the presence of an Elizabethan playhouse replica suddenly appearing through thick vegetation. Were one to consider the long and fascinating history of the park and its delights, the construction might not appear out of place anymore (Campitelli 2003). After all, this 'wooden O' stands next to Piazza di Siena, a hippodrome created in the late eighteenth century as a place that recalled the celebrated Piazza del Campo in Siena (hometown to the Borghese family), where the famous horse race known as the *Palio* has been hosted since the Middle Ages. Not far from it stands the magnificent Galleria Borghese, hosted in the Baroque palace erected at the beginning of the seventeenth century under the patronage of Cardinal Scipione Borghese in the fashion of Renaissance Tuscan suburban villas. Historical and geographical *otherness* is cited and comfortably accommodated within the green topography of Villa Borghese's ancient park, which mirrors Rome's unique capacity for recontextualizing, appropriating and repurposing diverse cultural objects.

Building a Globe replica in Italy's capital city was the bold idea of Gigi Proietti, a celebrated Roman actor, director and writer who passed away in November 2020. Having started his career in the mid-1960s, Proietti was, perhaps, the only Italian star who attracted a vast, trans-generational and steady audience of fans and followers on diverse media, from theatre to cinema and television. Therefore, he was given much credit when he suggested, at the celebration of the park's centennial as a public garden in 2003, that an Elizabethan theatre would be a welcome 'gift' to the city. The gift materialized courtesy of the Fondazione Silvano Toti, a charity founded by the Toti family, owners of an important construction firm, and under the auspices of Walter Veltroni, Rome's mayor at the time. Work started in June 2003 and was completed three months later when, in September, the theatre was inaugurated with a performance of *Romeo e Giulietta* directed by Gigi Proietti.

The theatre breaks with the tradition of proscenium arch stages of indoor venues still dominant in Italy, experimenting with an alternative performance space; at the same time, however, it aims at reaching the broadest audience possible. As Loredana Scaramella – one if its directors – puts it, the Globe is a theatre 'that cannot exist without some risks, that urges its actors to stand naked before the audience and expose their techniques, their souls; a theatre that is not meant for technological ways out or soft emotions; neither in its styles nor in its themes' (Pennacchia 2019: 94).

Impressive in itself and perfectly integrated within the natural environment, Rome's Globe is built from solid oak wood, with an outer circumference of 100 metres, and can hold up to 1,206 people. Its sustainable characteristics point to the socio-political value of a new performing space in dialogue with its green and historical context. From the project's inception, it was not considered 'a mere replica of the Globe in London ..., but a thoroughly new Italian performance venue' (Silvano Toti Globe Theatre Roma n.d.). It was Proietti's task to put into practice what at the time was only an encouraging good wish. Initially attracted by the fame of the Italian celebrity himself, his large audience gradually began to attend Villa Borghese's Globe per se, that is, as a part of their summer activities, and started to appreciate the selection of plays Proietti, as artistic director, offered them.

Rome has since added to its crowded cultural agenda a Shakespeare summer programme which is not a 'festival' but has the features of a festivalized theatrical event, in other words 'the artistic output [...] is turned into a significant *Cultural event*, framed and made meaningful by the presence of an audience and reviewers who will respond to the celebrated event' (Hauptfleisch 2007: 39). Indeed, Romans and visitors have gradually acquired a habit of coming to this outdoor playhouse, from the end of June to mid-October, to see a rich programme of Shakespeare plays in Italian and enjoy a participatory theatrical experience whose value is enhanced by the in-the-round space, the pleasantness of its natural materials, the garden's sweet air and the cosiness of the venue's bar which works as a space for meeting, relaxation and discussion that amplifies festivalized socializing.

Foucault's concept of heterotopia as 'real places ... which are something like counter-sites, a kind of effectively enacted utopia in which the real sites ... are simultaneously represented, contested and inverted' ([1984] 1986: 24) is useful in understanding the cultural meaning of the Globe Theatre in Villa Borghese as a relevant performance venue for Roman audiences. As Joanne Tompkins argues, theatre is precisely one of the 'enacted utopias' or 'counter-sites' (2014: 20–3) that are singled out by Foucault as examples of heterotopias. However, in order to narrow down this broad definition, Tompkins turns to the cultural geographer Kevin Hetherington, who interprets heterotopia as the differential space which opens between the two places included in the meaning of utopia: *eu-topia* (good place) and *ou-topia* (no place or nowhere), thus focusing on the 'relationship between spaces' more than on one single space (Hetherington 1997: ix). By bringing to the fore 'the relationship between performed worlds and the actual world beyond the theatre' (2014: 20), Tompkins contends that 'heterotopic theatre' reactivates the vital connection among audience, performance and location, thus rekindling, among other things, the political relevance of the theatre to local communities. Tompkins' heterotopic theatre refers explicitly to political theatre, however, and even though the Villa Borghese's Globe does not develop such a strong political ethos, it still exploits its eu/ou-topic collocation in the city to activate an equally compelling transformative power on the audience.

And very relevant, indeed, this Globe is to Roman citizens, according to statistics. Alongside the local audience, in fact, only a small number of theatregoers travel to Rome from other Italian cities for the season's events. Even fewer are the international visitors who come to watch a Shakespeare performance as part of their Roman holiday, because the productions are always in Italian, with the exception (only since 2015) of a single production in English per season, which is usually aimed at Italian school students.

While Shakespeare's Globe in London was seen, by some scholars, as a place that could only offer, and mainly to tourists, 'the easy delights of the heritage museum and historical theme park' (Kennedy 1988: 187; also Worthen 2004: 79–116), Villa Borghese's Globe has never elicited such harsh criticism. Nor has it ever been dismissed as a form of commodification of the past, if only because the theatre stands within a space – the park – which, as argued in the present chapter, mirrors the inclusive dynamics that traditionally characterize the city of Rome as made of several layers of history embodied in its diversified architecture.

The Globe in Villa Borghese has always been understood by Italian audiences (and the very few reviewers who wrote about it) for what it actually is: a new theatrical venue calling itself a Globe which, like other similar venues in the world, specializes in hosting Shakespeare productions which are, more often than not, *for all*, that is, productions aiming at being 'intellectually accessible' (Carson 2008: 122). 'Intellectual accessibility' is an important and not to be underestimated goal given that, in 2018, the playhouse was officially included within 'Teatro di Roma' – the theatrical circuit of the municipality of Rome – thus legitimizing it within the larger and diversified institutional offer of the capital city. This Globe's offer recalls the idealism of Tyrone Guthrie in Canada in the 1950s or Joseph Papp in New York in the 1960s, when they decided to present the audience with 'a democratic, non-elitist Shakespeare' (Lanier 2002: 156).

As well as being part of the Roman theatrical ecosystem, Villa Borghese's Globe is also constituted in relation to other Globes, and not only to Shakespeare's Globe in London.[13] It is conceptually related to the Neuss Globe in Germany, the Globetheater Diever in the Netherlands and the many Elizabethan-like venues around the world. Its value rests, however, on the *difference from* more than on the *similarity to* them because it presents very strong local peculiarities, Italian and Roman, not only in terms of location, audience, organization and investments, but – above all – of a shared artistic style in producing the plays, like, for instance, the purposeful quoting and recycling of Italian Renaissance art, the use of live popular music and folk dancing, as well as in resorting to the improvising acting tradition that goes back to the *commedia dell'arte*.

An overview of the theatrical seasons from 2003 to 2019, made possible by the creation of the Digitized Archive of the Silvano Toti Globe Theatre at Roma Tre University, shows that nineteen of Shakespeare's plays were produced for this stage (mostly by Politeama S.r.l.).[14] In terms of dramatic genres, only four tragedies, apart from *Romeo e Giulietta*, have been produced (*Giulio Cesare*, *Otello*, *Macbeth* and *Re Lear*) and two histories (*Riccardo III* and *Enrico V*). The lion's share belongs to comedies and romances: no fewer than twelve have been staged to date.[15] Moreover, Melania Giglio's *Sonetti d'amore* (*Love Sonnets*) has been performed since 2015; the latest additions, in 2020, are Daniele Salvo's thought-provoking and highly entertaining adaptation of the epyllion *Venere e Adone* (*Venus and Adonis*) and *#lostuprodilucrezia*, an open rehearsal show from *The Rape of Lucrece* directed by Marco Carniti.

While the interest of practitioners working at Shakespeare's Globe in London was mainly that of experimenting with original performance practices, one of the aims of the Silvano Toti Globe Theatre was to introduce Shakespeare to 'a wider audience of people mostly unacquainted with his works [and] to develop some familiarity with the original text' (Pennacchia 2019: 95). As the 'original text' had to be translated into Italian, some productions chose readily available translations by reputed scholars, such as Masolino d'Amico and Agostino Lombardo, or by professional theatre translators, such as Angelo Dallagiacoma; others used new translations which were made by the directors themselves for the performance at the Globe.[16]

The Borghese Globe also welcomes a variety of textual and stage configurations diversely related to Shakespeare, such as Andrea Camilleri and Giuseppe Dipasquale's *Troppu Trafficu ppi nenti* (2009). This was a co-production with *Teatro di Catania*, that playfully staged the supposed 'original' source-text of *Much Ado About Nothing*, in Sicilian dialect, suggesting that it was perhaps authored by Messer Michele Agnolo Florio, the writer who may have adopted the pen-name 'William Shakespeare' when he emigrated to England. Florio was again the protagonist, with Cervantes, of *Ghost Writer* by Stefano Reali, produced in 2019. Successful both at the box office and with the critics was *Edmund Kean* (2017), starring Gigi Proietti, who also penned the adaptation of Raymund FitzSimons' biography of the great Shakespearean actor. One-act shows for children (aged from four to eleven) have been produced since 2019, such as *Riccardino III* (*Little Richard III*) – a prequel of the play, when the three York brothers are still children – and *Le streghe di Macbeth* (*The Witches from Macbeth*) both written and directed by Gigi Palla, while the edutainment show *Playing Shakespeare* by Loredana Scaramella has been performed for high-school students since 2015. An Italian translation of the parodic work *The Complete Works of William Shakespeare (Abridged)* has been adapted by 'The Bignami Shakespeare Company' and has been running since 2019. Furthermore, the venue hosted other media, cinema in particular, as in the year of Shakespeare's birth anniversary (2014). Acknowledging the importance of Shakespeare in the film industry and its impact on theatre productions, Carlotta Proietti and Daniele Dezi organized the *Shakespeare Fest*, the first of a series of short-film contests where young directors presented their takes on the playwright and what his global myth means today to up-and-coming Italian film-makers.

Rome's Globe created a new habit of attending Shakespeare plays that certainly was not there before, at least not in Rome and not for such a wide audience, mostly made of young people. Box office figures confirm this: if season 2005 had 22,428 admissions, season 2017 almost tripled that number (63,598), with an average of 700 spectators per night. The summer season at the Silvano Toti Globe Theatre is undoubtedly one of the liveliest theatrical programmes in Italy, with over 50 per cent of the audience between thirteen and thirty-four years old. Moreover, the number of school students who watched the plays in 2019 reached 17,000,[17] a relevant figure in a country where theatregoing is not top of the list of national cultural activities and where there is a real necessity to develop new audiences, just as Gigi Proietti wished when he first conceived the project (Polidoro 2013: 49).

While the Silvano Toti Globe Theatre was not born with an Education department, like the Shakespeare's Globe, in order to broaden its educational mission beyond acting training, in 2018 the theatre started an ongoing collaboration – co-funded by the Fondazione Toti – with Roma Tre University on research and teaching projects, about the practical and theoretical uses of Shakespeare (in English and in translation) to facilitate the development of linguistic as well as relational abilities in teenagers through their bodily and emotional response to Shakespeare. The projects aim to familiarize students not only with theatre but, more specifically, with Shakespeare's civic and inclusive values.

Thus, in September and October 2019, the theatre opened its gates for the first time to workshops specifically addressed to high-school students that were co-designed by scholars and practitioners. The highly successful collaboration in such a meaningful venue and under the auspices of Shakespeare holds much promise for the future.[18]

Conclusion

As we have argued, Verona and Rome, two internationally prominent and renowned cities in their own right, regularly pay tribute to Shakespeare's genius by hosting festivals or festivalized theatrical events devoted to him. However, their approach to festivalizing Shakespeare differs in many respects.

Born after the Second World War as a response to the fascist appropriation of Roman vestiges, the Verona Festival has aimed at enlivening the city by relying on and commending its manifold and multi-layered cultural heritage, responding to the idea that 'the kind of space ... [theatres] occupy [is an] extremely important indicator ... of the social and cultural positioning of the theatre in its community' (Carlson 2013: 93). Locating the festival in a decentralized position by superimposing it on the ancient performative space, far from the refurbished Capulet's house-and-tomb scenarios, places it in competition with the idea of a city exclusively linked with Juliet's tale, spatially retold in a tourist-oriented jargon.

As for Rome, a city that is characteristically inclined to welcome and reuse cultural objects from all over the world, the sudden addition, in 2003, of a Globe replica in one of its historical parks with a Shakespeare-for-all cultural agenda, led to the development of a large audience fond of Shakespeare in the Italian capital city. The success of this theatrical model is confirmed by the fact that it entered the larger institutional theatrical circuit of the municipality of Rome, 'Teatro di Roma', and formed a partnership with Roma Tre University in order to collaborate on research and teaching programmes for students.

The primary aim of both Verona's Festival and the Rome's Globe Summer Season is not that of bringing people from all over the world to see Shakespearean plays (in Italian) – the two cities can, indeed, rely on many other artistic and cultural attractions to entice visitors – but that of honouring the cities, their people, and Italian theatre in the name of Shakespeare.

Notes

1. For a thorough study on the concept of festivalization, see Hauptfleisch et al. (2007).
2. The section on Verona is entirely by Lisanna Calvi. Thanks go to Giampaolo Savorelli, artistic director for four decades. The festival is currently directed by Carlo Mangolini.
3. The jazz component was inaugurated by Duke Ellington in 1970.
4. The only exceptions are *Timon of Athens*, *The Two Noble Kinsmen*, *Henry VI* and *Henry VIII*.
5. This refers to the tradition – dating back to the early nineteenth century – of people around the world writing to Juliet. For many decades a group of 'secretaries' belonging to a volunteer organization called 'Club di Giulietta' reply to the thousands of letters that arrive every year.
6. This tradition was revived in 2017 in collaboration with the National Institute of Ancient Drama (Siracusa).
7. See Bigliazzi and Calvi (2016).

8 The Veronese black shirts (*squadristi*) who died in the early 1920s during the so-called fascist revolution initiated the paramilitary and political movement that led to the March on Rome and Mussolini's rise to power (see Franzoni 1968).
9 This section's translations are Calvi's.
10 This production followed Zeffirelli's 1960 Old Vic staging of the play and preceded his famous film version.
11 This 'authenticity' may have inspired Zeffirelli's 1968 film.
12 The section on Rome is entirely by Maddalena Pennacchia.
13 A meeting between Gigi Proietti, in his capacity of artistic director of the Silvano Toti Globe Theatre, and Patrick Spottiswood, Director of Globe Education at Shakespeare's Globe, was organized on 14 November 2014 at the Roma Tre Palladium Theatre for *Joining Globes*, an event organized by Maria Del Sapio Garbero and Carlotta Proietti.
14 The Archive has been created thanks to the partnership between Politeama S.r.l. (of Gigi Proietti), which handles the exclusive management of the Silvano Toti Globe Theatre, and the Department of Foreign Languages, Literatures and Cultures of Roma Tre University. This ongoing scientific project, directed by Maddalena Pennacchia, started in 2018. In June 2021 the theatre was renamed Gigi Proietti Globe Theatre Silvano Toti. See https://bacheca.uniroma3.it/archivio-globe/chi-siamo/.
15 The only comedies and romances that have not been produced yet are: *The Two Noble Kinsmen, Love's Labour's Lost, Measure for Measure, All's Well That Ends Well, Pericles* and *Cymbeline*.
16 For a catalogue of productions, see Archivio Silvano Toti Globe Theatre Roma, https://bacheca.uniroma3.it/archivio-globe/esplora/.
17 Statistic data are among the materials of the Archive.
18 Notwithstanding the pandemic, Roma Tre University educational programme, in collaboration with the Globe in Villa Borghese, saw its second edition in October 2020. The programme was filmed and broadcast on the cultural channel of the national broadcasting company of Italy, RAI Cultura (see Pennacchia 2021).

References

Archivio Silvano Toti Globe Theatre Roma (n.d.), https://bacheca.uniroma3.it/archivio-globe/ (accessed 12 June 2020).
Bigliazzi, Silvia, and Lisanna Calvi (2016), 'Producing a (*R&*)*J* Space: Discursive and Social Practices in Verona', in Silvia Bigliazzi and

Lisanna Calvi (eds), *Shakespeare, Romeo and Juliet, and Civic Life: The Boundaries of Civic Space*, 238–59, London and New York: Routledge.
Bolla, Margherita (2016), *Il Teatro Romano di Verona* [*The Roman Theatre of Verona*], Verona: Cierre.
Campitelli, Alberta (2003), *Villa Borghese: da giardino dei principi a parco dei romani* [Villa Borghese: From Garden of Princes to Rome's Public Park], Rome: Istituto poligrafico e zecca dello stato.
Carlson, Marvin (1989), *Places of Performance: The Semiotics of Theatre Architecture*, Ithaca and London: Cornell University Press.
Carlson, Marvin (2013), 'The Theatre *ici*', in Erika Fischer-Lichte and Benjamin Wihstutz (eds), *Performance and the Politics of Space. Theatre and Topology*, 69–118, New York: Routledge.
Carson, Christie (2008), 'Democratising the Audience?', in Christie Carson and Farah Karim-Cooper (eds), *Shakespeare's Globe: A Theatrical Experiment*, 115–26, Cambridge and New York: Cambridge University Press.
De Cesco, Bruno (1979), *Un quarto di secolo con Shakespeare* [A Quarter of a Century with Shakespeare], Verona: Edizione del Comune di Verona.
Foucault, Michel ([1984] 1986), 'Of Other Spaces', *Diacritics* 16 (1): 22–7.
Franzoni, Lanfranco (1968), 'Un mancato restauro del Teatro Romano' [A Missed Opportunity for the Restoration of the Teatro Romano], *Vita Veronese* XXI (11–2): 421–4.
Franzoni, Lanfranco (1988), 'Il monumento e la sua storia' [The Monument and its History], in *Il Teatro Romano: la storia e gli spettacoli* [The Teatro Romano: The History and the Performances], 15–82, Verona: Comune di Verona.
Galetto, Alessandra (2009), 'Un'estate nel segno dell'originalità' [A Summer in the Name of Originality], *L'Arena*, 26 June. Available online: http://www.larena.it/home/altri/speciali/un-estate-di-eventi/teatro-romano/un-estate-nel-segno-dell-originalit-agrave-1.2658785 (accessed 15 May 2020).
Harvie, Jen (2009), *Theatre & the City*, Houndsmill, Basingstoke: Palgrave Macmillan.
Hauptfleisch, Temple, Shulamith Lev-Aladgem, Jacqueline Martin, Willmar Sauter and Henri Schoenmakers, eds (2007), *Festivalising! Theatrical Events, Politics, and Culture*, Amsterdam and New York: Rodopi.
Hetherington, Kevin (1997), *The Badlands of Modernity, Heterotopia and Social Ordering*, New York: Routledge.

Holderness, Graham, ed. (1988), *The Shakespeare Myth*, Manchester: Manchester University Press.
Isenberg, Nancy (2012), '"Caesar's word against the world": Caesarism and the Discourses of Empire', in Irena R. Makaryk and Marissa McHugh (eds), *Shakespeare and the Second World War: Memory, Culture, Identity*, 83–105, Toronto, Buffalo and London: University of Toronto Press.
Kennedy, Dennis (1998), 'Shakespeare and Cultural Tourism', *Theatre Journal* 50 (2): 175–88.
Lanier, Douglas (2002), 'Shakespeare Tourism and Festivals', in Douglas Lanier, *Shakespeare and Modern Popular Culture*, 143–67, Oxford: Oxford University Press.
Lefebvre, Henri ([1974] 1991), *The Production of Space*, trans. Donald Nicholson-Smith, Oxford: Blackwell.
Pennacchia, Maddalena (2019), '"But not love … ": An Interview with Loredana Scaramella about her Translation, Adaptation and Direction of *La bisbetica domata* (*The Taming of the Shrew*) at the Silvano Toti Globe Theatre in Rome (2018)', *JAFP* 11 (3): 91–106.
Pennacchia, Maddalena (2021), 'Younger Generations and Empathic Communication: Learning to Feel in Another Language with Shakespeare at the Silvano Toti Globe Theatre', *Shakespeare Survey* (74): 131–8.
Polidoro, Paola (2013), '*Romeo e Giulietta* per aprire il Globe' [*Romeo and Juliet* and the Opening of the Globe], *Il Messaggero*, 10 July: 49.
Ricci, Serafino (1895), 'Il teatro romano di Verona: studiato sotto il rispetto storico ed archeologico, con la biografia di Andrea Monga' [Verona's Roman Theatre: An Historical and Archeological Study, with a Biography of Andrea Monga], in Serafino Ricci, *Miscellanea di Storia Veneta* [Sundry Texts about the History of Veneto], 1–202, Venezia: Visentini.
Sanders, Julie (2006), *Adaptation and Appropriation*, London and New York: Routledge.
Sestito, Marisa (1978), '*Julius Caesar*' *in Italia (1726–1974)*, Bari: Adriatica.
Shakespeare, William (2012), *Romeo and Juliet*, ed. René Weis, London: Arden Shakespeare.
Silvano Toti Globe Theatre Roma (n.d.), https://www.globetheatreroma.com/ (accessed 2 August 2021).
Tompkins Joanne (2014), *Theatre Heterotopias: Performance and the Cultural Politics of Place*, Basingstoke and New York: Palgrave Macmillan.

Wertmüller, Lina (2004), 'Nota del regista' [Director's Note], in *Estate Teatrale Veronese 2004 – Programma degli spettacoli* [Verona Summer Festival 2004 – Programme of Events]: 36.

Worthen, William B. (2004), 'Globe Performativity', in William B. Worthen, *Shakespeare and the Force of Modern Performance*, 79–116, Cambridge: Cambridge University Press.

8

The Gdańsk Shakespeare Festival: Four centuries of travelling theatre in Poland

Urszula Kizelbach and Jacek Fabiszak

The Gdańsk Shakespeare Festival is one of the largest Shakespeare festivals in Europe. Its pioneering edition 'Shakespeare Days' began in 1993 as the materialization of a man's dream. The first edition of the festival proper was in 1997, and it has been continuously organized since then under the patronage of the Theatrum Gedanense Foundation and of the Gdańsk Shakespeare Theatre (GST) later on. It is an 'establishment' festival (Engle et al. 1995: 17), developed over more than two decades, employing professional personnel (actors and educators), enjoying the patronage of both theatrical institutions and local authorities (Gdańsk City Hall), and receiving funding from sponsors and grants. This chapter discusses the unique character of the Gdańsk Shakespeare Festival: its origins, its exclusive focus on a single author – which does not preclude the variety of its programme – its particular timing, as well as the location of the GST, its main venue, which can be traced back to the seventeenth century when Gdańsk was an influential Hanseatic merchant city with well-established theatrical traditions. One of the specificities of the festival consists in its seasonal interconnection with the GST, whose year-long activity both includes and overflows the summer celebrations. Particular attention will be paid to the crucial role of the Education Department of the GST in the festival and beyond. To better illustrate Gdańsk's valuable contribution to the world of Shakespeare festivals, the chapter focuses on representative case studies of productions performed in the most recent editions of the festival from 2014 to 2019.[1]

Modern-day celebrations of the early modern tradition

The Gdańsk Shakespeare Festival continues a long-standing tradition (1590–1650) of English actors playing on the Continent in the cities and regions of Gdańsk, Elbing, Königsberg, Pomerania or Livonia as part of their Baltic Route. Faced with Puritan opposition and growing competition from boy acting companies at home, the *Englische Kömedianten* left for the Continent to gain international recognition or to escape an unstable economic situation in England. In spring and autumn, they habitually returned to Leyden, Amsterdam, Utrecht and Gdańsk to play on special occasions, during local celebrations, weddings or fairs, such as Gdańsk's St Dominic's Fair in August and St Martin's Fair in late autumn. Lured by fame and money, the English players made frequent visits from 1600 to 1619 and from 1636 to 1654. The first acting company may have arrived as early as 1587 and were said to have been the same players who performed a *Spiel mit Springen* at the Danish court at Elsinore in 1586 (some of the names included Thomas King, George Bryan, Rupert Pesten, Will Kempe and Daniel Jones). More tangible evidence comes from the year 1615 when a certain John Spencer applied to the City Council asking for permission for his actors to play in *Fechtschulen* (fencing schools) in Gdańsk where their 'Antecessor vor dreyen Jahren' had been performing (Limon 2009: 2–6). The GST, which now serves as the main theatrical venue for the festival, was built to commemorate the Fencing School that hosted the English players and was witness to their theatrical art in early seventeenth-century Gdańsk.

The Gdańsk Shakespeare Days, a city event launched in 1993 under the auspices of the Theatrum Gedanense Foundation, provided several days of intense theatrical experience for the audience. It also served as a cultural platform for exchanging creative thoughts among artists, directors and critics. In 1997 the Shakespeare Days were transformed into the Gdańsk Shakespeare Festival to celebrate the thousandth anniversary of the foundation of the city. The millennial celebrations commemorated the first mention of Gdańsk in the historical chronicles (*The Life of St. Adalbert*), which describe the baptism of many Gdańsk dwellers by St Adalbert in April 997 CE. The modern-day festival is organized at the time of St Dominic's Fair when it was customary for the English actors to play in Gdańsk back in the early modern period. In 2020 the city celebrated the 760th anniversary of St Dominic's Fair, organized from the last days of July until mid-August. The fair has not changed much since the old times: people buy, trade and bargain in the stalls, different languages can be heard and the Babelic streets bustle with life and theatre. From fair to 'urban' festival (Falassi 1987: 3), the event has retained strong ties with the city's seventeenth-century theatrical tradition.

The historical origins of the Gdańsk Shakespeare Festival may account for its development both at local and global levels. It is global because of Shakespeare's global outreach and because since its first edition the festival has hosted theatrical groups from all over the world. The Prince of Wales is the honorary patron of the GST; Prince William and Kate Middleton visited the theatre during their trip to Gdańsk in 2017. 'Shakespeare always reminds us how much we have in common because the language he uses and the problems he describes are universal', Professor Jerzy Limon, the festival's director and the founding father of GST, said in an interview for the BBC a week before the theatre's inauguration in 2014.[2] The festival's local character is determined by the audience, the inhabitants of the Tricity (Gdańsk, Gdynia and Sopot) and its surroundings, conveniently located at the seaside and connected by fast rail. Every year, the festival audience also includes thousands of Gdańsk's Polish tourists.

The year 2014 was special in the festival's history because the performances were partially held in the newly constructed venue of the GST.[3] The black-brick theatre building was designed by a Venetian architect, Renato Rizzi, and modelled on the London Fortune. Jerzy Limon decided that the theatre would not have a permanent company but that it would be open to many forms of performance and stage art. Today, the GST serves as an important theatrical centre in the city and is home to artistic, educational and cultural events. Since its foundation, GST has been the hub of the Gdańsk Shakespeare Festival and a reminder of the festival's missions: to cultivate high standards in theatrical art, to educate its audiences culturally and to provide high-quality entertainment on a local and global scale.

'This is very midsummer madness': festival structure and programme

The festival is composed of two meta-events, both taking place in the same week(s) of the midsummer Dominican Fair, but at different hours: the main programme and its fringe alternative ShakespeareOFF. The former addresses a mainstream audience and offers theatre productions from well-established companies and institutions, staged in the theatre venues all over the Tricity. The most prestigious tradition within the main programme is the competition for the best Polish Shakespeare production of the season, which is awarded the prize of the Golden Yorick. Every year since the competition originated in 1994, the three best Polish performances are selected for the finals to be shown later at the festival. An independently appointed jury decides on the winning performance to be awarded the Golden Yorick at the end of the festival. In the 2018/19 theatrical season, for example, fourteen Polish productions applied for the competition and the three finalists were: *Hamlet*, directed by Maja Kleczewska (The Polish Theatre, Poznań); *Twelfth Night*, directed by Łukasz Kos (Juliusz Osterwa Theatre in Lublin); and *The Merchant of Venice*, directed by Szymon Kaczmarek (The Witkacy New Theatre in Słupsk) – the winner. The jury was impressed by the consistent interpretation of this drama and highlighted the fact that it provided 'food for the Polish thought'. 'Kaczmarek treats Shakespeare's play as if it was written today – in the world haunted by the monsters of anti-Semitism ... and many stereotypes poisoning the society', said Łukasz Drewniak, the competition's selector, on the festival website.

A ten-year-old initiative invented by the festival organizers, ShakespeareOFF is part of city life and takes place in less conventional venues, such as parks, streets, cafés and courtyards. Its programme proposes more experimental, 'off-road' theatre in the form of happenings and artistic events, either based on Shakespeare's works or somehow inspired by Shakespeare, by independent artists and groups from Poland and abroad. It popularizes alternative forms of theatre in Poland and promotes young and talented individual artists and groups. The programme addresses all kinds of audiences – art and theatre critics, theatre aficionados and mainstream audiences. There are many late evening shows, especially in the streets or in pubs, but performances are organized all day long. Since 2016, the organizers have added a new element within ShakespeareOFF: a competition running in April, ahead of the festival, for the most original alternative theatre project. In 2020, for the first time in ShakespeareOFF's history, the jury offered funding to support the production of the best project so it could premiere during the upcoming edition of the festival.

The Gdańsk Shakespeare Theatre

The GST is a sophisticated combination of tradition and innovation since it revives the memory of Gdańsk's early modern history while providing theatre directors with state-of-the-art technology. Its protean stage easily transforms into an Elizabethan platform, a theatre-in-the-round or the classical black box. Choosing the type of stage always depends on the director's decision, even though the auditorium – which can accommodate up to 595 spectators – partially remains a faithful copy of the traditional Elizabethan galleries. The pit contains removable seats and can make room for a standing audience in the fashion of Elizabethan groundlings surrounding the thrust stage in the daytime, as was the case with Paweł Aigner's lighthearted and very dynamic matinee production of *The Merry Wives of Windsor* (Kizelbach 2016). For Oliver Frljić's Croatian *Hamlet* (2017), the stage was folded, so the actors sat at a large table 'in the pit', with the audience surrounding it on all four sides.

The venue also lends itself to acoustic reconfigurations. The 2014 edition of the festival hosted *Othello: The Remix* by Chicago Shakespeare Theater and Richard Jordan Productions Ltd, programmed at the 2012 Globe to Globe, in which Shakespeare's plays were staged in many different languages by companies from different countries. In this combination of Shakespeare and hip-hop performed by the Q Brothers, the model of the Elizabethan platform proved most successful – due not only to the energy of the performers (who were able to rouse elderly spectators) but also to the possibilities offered by the theatrical space, where the music and singing sounded as in a genuine concert hall.

The GST is equipped with an electrically powered roof which opens to the weather, thus affecting the staging of many performances. In 2014 Javor Gardev's *Hamlet* from the National Theatre in Sofia was specifically accommodated to the open-air amphitheatre. The opening roof of the theatre became part of the production's stage design. The play began in the late afternoon and the audience needed to see a starry sky in the evening at key moments of the play. The roof opened twice: once during Claudius' confession (Claudius looking up to the sky and praying) at the end of the first part, and for the second time at the end of the play, when it opened for three minutes, noiselessly; the only sign of it being opened was the chill from the slight evening cold the audience felt inside the theatre.

FIGURE 8.1 *The upper galleries of the Gdańsk Shakespeare Theatre with an open roof (night view). Photograph by Dawid Linkowski. By permission of the Gdańsk Shakespeare Theatre.*

It has become a tradition since the GST venue was erected that in the middle or at the end of successful performances the rooftop opens to celebrate well-received plays or to highlight important moments during the show. At the 2017 Shakespeare Festival, the roof of the theatre opened to honour Declan Donnellan's *Measure for Measure*, performed by the actors of the Pushkin Theatre in Moscow. This London- and Moscow-based production with its flexible scenography (three black-and-red cubes serving as different types of space, namely prison, brothel, monastery), with its skilful operating of the stage lighting of the upper gallery, and the tunes of the waltz by Pavel Akimkin, earned its Russian acting crew a thirty-minute standing ovation. The director's sixty-fourth birthday was celebrated on stage with a birthday cake. The roof also opened at the culminating points of Jan Klata's Polish production of *Hamlet* during the 2014 edition of the festival to refer to a star called 'Hamlet', referenced in the poem 'Elegy of Fortinbras' by Polish poet Zbigniew Herbert. Klata's *Hamlet* shown on the GST stage did not reference the Elizabethan stage conventions and conditions because it was originally meant for traditional stages. The only exceptions were the moments when the roof was opened, for example the mousetrap scene, which was watched by Claudius and Gertrude from the upper central gallery (the actors playing close to the audience, rather than an actual Elizabethan convention).

The new theatre venue in the centre of Gdańsk made the festival more accessible to the audience. Until 2014, the festival audiences had to commute between Gdańsk, Gdynia and Sopot, sometimes on the same day, to be able to watch their favourite plays, which were staged in the three cities at different hours. The usual venues for the performances from the main programme were the Wybrzeże Theatre in Gdańsk, the Music Theatre in Gdynia and the Kameralna (Chamber) Stage in Sopot. These days, the GST together with the Wybrzeże Theatre (Main stage and Malarnia stage) are capable of hosting the majority of performances from the main programme. Both theatres are conveniently located in the city centre and are a three-minute walk away. This way, the key performances within the main programme can be attended in one city, which rules out the problem of hectic commuting.

Still, the unique character of the festival consists in its variety not only in terms of its artistic programme but also of its theatrical space(s). Thus, the 2014 Shakespeare Festival used not only the long-awaited GST but also the main stage of the Wybrzeże Theatre, which hosted the winner of the Golden Yorick – Katarzyna Deszcz's *The Taming of the Shrew* from Stefan Żeromski Theatre in Kielce (Fabiszak 2015: 163–4) – and the Kameralna Stage in Sopot for *Diagnosis: Hamlet*, a puppet show by Companyia Pelmànec, Spain. Malarnia, the studio of the Wybrzeże Theatre, hosts smaller-scale, often experimental productions, such as *Shakespeare Laboratory* by the Bolshoi Puppet Theatre from St Petersburg. For this highly symbolic series of mini-etudes, the Russian actors used their imagination and stage conventions to present scenes from Shakespeare's plays. The fight between the Capulets and the Montagues in *Romeo and Juliet* was performed as a fight of pins on the table (utilizing magnets under the table), and Ophelia poetically drowned in a bucket of water spilt on the stage.

ShakespeareOFF: street and site-specific theatre

The ShakespeareOFF programme used to be traditionally located in the TwO Windows Theatre: a street theatre at the heart of historical Gdańsk, where the acting space encompasses a small stage raised in front of two windows on the ground floor of an old tenement house on Długa Street (the auditorium, like the stage, is literally situated in the street). The street attracted the inhabitants and tourists who would first incidentally stumble upon the windows but after a few years would purposefully plan to spend part of their evening there, watching unconventional Shakespeare. Today, ShakespeareOFF prides itself on luring wider audiences in various localities and spaces in the city, such as parks and cafés. The list of titles within the programme lengthens every year, and the levels of artistic expression and originality prove more startling with each new edition of the festival. Within a wide scope of ShakespeareOFF happenings and performances, so far there have been short fringe productions, for example performing scenes from Shakespeare's plays or monodrama, as well as staged readings of poetry, puppet shows or film screenings.

In 2016 ShakespeareOFF included thirty-four performances and events presented by over a hundred artists from Poland, Romania, Great Britain and Australia. Among them were plays prepared by theatre adepts, for example *Much Ado About Nothing*, a diploma performance staged by the students of the Faculty of Dance Theatre at State Theatre School in Bytom. The play by Brian Michaels concentrated on the oppression of women in a world dominated by men and was performed in a popular Italian pizzeria in Gdańsk. *Shakespearations* was an hour-long improvisation with music (keyboard), which took place at an art café in Sopot on two festival days. The performers improvised scenes from Shakespeare's plays, suggested by the audience. Some members of the audience would propose a character and setting of the scene, and the actors would act it out using traditional Shakespearean trademarks, such as poison, soliloquy, madness or multiple deaths on the stage. Agnieszka Skawińska's *Lady M.* was a fifty-minute-long monodrama performed on the stage of Gdynia Główna Theatre, which focused on the situation of contemporary women. A solo performance by Brett Brown, directed by Philip Parr, looked at the complexity of Shakespeare's Henry V as a monarch and as a man. The actor pondered on both Henry's popularity and military glory at Agincourt, and his loneliness as a human being. This hour-long drama was acted out in the street, in front of the TwO Windows Theatre.

ShakespeareOFF's competitive section helped enhance the whole programme's international recognition and prestige. Its curator, Katarzyna Knychalska, and judges ensure the quality of the festival as well as the highest artistic quality of the shows competing in the finals. The 2019 edition of ShakespeareOFF invited individual artists, students of theatrical schools, as well as alternative and professional theatre groups from all over the world. There were twelve finalists in the competition at the Shakespeare Festival that year, among them: Caroline Pagani with *HAMLETELIA* (Italy); the Royal Academy of Dramatic Art with *Julius Caesar* (UK); Hubert Michalak/Tricklock Company with *The Shortest Shakespeare in the World* based on *As You Like It* (Poland/USA); and second-year students of the Aleksander Zelwerowicz National Academy of Dramatic Art in Warsaw with *Shakespeare's Ghosts*, based on *Julius Caesar, Macbeth, Hamlet, Romeo and Juliet* and *The Two Gentlemen of Verona. Shakespeare's Ghosts* was a fifty-minute performance staged in the TwO Windows Theatre, which combined various means of artistic expression: dance, music, fighting on stage, drama and poetry. Yet, ShakespeareOFF does not function as a separate event from the festival. It serves as an extension of

FIGURE 8.2 *Photo impression from ShakespeareOFF during the 23rd Shakespeare Festival. Photograph by Dawid Linkowski. By permission of the Gdańsk Shakespeare Theatre.*

the main programme and invites mainstream audiences to see more experimental productions which relate to the titles from the main programme and go beyond it.

Cultivating high standards in theatrical art provides the festival, and beyond it the GST, with fertile ground for developing ambitious cultural and educational programmes, thus reviving the Elizabethan spirit of theatre for all people.

Civic education and social commitment

Part and parcel of the GST's civic and cultural role, its Department of Education takes an active part in preparing the festival and organizing accompanying cultural and educational events. It is important to note that the educational section of GST works all year round and is aided by volunteers, trainees and co-workers. It aims to spread knowledge about Shakespeare and Elizabethan drama, but also to teach young people that the theatre is a friendly space, open to anyone. One of many civic projects run by the department is the so-called 'Theatre Solitaire' (*Teatralny Pasjans*). The project addresses three groups of people: students from schools in the region, people with disabilities and senior citizens. Each group receives the professional support of a theatre director and prepares their own staging of a given play by Shakespeare or other (including Polish) dramatists. On the day of the competition finals, each group presents their performance before exchanging about their experience with the other groups. Such performances are very popular and attract wide audiences. Another interesting project called 'Theatre Chemistry' (*Chemia Teatru*) addresses students aged from twelve to nineteen, who wish to expand their interests in art and science subjects. The workshops are prepared for student groups under their teachers' supervision. There, the participants learn, for example, how to make an invisible letter, a genie in a bottle or theatrical fog, using chemistry and physics. The classes give the students a chance to share in the art of theatre, as they can create their own stage props.

The regular educational venture at the festival is the Summer Shakespeare Academy, another time and space in which students, teachers and anybody willing can participate in workshops, rehearsals and lectures offered by actors, individual artists, educators and visiting scholars. The initiative was launched in 2005 as part of a pilot project, 'Summer Academy of Theatre and Drama', in cooperation with German Shakespeare Globe Zentrum, Associazione Lunaria Onlus and London Metropolitan University, and it has continued in its present form since then. Attending workshops, lectures and meetings with artists after performances is admission free, but requires previous registration when the theatre company is famous. Pre-performance rehearsals are also open to the public interested in the theatre-making process and willing to buy a ticket. While the core formula of the Summer Shakespeare Academy includes workshops, meetings with artists and rehearsals open to the public, the Academy never looks exactly the same – its scope (discussion panels, theatre workshops, accompanying educational events) is more varied every year.

For example, within the Summer Shakespeare Academy of the 2015 edition of the festival, the audience had an opportunity to ask questions during meetings with directors and actors of, among others, Bral School of Acting (Poland), Baltic House Theatre (Russia,

Germany), The Tiger Lillies (UK, Denmark) and Rustaveli Theatre Tbilisi (Georgia). Additional events included open rehearsals, for example, Flute Theatre's *Hamlet: Who's there?* or *Macbeth* by Baltic House Theatre, both performed at the GST as part of the main programme. The workshops on acting and theatrical art included techniques of reading, interpreting and acting a role (Thinking Through Shakespeare), working on the body (The Body as a Vehicle for an Actor's Intuition) and even theatre therapy (Shakespeare Theraplay). Paulina Kwiatkowska, a certified art coach, also gave a lecture on art-coaching for artists, which was followed by a panel discussion and a free trial art-coaching session. The idea behind the Shakespeare Academy is to give audiences a chance to learn from highly expert theatre scholars and practitioners and acquire new practical skills and knowledge about Shakespeare, theatre and drama.

The Summer Shakespeare Academy continued in 2016, with great success, as, apart from workshops and meetings with artists, the festival team organized an international seminar for teachers, trainers and educationalists, which involved thirty hours of classes and tutorials with theatre experts from Poland, Great Britain and Norway (Mażka Wojciechowska, Tanya Roberts, Einar Dahl). At the 2019 edition of the festival, the audience attended lectures by both an early modern theatre scholar (Professor Jerzy Limon's talk on Shakespeare's contemporaries: Francis Beaumont's *The Knight of the Burning Pestle*) and a translator (Filip Krenus' talk on translating a Croatian Renaissance classic *Dundo Maroje* by Marin Držić into English). The Croatian and British actors (House of Marin Držić, Marin Držić Theatre and Midsummer Scene in Dubrovnik), who performed *Uncle Maroye Re-Examined*, answered the audience's questions at the post-show talk. Tickets were sold for open rehearsals before plays, for example *Rosencrantz and Guildenstern Are Dead* directed by Tapasztó Ernő (Hungary) and Aradi Kamaraszínház (Romania) with live music by The Tiger Lillies (UK), or the youthful, contemporary version of *Romeo and Juliet* performed by the Yerevan Chamber State Theatre (Armenia). For the audience's benefit, the Department of Education at GST decided that from 2018 they would appoint an educator from their team to provide a short introduction about the history of the performance and a few words about the original Shakespeare text before every open rehearsal. Each edition of the festival publishes its own gazette, *Shakespeare Daily*, with articles about performances written by both the festival organizing team and by professional theatre critics.

The 2017 Shakespeare Festival was special for educational and academic reasons since it was accompanied by the biennial conference of the European Shakespeare Research Association (ESRA). The conference was jointly organized by the University of Gdańsk and the GST and, as the organizers noted, it was a unique meeting of international theatre practitioners (directors, actors, choreographers) and academics (scholars, translators and theatre and film critics). The conference's theme, '(An)atomizing Text and Stage', encouraged reflection upon Shakespeare's profound influence on European theatre today. The conference opened on the stage of the GST with Luk Perceval's talk about his successes and failures as a director, stressing the prominence of 'the three witches' motif in his life and in his productions. Both festival and conference were inaugurated by *The Island*, an adaptation of Shakespeare's *The Tempest* performed by Song of the Goat Theatre. Grzegorz Bral's School of Acting teaches its actors creative boldness, and their performances are usually a mixture of oriental music/song, dance, poetry and pantomime. The festival hosted thirty companies and artists from ten countries (from as far away as China), who presented shows, stand-ups, workshops and offered meetings with the creatives.

The 2017 edition of the festival allowed academics to continue, during the conference, the discussion on reviewing Shakespeare from a continental European perspective – a discussion that began at the 2011 World Shakespeare Congress in Prague. The discussions by panellists and members of the audience concerned mostly the countries they knew best (Italy, Poland, Germany, Romania) and embraced both historical and cultural points of view (Fabiszak 2016). They tried to establish if and how Shakespearean productions were covered by the media in those countries, if reviews opened onto political issues or contemporaneous concerns, such as migration, terrorism, or if the reviewing formats provided a wider outreach (academic, press, Facebook, Twitter, blog). The panellists underlined that contemporary Polish directors, for example Jan Klata, Maja Kleczewska, Krzysztof Garbaczewski, followed the tenets of 'postdramatic theatre' (Lehmann 2006) and their plays were often socially engaged. 'Postdramatic' aesthetics resonates with postmodernist thinking and involves the 'deconstruction' and 'narrative fragmentation' (Lehmann 2006: 13) of the dramatic text, which no longer forms a monolithic part of the performance. This type of drama is fond of using non-theatrical locations, such as factories, post-industrial and public utility spaces. For example, Jan Klata located his *H.* (2004) in the derelict Gdańsk shipyard, the birthplace of *Solidarność* (the first non-communist trade union in Poland) and Maja Kleczewska's *Hamlet* (2019) was staged in the deserted post-industrial building of an old slaughterhouse in Poznań. The functions of both venues referring to joining and disjoining, assembling and dismembering, proved them particularly well suited to the stage directors' postdramatic aesthetics as they tampered with Shakespeare's text, deconstructing and reconstructing it. Klata thus justified his choice of the play's venue, which talks about old patriotic values and how they were forgotten in the new capitalist reality:

> When Shakespeare wrote 'something is rotten in the state of Denmark', surely he didn't mean the Danes but the English. And so do I; when I read the play I think about my own country ... I wanted a place that would captivate the Polish national spirit and be a repository of historical and social processes. The Gdańsk shipyard seemed to me an ideal place ...
> (Klata qtd in Mokrzycka-Pokora 2015)

Jan Klata, who was present at the 2017 edition of the festival and put on a workshop there, is a frequent and welcome guest at the festival. His socially and politically engaged productions have earned him the title of 'an expert on Polishness' (Kwaśniewska 2012: 70). They evoke a gallery of debates on current social issues, such as the Polish national identity (*H.*, 2004), the stereotypes about Germans and the Polish martyrological approach to history (*Titus Andronicus*, 2012), excessive consumerism and lack of tradition in the modern world (*Hamlet*, 2013), Polish Catholicism (*King Lear*, 2015) and political hypocrisy (*Measure for Measure*, 2018). His meetings with the festival audience adopt a similar debate-like formula, and Klata always eagerly discusses the function of the theatre today. He says loud and clear that theatrical institutions should be engaged in modern problems, both social and political (his production of *King Lear* featuring Jerzy Grałek's Lear dressed in papal robes won the Golden Yorick in 2015). He waged war on audiences who treat the theatre only as a source of entertainment, wishing for serious audiences as he talks about serious matters.

His short artistic manifesto remains unchanged: 'An artist needs food and [an] enemy. I have food, and I'm glad it's war' (Klata qtd in Drewniak 2005). It seemed impossible, even in Shakespeare's times, to separate theatre from political influence. The Shakespeare Festival hosts, and will surely continue hosting, politically engaged plays. However, it has never been a festival policy to promote politically engaged productions or manifest its political stance. The festival organizers are interested in promoting what Jerzy Limon once called 'a good theatre', that is, a high-quality theatre, whose aim is to accurately reflect human nature and the times we live in.

The latest edition of the festival proved it, and one example was Maja Kleczewska's Polish and Ukrainian *Hamlet/Гамлет*, staged in the Gothic building of St John the Baptist's Church, which qualified for the finals in the Golden Yorick competition. Her production expertly combined in a postdramatic fashion the elements of stage design, light, soundtrack, video art and the actors' play, thus resembling a 'contemporary simultaneous setting theatre' (Obarska 2019) – the kind of theatre used in the Middle Ages to stage parallel biblical scenes in liturgical drama. There were two simultaneous plans of action – one focusing on Hamlet, the other on Gertrude, with at least three large spaces (the courtyard, Gertrude's bed-chamber, the dining hall) and the headphone-wearing audience following the actors. The performance involved a lot of multitasking but members of the audience were free to choose which actor, and plot, they wanted to follow and they could switch between channels in the headphones (this made it possible to be in one place and listen to a parallel scene in another room).

Kleczewska's *Hamlet* told a story about the end of Western civilization, showing actors who walked like zombies and recited verses from Heiner Müller's *Hamletmachine*. She introduced 'collective Fortinbras' (Obarska 2019), who was not a saviour from Denmark but an invader from outside. Fortinbras related to the present context of multicultural societies and the European migration crisis: two actors, a Senegalese and an Indian, and a South African actress with Polish roots, played the uncontrollable element of Fortinbras, who claimed his right to this land in various languages. Fortinbras' powerful dance, song and imposing costumes all indicate his/their entrance into the ruins of Europe and represent the multicultural world that the Europeans are afraid of (Obarska 2019). Kleczewska has said recently that 'Hamlet is a machine that drives the next generations, humanistic thoughts, and will never stop' (qtd in Ostrowska 2019). The 2019 *Hamlet* aspires to be part of the global cultural code – Shakespeare – and its role is to foster humanistic thought in modern societies (Ostrowska 2019). The ethos of the Shakespeare Festival in Gdańsk expresses very similar sentiments.

Perspectives on the festival

The Gdańsk Shakespeare Festival was honoured with a prestigious EFFE Award (Europe for Festivals, Festivals for Europe) in 2017.[4] The EFFE Award is a confirmation of the festival's exceptional role in cultivating creative explorations in the field of the arts and promoting high-quality theatre, and of its involvement in the cultural education of societies.[5] Apart from the high artistic quality and variety of performances, the nomination for the Gdańsk Shakespeare Theatre was a result of its active cooperation with the theatres and cultural institutions in the European region.[6] So far, the Gdańsk Shakespeare Festival has presented 873 performances and shows by 239 theatre groups from forty-four countries. The festival's many theatre stages in Gdańsk, Gdynia and Sopot have hosted productions by over 250 directors including, among others, Peter Brook, Luk Perceval, Lev Dodin, Eimuntas Nekrošius, Oskaras Koršunovas, Roberto Ciulli and Robert Sturua.

The structural formula and the cultural and educational missions of the festival continue. The organizers focus on providing high-quality entertainment for local and global audiences in various forms and locations of the Tricity. The Gdańsk Shakespeare Festival's ambition in the future is to broaden the thematic variety of the programme to reach even wider audiences. 'Shakespeare's Contemporaries' is a new section in the main programme, whose aim is to popularize Elizabethan and Jacobean drama by other playwrights, such as John Webster or Thomas Middleton. This initiative is driven by Professor Limon, who explains:

> The Elizabethan age was an extraordinary time of the flourishing of the theatre, not only in England but in other European countries, such as Spain, France, Germany ... The idea behind Shakespeare's Contemporaries is to show other historically

significant theatrical phenomena to more accurately mirror the specificity of the Elizabethan times.[7]

The first edition of 'Shakespeare's Contemporaries' was launched in 2019 and included the Croatian classic *Uncle Maroye Re-Examined*, as well as Francis Beaumont's *The Knight of the Burning Pestle* performed by Cheek by Jowl and the Moscow Pushkin Drama Theatre. Both performances were sold out.

In light of the current closures of theatres in Poland and Europe because of the Covid-19 pandemic, the festival was rescheduled for the second half of November 2020. This is the second time in the festival's twenty-four-year history that the date has been changed from the usual summer date to later in the year (the first time was in 2014, the year of the GST opening when the festival was moved to the autumn and was synchronized with the opening ceremony). Much as the festival was temporarily suspended, the Gdańsk Shakespeare Theatre continues its work online. Its *SzekspirOn//line* series offers online screenings of the plays, accompanied by Jerzy Limon's talks and lectures by critics discussing not only the plays in question but also Shakespeare's life and the Elizabethan drama. *Hamlet*, *Macbeth* and *The Merry Wives of Windsor*, equipped with critical commentary, are just a few screenings proposed by the GST.[8]

Thus, despite the world pandemic, the festival continues its cultural mission and remains a locus for humanistic European values in Poland. In recent years, the festival has offered its audiences a less varied main programme due to limited funding. This fact was quickly picked up by the local newspapers and made the headlines: 'It was modest, but with class'[9] – was one of the commentaries on the 2017 edition of the festival. Despite these temporary setbacks, the organizers work hard and do not give up, as fortune is fickle. Jerzy Limon knows it best – in an interview for a local paper he reminds us of 'Fortune, this capricious Lady, whom Shakespeare repeatedly mentions', and he notes that She has always regarded the theatre with a favourable eye.[10]

In 2021, a jubilee, the twenty-fifth edition of the festival took place, for the first time without Professor Jerzy Limon as its director. This chapter is dedicated to the memory of this true Renaissance man (1950–2021).

Notes

1. We wish to thank three very special women at the GST, who provided us with important 'insider' information about the organization and running of the festival: Magdalena Hajdysz, Press Officer; Anna Ratkiewicz, Head of the Education Department; and Marta Nowicka, Specialist on Education in the Education Department and Grant Expert. Their daily work makes the festival grow stronger every year, and the GST and its cultural and educational initiatives are gaining widespread publicity in Poland and abroad.
2. Read and watch more at https://www.bbc.com/news/world-europe-29250459 (accessed 2 December 2020).
3. The building of GST began in 2011 as its funding only became possible after Poland joined the EU in 2004. The EU covered three-quarters of the £18 million cost (€23 million), with the remainder provided by local authorities. The local government gave up a valuable piece of real estate on the outskirts of the Old Town as a location site for the new theatre.
4. The EFFE label is the European Festivals Association's (EFA) mark of recognition for Europe's most exciting arts festivals, which is awarded by EFA with the support of the European Commission and the European Parliament.
5. For further information, see the festival site: https://www.festivalfinder.eu/effe-label (accessed 2 December 2020).
6. The Gdańsk Shakespeare Festival is an integral part of the European Shakespeare Festivals Network (ESFN), which supports and develops cultural cooperation in Europe and all around the world. ESFN was founded on the initiative of the Gdańsk Shakespeare Festival in 2010 and has its main office in Gdańsk. The festival network includes the following countries: Armenia, the Czech Republic, Denmark, France, Germany, Hungary, Macedonia, Poland, Romania, Serbia, Spain and the United Kingdom. For further information, see: http://esfn.eu/ (accessed 2 December 2020).
7. Read more in Professor Jerzy Limon's interview on the Shakespeare festival website at http://festiwalszekspirowski.pl/en/shakespeares-contemporaries/ (accessed 2 December 2020).
8. Read more on the GST website at https://teatrszekspirowski.pl/uncategorized/szekspiron-line-wesole-kumoszki-z-windsoru/ (accessed 2 December 2020).
9. Read more on the official website of the city of Gdańsk at https://www.gdansk.pl/wiadomosci/festiwal-szekspirowski-jeszcze-sie-nie-poddal-bylo-skromnie-ale-z-klasa,a,85080 (accessed 2 December 2020).
10. Read more on the official website of the city of Gdańsk at https://www.gdansk.pl/wiadomosci/festiwal-szekspirowski-jeszcze-sie-nie-

poddal-bylo-skromnie-ale-z-klasa,a,85080 (accessed 2 December 2020).

References

Drewniak, Łucasz (2005), 'W oku salonu' [In the Theatre Salons], trans. U. Kizelbach and J. Fabiszak, *Przekrój*, no. 8. Available online: http://www.e-teatr.pl/pl/artykuly/9329,druk.html (accessed 28 October 2019).

Engle, Ron, Felicia Hardison Londré and Daniel J. Watermeier, eds (1995), *Shakespeare Companies and Festivals: An International Guide*, Westport, CT and London: Greenwood Publishing Group.

Fabiszak, Jacek (2015), '"So Curst and Shrewd a Play": *The Taming of the Shrew*, dir. Katarzyna Deszcz. Stefan Żeromski Theatre, Kielce, Poland', *Multicultural Shakespeare: Translation, Appropriation and Performance* 12 (27): 160–5.

Fabiszak, Jacek (2016), 'Andrzej Wajda's Two *Hamlets* and One *Macbeth*: The Director's Struggle with Shakespearean Tragedy in the Changing Contexts of Polish History', *Anglica: An International Journal of English Studies* 25 (3): 97–106.

Falassi, Alessandro (1987), *Time Out of Time: Essays on the Festival*, Albuquerque: University of New Mexico Press.

Kizelbach, Urszula (2016), '*The Merry Wives of Windsor* (2015): Shakespeare Reloaded in the Gdańsk Shakespeare Theatre', *Reviewing Shakespeare*. Available online: http://bloggingshakespeare.com/reviewing-shakespeare/merry-wives-windsor-directed-pawel-aigner-gdansk-shakespeare-theatre-gdansk-poland-2015/ (accessed 15 August 2017).

Kwaśniewska, Monika (2012), 'Od Buntownika do Eksperta. Medialne Wizerunki Jana Klaty' [From a Rebel to an Expert. Media Images of Jan Klata], trans. Urszula Kizelbach and Jacek Fabiszak, *Didaskalia* 111: 69–77.

Lehmann, Hans Thies (2006), *Postdramatic Theatre*, trans. Karen Jürs-Munby, London and New York: Routledge.

Limon, Jerzy ([1985] 2009), *Gentleman of a Company: English Players in Central and Eastern Europe 1590–1660*, Cambridge: Cambridge University Press.

Mokrzycka-Pokora, Monika (2015), 'Jan Klata', trans. Urszula Kizelbach and Jacek Fabiszak. Available online: http://culture.pl/pl/tworca/jan-klata (accessed 12 October 2016).

Obarska, Marcelina (2019), '*Hamlet*, reż. Maja Kleczewska' (*Hamlet*, dir. Maja Kleczewska), trans. U. Kizelbach and J. Fabiszak. Available online: https://culture.pl/pl/dzielo/hamlet-rez-maja-kleczewska (accessed 17 October 2019).

Ostrowska, J. (2019), 'Silent disco party, czyli jak zrobić głośny spektakl' [Silent Disco Party, or How to Make a Play People Talk About], trans. U. Kizelbach and J. Fabiszak. Available online: http://teatralny.pl/recenzje/silent-disco-party-czyli-jak-zrobic-glosny spektakl,2783.html (accessed 3 July 2019).

9

From a schoolyard play to civic festival: Shakespeare in the Bulgarian village of Patalenitsa

Boika Sokolova and Kirilka Stavreva

The road to Patalenitsa

Late summer afternoon, shimmering in luscious light. Pan-European Corridor 8, between the Black and Adriatic Seas, has now joined Corridor 4 – the ancient East–West road from Asia to the heart of Europe. The motorway skims close to our destination – the only village in Europe with a homegrown Shakespeare festival – but does not quite deliver. Like the festival that we are about to join, the approach diverges from the well-trodden path. One sharp turn south, a two-lane road plunges toward the softly undulating Rhodope Mountains, through a luminous field of sunflowers, their heads bowing deeply. In the distance, the village of Patalenitsa hovers, at a crossroads between valley and mountain, past and present, tradition and experiment. It is a crossroads sought out by theatregoers drawn from across Bulgaria by their friends' reports; by journalists and luminaries from the nearby cities of Pazardjik and Plovdiv; by the theatre guild of the capital Sofia; and by the authors of this chapter, two Shakespeare scholars and their families – one based in London, the other, in the American Midwest – who have finally managed to synchronize their schedules to witness this improbable theatre feast. For all these, Patalenitsa Shakespeare has become a destination. For the village schoolchildren, youth and their parents and grandparents, for the three generations of the family that started putting on performances of Shakespeare here, for the elementary school principal who has transformed the school playground into a theatre and the classrooms into costume- and prop-shops, this festival has become an indelible part of their civic identity. For the Bulgarian acting students and young theatre professionals, and for the theatre students and teachers from British universities who return to Patalenitsa year after year, following in the footsteps of a beloved teacher-director, this has become a living-and-learning community. As a destination *and* a community festival, as a grassroots theatre event that has grown into an international collaboration of young actors, as an altruistic venture with rewarding professional and human development, at once edifying and entertaining, Patalenitsa Shakespeare challenges established dichotomies in the critical discourse of theatre festivals (Engle et al. 1995: xvii).[1]

On the afternoon of 27 July 2019, two festivals are underway in Patalenitsa, population *c.* 1,500. Around the corner from the eighteenth-century church of the Assumption of the Holy Virgin, dancers and singers of all ages, in traditional dress, are milling around souvenir-, toy- and food-stalls lining up a square. This is the local fair that for some fifty years has marked the Feast Day of St Panteleimon, protector of the village. Up the street – a different festival. An arrangement of posters on the schoolyard fence invites all to a 9.00 pm performance of *A Midsummer Night's Dream*, on behalf of the Shakespeare Theatre School 'Petrovden', the 'Konstantin Velichkov' elementary school and 'Theatre House and Friends'. Inside the schoolyard, towering trees shelter a graceful exhibition of costumes, props, masks and posters from previous productions;[2] musicians tune their instruments under a white canopy; director Terrie Fender contemplates the simple green-floored stage canopied by gauzy fabric, now tinted peach by the setting sun; a videographer with a flowing white beard tests his equipment; actors exchange hugs after their warm-up. The Patalenitsa Shakespeare Festival is about to deliver its twentieth-anniversary performance.

Participants in the two festivals mingle, then part their ways. Actors and theatre audience members swing by the village fair to pick up a fan for the warm evening or some candy floss before heading back to the schoolyard; fairgoers pop by the school, curious about the chants and clamour from the pre-performance bustle; some will stay on to claim their free theatre seats a good hour ahead of time; others will opt for the folk songs and dances. People commit their evening to a festival of their own as the doubly charged spirit of celebration hovers over the village.

What kind of festival?

Artistic saturation is a familiar quality of summer festival culture. Oftentimes, festivals beget festivals, as in the case of the genesis of Bulgaria's biggest international theatre event, 'Varna Summer', designated as a Remarkable Festival by the European Festival Association in 2017. Launched in 1993, it tapped into the successes of a venerable music festival established in 1926, and an annual international ballet competition dating from 1964, both bearing the same name. Nowadays, between May and August, Varna is Bulgaria's capital of cultural tourism, hosting literature, folklore, jazz and film festivals with a rich cultural programme for tourists and citizens of this Black Sea city. Shakespeare is a prominent, though by no means obligatory presence on the roster of 'Varna Summer'. The twenty-seven years of the festival have seen over 680 live theatre productions, thirty-five of which were of plays by or after Shakespeare, locally and internationally produced (International Theatre Festival 'Varna Summer' 1993–2019).

Another prominent destination of cultural tourism in Bulgaria is the city of Plovdiv, whose Roman amphitheatre is the hub of spectacular summer theatre and music performances. In 1999, this second-largest Bulgarian city hosted the European Month of Culture featuring multiple concurrent events: opera, ballet, classical guitar, folklore and cinema. Thanks to the sponsorship of the European Union, from 28 May to 1 August, some five thousand artists from around the world converged in the city to present 250 live events and exhibitions, on top of more film screenings and youth programmes. Among the forty-five theatre performances, 'Plovdiv '99' featured a week dedicated to *Hamlet* with seven productions of the play by world-famous directors: Robert Sturua, Peter Stein, Eimuntas Necrošius, Bulgarian experimental directors Liliya Abadjieva, Nikolai Georgiev and Stavri Karamfilov, and puppetry director Sabi Sabev (Dragostinova 1999; Kalinkova 1999). In 2019, Plovdiv was selected as European Capital of Culture. In the extensive and rich programme offered in that year, Shakespeare was represented by three productions from Patalenitsa.

With their attractive locations, high-profile and high-cost productions, star performers and well-heeled audiences, 'Varna Summer' and 'Plovdiv '99' are prime examples of destination cultural tourism. The humble schoolyard location of Patalenitsa Shakespeare in a village off the beaten track, its meagre and perpetually insecure local funding, the pro bono work by the creative teams, all place it in a completely different cultural category. And yet, having started as a single yearly school performance, it has managed to evolve into a fully-fledged, multi-production professional undertaking. Though it is still uneasy under the mantle of 'festival' thrown around its shoulders by critics and journalists, it manages to wear it with a difference. Fuelled by resilient idealism, Patalenitsa Shakespeare, remarkably, has attracted both a local and an international following, which has sustained it over the course of two decades. This, we suggest, is a new kind of festival, a civic festival, with several results. On the one hand, it has succeeded in rejuvenating the village in the economically, culturally and psychologically trying period of the post-communist transition.[3] By transforming the tradition of the school play (going back to the Bulgarian Enlightenment), it has awakened the community spirit, engendering an interest in local history and a commitment to inclusivity. The other major effect of the Patalenitsa festival – the only Shakespeare theatre festival in the country – is that it has changed a parochial community into a more outward-looking one, at the same time nurturing a multicultural and self-sustaining theatre summer colony.

Patalenitsa Shakespeare is a unique example of a collaborative altruistic endeavour of Bulgarian and international theatre practitioners and educators who donate their time and expertise to producing professional-quality theatre, using as a rehearsal room and stage the yard of a village school. There are no honorariums; board and lodging, as well as production materials, are financed through small municipal grants and donations from local companies. The festival runs on enthusiasm and professional dedication.

Patalenitsa Shakespeare originated as a refusal to accept the predicament of Bulgarian post-communist theatre thrown, as it was in the early 1990s, to the dogs of consumerism, dismantled, and starved of funding. In these circumstances, two theatre professionals left the theatre establishment to go back to the source of theatre as a space for fostering community. From the start, this was a venture based on profoundly ethical principles.[4] Those who have worked in Patalenitsa recall becoming part of the 'creation of an ideal society' (Russell Bolam qtd in Baichinska et al. 2019: 91). They speak of the value of 'total professional honesty' (Trevor Rawlins qtd in Baichinska et al. 2019: 77), of 'celebrating the spirit of freedom' (Penka Kalinkova qtd in Baichinska et al. 2019: 4), of cultivating 'personal honour and decency' (Lubomir Tarpov qtd in Baichinska et al. 2019: 6), and the freedom to 'express the truth of the human soul' (Rex Doyle qtd in Baichinska et al. 2019: 50).[5] Audiences, on their part, do not travel to Patalenitsa only to enjoy a well-crafted theatrical product, but to partake in the unadulterated joyousness of theatre-making that creates a sense of community.

Shakespeare enters post-communist village life

Patalenitsa Shakespeare was born in 1999, eight years into the seismic political and economic transition following the fall of communism. The Bulgarian 1990s were marked by the blight of rampant capitalism, unemployment, the unravelling of systems of social provision, such as education and healthcare, the almost complete dereliction of funding for the arts and a general loss of moral compass (Sokolova and Stavreva 2017: 1–7). Basic social structures began to crumble. Communities and families came under enormous strain while many of their working members were pressed into economic emigration. The public sphere was flooded by mass media owned by newly made tycoons, marketing the latest objects of desire. Writer Vladimir Zarev sums up the situation:

The last twenty-five years saw the dismantling of the immune systems of statehood, the corruption of the police and the judiciary, the abrogation of morality, the demise of social justice. The product of the work of several generations of Bulgarians was stolen, and even worse, made to look completely meaningless; what had been created by them was pilfered, or handed over to party flunkies. Morally, the situation was aggravated by branding the intelligent, and most importantly, honest person, a fool, while the thief and self-confessed impostor became the hero of our time and the centre of media attention.

(Zarev 2014)

In this context, the decision of a team of three professionals to mitigate the multiple traumas of local children growing up in conditions of economic hardship, family separation and even abandonment by creating an inclusive theatre community and by teaching the children to a high standard of linguistic and artistic expression through the medium of Shakespeare's plays, amounted to an extraordinarily courageous ethical act.

The team was headed by Hristo Tserovski (1956–2002), a charismatic theatre director who had been at the helm of the Plovdiv Drama Theatre and worked as Professor of Theatre at the University of Plovdiv. He moved to Patalenitsa with his wife, Inna Tserovska, a set and costume designer and principal grant writer, now the manager of the Shakespeare Theatre School 'Petrovden' and the driving force behind the complex organization of the summer performances.[6] The third member of this extraordinary team is Nikola Kolev, principal of the local school, chief photographer and troubleshooter.

An important decision made at the very beginning was to invite theatre students from the University of Plovdiv to perform alongside the children, immediately raising performance standards. Throughout the production cycle, directors treated the schoolchildren and the theatre students as equals, shaping a finely integrated ensemble (Dimitrov 2014). Children recognized the value of this experience, returning to their weekly Saturday acting workshops year after year, and growing as actors during the month-long summer rehearsals for the play. This was, in itself, a rare phenomenon: children studying theatre and Shakespeare with professionals, the professionals embracing the opportunity for pedagogical and intergenerational collaborative work.

Patalenitsa Shakespeare started in 1999 as a small project on 'Social Problems and Drama', sponsored by the Open Society Foundation (Baichinska et al. 2019: 4), which quickly outstripped its original scope and came to define the village as much as its heritage of ancient churches and monasteries. The activities around the summer Shakespeare performances have energized a long-term commitment to social inclusion. Creative collaborations among Plovdiv University theatre students, schoolchildren from 'Petrovden' and children and adults from day centres for people with disabilities in the nearby city of Pazardjik have resulted in the writing of new plays and in award-winning productions. Schoolchildren conducted independent research into local history to create these plays, an example of communal theatrical storytelling. To their emotional audiences, they told stories of the past with wit and humour, stories that, in the words of director Vyara Nacheva, suggested 'to each theatre-goer that they should help their children make choices about everyday life and ideals with dignity' (Baichinska et al. 2019: 102).[7]

To meet the needs of the yearly Shakespeare productions the school yard was adapted, acquiring, in 2002, a small open stage and some permanent raked seating. In 2006, Patalenitsa opened the first community cultural centre built in the country since the 1970s – a testimony to local initiative and the growing significance of theatre culture in the village as opposed to the mandated establishments of this sort from the communist period. This centre has an indoor auditorium; though not used for the Shakespeare performances, which always take place outdoors, it offers rehearsal space in inclement weather.

The purposeful integration of theatre and local history started with the first performance of *Romeo and Juliet* in 2000. Tserovski chose to move the final scene of the play from the schoolyard to the twelfth-century church of St Dimitar up the street. According to legend, in the late fourteenth century, when the Ottoman invasion reached this part of the medieval Bulgarian kingdom, the local people buried the church under a mound of earth. It was discovered by chance in 1840 and declared a cultural monument in 1956. This space of cultural memory, not a hundred metres from the school, was again put to use for a 2013 promenade performance of a collage of Shakespeare love scenes, entitled *To Love or Not to Love*, scripted and directed by Sterre Maier and Jenny Clarke of the Guildford School of Acting, UK. In 2015, Trevor Rawlins' *Romeo and Juliet* commemorated Tserovski's inaugural production by, once again, setting the final scene in the church.

During the winter of 2001, a film crew shot a documentary for which *Romeo and Juliet* was revived in winter conditions. Performed, this time, in the snow-covered school yard and in the medieval church, the performance was attended by the local people. *Shakespeare, the Balkan Way*, directed by Vassil Barakov, was aired on the main Bulgarian TV channel, and went on to garner the highest prize at the International Festival for TV Films in Plovdiv.[8] The high artistic quality of the film contributed significantly to raising the national profile of Patalenitsa Shakespeare.

What nobody expected was that the first foray into Shakespeare in the open would attract an audience of around 300, mostly theatre professionals, colleagues of the students involved in the play and journalists. The locals, though significantly outnumbered in the audience, were present throughout the production process. Todor Dimitrov, both Patalenitsa Shakespeare director (*Hamlet* in 2003 and 2017, *A Midsummer Night's Dream* in 2004) and actor (Leontes, *The Winter's Tale* in 2012), gives a colourful description of the schoolyard rehearsals:

> Young people hang around here in their spare time, date, share a beer, talk about their problems. All of this is taking place while rehearsals go on and somehow the two begin to enter a sort of symbiosis. Until, that is, these young people start paying attention to us, retain some of the lines, the monologues, begin to anticipate what actors are about to say next. Big kids, little kids show up on their bikes, mothers with their infants stop by, and thus, the show starts living with the daily life of the village well before opening night. These people will then show up at *both* our performances.
>
> (Dimitrov 2014)

Russell Bolam, director of the 2017 production of *The Taming of the Shrew*, concurs: 'Among the many reasons why I love the Patalenitsa Shakespeare festival is that one lives with the model society we attempt to create. Performance participants are always right by each other. The model society of the rehearsal shares the space of the real society of the village. These lines blur in a very exciting way' (Baichnska et al. 2019: 91). One might conclude that the average Patalenitsa teenager is exposed to more Shakespeare than most children in the world, though the situation should not be romanticized. Local people have yet to comprise the majority of the audience. Still, as the company veteran Pavlina-Kalina Tserovska suggests, 'if you ask the villagers today, "Who is Shakespeare?", they will answer "My people!"' (Tserovska 2014).

Open theatre

For the duration of its existence, Patalenitsa Shakespeare has been theatre in the open: open to the stars and the elements, to anyone who might stroll into the shady schoolyard during rehearsals and performances. It has also been something larger than that, an Open Theatre, where the professional and communal, the new and traditional, the national and international enrich one another. In 2009, the summer Shakespeare performances entered a new phase by integrating a different theatre tradition. The production of *Pericles* that year marked the beginning of a collaboration with Rex Doyle, a distinguished British director, actor and pedagogue from the Guildford School of Acting, who took over the planning of productions and the summer rehearsals. A pioneer of Youth Theatre in the United Kingdom, a man who had performed Shakespeare in culturally diverse locations, Doyle's experience, professionalism and open disposition made him the perfect leader at this juncture in the evolution of Patalenitsa Shakespeare ('Rex Doyle Obituary' 2015). Under his guidance, performances took a turn to professionalization with a predominance of actors and acting students in the cast. This, along with the intercultural collaborative element, brought higher visibility and raised production values, prompting journalists to start referring to the already well-established community event as a festival.

In 2010, Doyle was joined by Guildford colleagues and later, students, who continued his work after his death in 2015. Thus, an event which had come to life through local pioneer enthusiasm and personal determination acquired a new cross-cultural identity as it evolved through its second decade. Importantly, the altruism of theatre practitioners and organizers remained unchanged in this new phase. It is evident in an interview, given by Doyle for Bulgarian television:

> Interviewer: Why have you come to this Bulgarian village?
> Doyle: To direct young people who perform Shakespeare.
> Interviewer: How much are you paid?
> Doyle: Nothing.
> Interviewer: Why are you doing it then?
> Doyle: Because it makes me happy ... Happy that I can create theatre together with these people. We are free from the control of politicians or anybody else – we are wandering artists. We have no money, rarely have a home, don't even have a playhouse – simply a school yard ... But we're doing all this because we wish to express ourselves through somebody's play and in the process to reach the truth of the human soul. I think that Shakespeare is one of the best ways of doing that.
> Interviewer: Theatres are in a deep crisis nowadays.
> Doyle: I know. So I've been hearing, but look out the window. This is a really small village, but look who comes to the play, who is sitting on the benches outside? Children, all children ... What we are doing here is deep and far-reaching.
>
> (Baichinska et al. 2019: 50)

Altruism in Patalenitsa goes hand in hand with professionalism. By sustaining its foundational principles which seem to be close to the hearts of many, Patalenitsa is beginning to emerge as a summer centre for cross-cultural actor training, attracting established Bulgarian and international professionals, as well as students from the Guildford School of Acting, the National Academy for Theatre and Film Arts (NATFA) in Sofia and young actors from Britain and Bulgaria ('Teatralni mostove' 2013).

In addition to putting the performances on a firmer professional footing, Doyle added a new element to the production process. Reviews of his *Pericles* (2009) single out the live instrumental and vocal music (Darik 2009). For the 2014 production of *The Tempest*, the British collaborators, among whom were students of musical theatre, helped develop a sophisticated musical component as a signature narrative device. Music has since become a distinctive feature of all productions. Another development was the integration of Laban movement techniques in the production process.[9] Along with the music, dance and dynamic movement have become an artistic emblem of Patalenitsa Shakespeare.

Production work, always based on mutual openness among Bulgarian and British, amateur and professional cast and crew members, has generated finely integrated ensembles. Each month-long summer season begins with a focused series of workshops, integrated in the rehearsals and culminating in two performances. This workshop-based production approach has also yielded standalone professional development sessions in movement, rhythm and set design. Some of these were conducted outside the production cycle and involved theatre students from various institutions.[10] In this way, the skills developed by the ensembles in Patalenitsa started to be taught beyond the framework of the festival. The popularity of its intercultural theatre work and the professional development outreach have paved the way to a self-sustaining theatre ecology, with the number of professionals attracted to the place growing every year.

A festival for new generations

The year 2017 marked the latest phase in the evolution of Patalenitsa Shakespeare. Actors who had taken their first steps on its stage as children started to graduate from theatre academies, and connect their creative home to new professional networks. The schoolyard stage in the little village began to emerge as the hub of Shakespeare performance in Bulgaria. Press coverage started referring regularly to the yearly performances as a festival. The number of productions and participants grew. Three plays featured that season, two created on site – *Hamlet* (director Todor Dimitrov's second engagement with the play in Patalenitsa) and *The Taming of the Shrew* (directed by Russell Bolam) – as well as the first visiting production from NATFA, *The Comedy of Errors* (a graduate production, directed by Martin Kiselov). For the first time, audiences were able to attend multiple Shakespeare productions over the course of three weeks.

The 2018 season included two plays: the locally produced *Merchant of Venice*, directed by Kalin Angelov, and *A Midsummer Night's Dream*, directed by Margarita Mladenova – a NATFA visiting production. *The Merchant of Venice*, like *Hamlet* and *The Taming of the Shrew* of the previous year, was emblematic of the growth of Patalenitsa. All these plays had been done in the early 2000s by the schoolchildren; now, the same school yard was the site of professional performances. *The Merchant* was a roaring success, employing in equal measure text and live music (Angelov 2018). It was advertised on radio and TV channels, which have started to follow the Patalenitsa Shakespeare events regularly. The guest production of *Dream* was the vision of one of Bulgaria's most influential theatre directors. Her streamlined conceptual style and emphasis on physical acting honed in studio environments met the challenge of performing in the open, enriching the experience of her theatre students. Thus, Patalenitsa is becoming a stepping stone to the professional stage for a budding generation of actors, a litmus test for their capacity to cope with the challenges of space, text and music, for their Shakespeare-worthiness.

Locally, 2019 was a special year. The nearby regional centre, Plovdiv, which had won the title of European Capital of Culture, mounted a rich programme of events. Unsurprisingly, the continuing presence of Patalenitsa Shakespeare was recognized by including its productions in the schedule of the festivities. For the event, which coincided with the twentieth anniversary of Shakespeare performances in Patalenitsa, *The Merchant* of the previous season was revived. That year, the guests from NATFA came with Penko Gospodinov's production of *Romeo and Juliet*, staged in Weimar-republic style of Dark Cabaret, full of menace. The culmination of the fortnight-long celebrations was a spectacular and musically rich *A Midsummer Night's Dream*, directed by Terrie Fender of Falmouth University, UK.[11] Fender, a professional with rich acting and pedagogical experience, is continuing the work of developing creative and ensemble work started by Rex Doyle. The young actors of Patalenitsa, in the meantime, dream about building a new theatre in this Shakespeare festival village.

***

FIGURE 9.1 *Velizar Emanuilov (Demetrius), Nikolai Vladimirov (Lysander), Maria Panayotova (Helena) and audience members at the July 2019 production of* A Midsummer Night's Dream *in Patalenitsa, directed by Terrie Fender. Photograph by permission of Nikola Kolev.*

In the velvety night of 27 July 2019, those who had taken the road to Patalenitsa partook in a feast of communal delight (Figure 9.1). As the play unfolded onto 'the [baize] green plot' (3.1.3) of the stage and Demetrius struggled to shake off Helena and 'alone [...] go' (2.2.91), an unexpected explosion of fireworks illuminated the skies. This marked the end of the St Panteleimon fair, the other local festival concurrent with the performance. As the young actor extempore threatened to leave the girl to 'the mercy of these wild fireworks' and the audience roared with laughter under the blazing skies, the feeling of there-ness, of nature, audience and stage blending, was like nothing else we had experienced in a lifetime of theatregoing. What a way to cut your teeth as an actor! The emotion of Patalenitsa is expressed by no one better than one of its 'children', now designer and producer, Pavlina-Kalina Tserovska: 'At every performance I look up: the sky is not a sky, the stage is not a stage … it is a bare place that teaches you about yourself' (Tserovska 2014).

A year later, the unexpected struck with the onset of the Covid-19 pandemic. Schools and theatres closed, public events shut down, life was put on hold. Nobody expected the twenty-first edition of the festival to take place. Yet a team of six actors, designers and a small support crew quarantined together in Patalenitsa, and in just two weeks managed to produce a stunning appropriation of *Measure for Measure*, directed by Kalin Angelov. It was performed in front of a miniscule, physically distanced audience in the medieval church of St Dimitar, but had an unusually wide reach, since it was streamed on the festival's Facebook site and later broadcast on a local TV channel. In an hour-long cut of the play collaged with Shakespeare sonnets, Hamlet's most famous soliloquy and the aubade from *Romeo and Juliet* – as a starting point of Claudio and Juliet's plot – the production stripped *Measure for Measure* to its tragic core about the impunity of political power and the way it blights the lives of the young. Removing the character of the Duke allowed Angelo's plan to run its devastating course. There was no chance that Claudio would remain alive in this version. Live contemporary musical numbers provided poignant punctuation to the dramatic narrative, while the Viennese social scene was cut. At the end, baby in arms, Juliet stood alone by the church altar – a mirror image of the medieval fresco behind her. This minimalistic, elegant production of a play about the abuse of power formed an artistic complement to the political protests sweeping the country in the midst of the pandemic. Attended mostly by young people and running throughout the summer of 2020, these demonstrations targeted the decades-long abuse of the law by the same male politicians appointed to uphold it. This routine abuse and related normalization of corruption – the local equivalent of the play's excised Vienna scenes – was met by the creative team's own mode of resistance.

Born in the midst of the early crises of post-communism, the Patalenitsa Shakespeare festival continues to provide a corrective to surges of social despair. Now inscribed not only into village life but in the ecology of Bulgarian theatre, it brings together a community that identifies with Bulgarian historical bonds and with a globally open culture represented by the actors, directors and designers who reimagine Shakespeare every summer, sometimes against impossible odds. This unique, civic festival is a joyful celebration of creativity and a model of resilience countering a dispiriting reality. Patalenitsa empowers young actors, makes them professionally capable of resisting the relentless pressures and volatility of our time, teaches them to take their audiences to places where they encounter selves they would like to be. Every year, theatre-makers and theatregoers return to experience *communitas* under the stars. And even when audiences are locked away, these unstoppable creatives reach out to them through modern media technologies, connecting spectators to theatre performed in an ancestral liturgical space, yet filled with the passions and hopes of the present day.

Notes

1   Theatre festivals are typically discussed as either destination or community. Well-established destination festivals, such as those in Avignon, Craiova, and Gdansk, harness star-studded casts and high production values to attract affluent, well-educated, middle-aged audiences, able to travel from considerable distances. The sometimes short-lived community festivals, in turn, are free; their 'rougher', often more playful productions attract diverse local audiences, children, families, senior citizens.
2   Since 1999, twenty Shakespeare plays and adaptations (eight comedies, three tragedies and three romances, several of them revisited) have been produced in Patalenitsa by Bulgarian and British directors. Since 2016, the festival has also included visiting Shakespeare productions from theatre institutions of higher education.
3   For a fuller discussion of the façade democracy of the Bulgarian post-communist transition, see Sokolova and Stavreva (2017).
4   The idea of making theatre with children, as well as the principle of its execution, were originally suggested by theatre designer Dimitar Bozhkov: 'It doesn't matter where you will be making theatre, the important thing is that you do it decently' (Baichinska et al. 2019: 4).
5   All translations from Bulgarian are the authors'.
6   The name 'Petrovden' (St Peter's Day) was chosen spontaneously by the children participating in the first performance, which coincided with the saint's feast day (Baichinska et al. 2019: 4).
7   The locally created plays included *Legends of Batkun and Patalenitsa* (2005) and *Our Folk* (2006). In 2009, *The Little Prince* was staged (Baichinska et al. 2019: 100–1).
8   The film can be watched on YouTube in two fifteen-minute sections, at https://www.youtube.com/watch?v=rddjw8wMAmI and https://www.youtube.com/watch?v=bfFW7Ibann0.

9 The work of Rudolf Laban (1879–1958), a movement theorist, choreographer and dancer, has been used, since the 1980s, in theatre performance to diversify the movement expressiveness of actors and help them physicalize character portrayal.
10 In the autumn of 2013, students and professors from Guildford, NATFA, as well as young Bulgarian actors gathered in Patalenitsa to study the rhythms of Balkan music, Laban movement technique and a variety of innovative cultural practices; they then shared their experience at meetings with students and young creatives in Plovdiv and Sofia. The project was sponsored by the program 'Youth in Action, Youth for Europe: Theatre Bridges'.
11 The music for the production was developed by Danielle Meunier, who was also voice coach.

References

Angelov, Kalin (2018), 'Shekspirova teatralna shkola "Petrovden" za parvi pat shte predstavi muzikalen spektakal [Shakespeare Theatre School "Petrovden" Will Stage a Musical Performance for the First Time]', *Pzinfo.com*, 19 July. Available online: https://pz-info.com/шекспирова-театрална-школа-петровд-3 (accessed 20 December 2019).

Baichinska, Svetlana, Pavlina-Kalina Tserovska, Elena Tserovska and Inna Tserovska (2019), *Pod kupola nebesen: 20 godini Shekspirova Patalenitsa* [Under the Dome of Heaven: 20 Years of Patalenitsa Shakespeare], Sofia: BG Reklama i dizain.

Darik [Finansi] (2009), 'Britanetz postavi Shekspir v pazardjishkoto selo Patalenitsa [A British Director Stages Shakespeare in the Pazardjik-Region Village of Patalenitsa]', 27 July. Available online: https://financebg.com/британец-постави-шекспир-в-пазарджиш/ (accessed 28 December 2019).

Dimitrov, Todor (2014), Personal communication, 21 January.

Dragostinova, Elena (1999), 'Plovdiv '99'. *Kultura* 21, 28 May. Available online: https://newspaper.kultura.bg/media/my_html/2081/c_plvd.htm (accessed 2 August 2021).

Engle, Ron Felicia, Hardinson Londré and Daniel J. Watermeier (1995), *Shakespeare Companies and Festivals: An International Guide*, Westport, CT: Greenwood Publishing Group.

International Theatre Festival 'Varna Summer' (1993–2019), Archive. Available online: http://viafest.org/varna/en/archive/ (accessed 21 October 2019).

Kalinkova, Penka (1999), 'Plovdivski dnevnitzi: Energiite Hamlet [Plovdiv Diaries: The Hamlet Energies]', *Kultura* 27, 9 July. Available online: http://newspaper.kultura.bg/bg/article/view/2733 (accessed 21 October 2019).

'Rex Doyle Obituary' (2015), *Guardian*, 2 June. Available online: https://www.theguardian.com/stage/2015/jun/02/rex-doyle-obituary (accessed 2 September 2019).

Shakespeare, William (2017), *A Midsummer Night's Dream*, ed. Sukanta Chaudhuri, London, New Delhi, New York and Sydney: Bloomsbury Arden.

Sokolova, Boika, and Kirilka Stavreva (2017), '"The readiness is all," or The Politics of Art in Post-Communist Bulgaria', *Toronto Slavic Quarterly* 60: 1–17. Available online: http://sites.utoronto.ca/tsq/60/SokolovaStavreva1_60.pdf (accessed 15 September 2019).

'Teatralni mostove v s. Patalenitsa—mladezhki obmen po programa "Mladezhta v deistvie"' [Theatre Bridges in the Village of Patalenitsa: A Youth Exchange Sponsored by the Program 'Youth in Action'] (2013), *PAmedia*, 13 November. Available online: http://pa-media.net/news.php?extend.5834 (accessed 7 July 2020).

Tserovska, Pavlina-Kalina (2014), Personal communication, 20 January.

Zarev, Vladimir (2014), 'Ili shte poletim, ili shte se srinem v propastta' [We Will Either Fly, or Fall into the Abyss], *Trud*, 6 December.

10

The Gyula Shakespeare Festival (Hungary): Local, national, European, global

Júlia Paraizs and Ágnes Matuska

When preparing the tenth anniversary of the Gyula Shakespeare Festival's founding to be celebrated in 2015, the managing director of the Gyula Castle Theatre and founder of the festival, József Gedeon (1956–2016) shared the following:

> The idea of the Shakespeare Festival came about as I am a great admirer of Shakespeare and England, and since 1999 we have started [the season] with a Shakespeare production in the Castle Theatre. I look for directors who approach Shakespeare's works in new ways. Shakespeare is so profound, so multilayered, his *oeuvre* is so extensive that there is almost everything in it that one needs to know about life: he writes about everything from relationships to politics to an unparalleled degree of depth. Shakespeare is very popular in Hungary; maybe, apart from England, we have the highest number of new productions in Europe, forty to fifty, but it used to be even higher. The considerable national activity, set side by side with an international festival, offers the opportunity to assess the state of our theatrical culture today.[1]
>
> (Balogh 2013: 19–20)

Whereas his reasons ranged from personal experience to Shakespeare's aesthetic supremacy and universality, Gedeon justified the dedication of an annual festival to Shakespeare as an instrument for disseminating new forms of theatrical creativity, placing national performance activity within a larger international perspective. Gedeon's initiative has most often been praised along these lines: at the beginning, for presenting theatre on a European scale (Jászay 2005; Csáki 2006); later, on the occasion of the tenth anniversary, for organizing the first international theatre festival in Hungary which has regularly been showcasing '*mainstream* theatre' (Koltai 2013: 157, his italics); for presenting important or interesting, fashionable or exotic international Shakespeare productions (Zappe 2013); and for becoming part of the international theatre festival circuit (Attila Vidnyánszky qtd in Koltai 2013).

Another ambition from the start has been to incorporate the Shakespeare Festival into the life of the town, to make it contemporary (Koltai 2013). As a curator on Gedeon's artistic advisory board, András Nagy, put it, the fifteenth-century brick castle in Gyula is particularly suitable for such an undertaking 'with its stout walls, big sky, the surrounding moat, and the tireless cicadas' (Koltai 2013: 157). The castle in Gyula is the icon of its distinguished history; its use as a theatrical space since the 1960s has made it more than a site of national heritage. It is in this light that Nagy, who was the director of the National Institute for Theatre History at the time of the festival's founding, talks about 'the completeness of experience': 'Theatre, primarily, but also sounds, images, even flavours and scents, the illusion of the senses, because without these the *world* would not be *complete*. That is, *theatre*, as Shakespeare had seen it once' (Koltai 2013: 157, italics original). As another curator on Gedeon's board, the doyen of Hungarian theatre critics at the time, Tamás Koltai, remarked, Gedeon achieved this by making the festival a multi-arts cultural event, offering a wide range of activities related to the onstage events (ranging from mainstream to independent theatre productions), including theatre workshops, an academic conference open to the public, films, stage recordings, 'Shakespeare-time cuisine' in local restaurants (Koltai 2013: 157) and an art exhibition.

This chapter explores the local, European and global dimensions of the festival which have shaped it from the beginnings in 2005 to the present day, focusing on three pivotal moments. First, we look at the founding of the festival in 2005 and the production inaugurating the first edition, directed by Attila Vidnyánszky, *Shakespeare's Laurel Wreath*, which articulated important aspects of the festival's ethos in its attention to the locality of the performing space. Next, we explore the meaning of 'European' for the Gyula Shakespeare Festival through a case study, Oskaras Koršunovas *Miranda* based on *The Tempest* and produced by the Castle Theatre as part of a European cooperation. Last, we approach the global aspects of the international Shakespeare Festival in Gyula through the multicultural co-production of Teatro Potlach (Italy) and the Castle Theatre. Investigating the local, we argue that Gyula's own theatrical tradition and the change in the Castle Theatre's management have been instrumental in shaping the festival's annual editions from 2005 to 2020. In charting the European aspects of the festival, we will be focusing on two features that have come to the forefront: the significance of negotiating the Eastern European experience in a new Europe symbolized by the European Union, and cross-border cultural relations with a special interest in minority cultures. With its rising international fame, the festival has also become part of Shakespeare's globalized world, foregrounding questions about authenticity in both local and global performances.

The local context of an international festival

Although Shakespeare has been read, studied and performed with enthusiasm since the late eighteenth century in Hungary and, for over a century, a number of Shakespeare plays have been part of the national secondary school curriculum, Gedeon's vision was called a 'bold venture' both in the national (Balogh 2013) and international press (Irmer 2008). Gyula is a historical spa town in the southeast corner of Hungary close to the Romanian and the Serbian border. It is situated in a non-metropolitan, agricultural area without a university, and inhabited by 30,000 people. After the Ottoman rule (1566–1694), the town was repopulated with Hungarians, Germans and Romanians. Since Hungary's Romanian minority is concentrated in and around Gyula, the town has a Romanian primary and secondary school. Gyula and its castle stood for a regional stronghold, and until the middle of the twentieth century it was the Békés county capital, but after the war the power shifted to Békéscsaba. Today the town's most important service industry is tourism, centring around the Gyula Castle Spa and the fifteenth-century brick castle built in Verona style, situated in the middle of a grassy park, next to a boating lake. The town also has a theatre owned by the town council: *Gyulai Várszínház* (Gyula Castle Theatre). For six weeks each summer, the castle's courtyard turns into the main venue of the arts festival organized by the Castle Theatre. Although summer is the theatre's high season, the Castle Theatre is not a summer theatre: in the winter months the theatre is kept alive by staging productions in a two-hundred-seat chamber playhouse. With a lot of guest performances not specifically designed for the open-air stage in the castle, other performance spaces also had to be found for the summer festival's programme: a proscenium stage in the building of the town's cultural centre, a chamber theatre with a platform stage housed in the administrative headquarters of the festival and the town's sports hall.

Gyula cannot rely on the cultural prestige and touristic appeal of metropolitan areas, nor can it rely on historical evidence to establish spatial connections between the early modern stage of Shakespeare and the world of contemporary theatres like Shakespeare's Globe Theatre in London or the new Shakespeare theatre in Gdańsk.[2] But what Gedeon's Shakespeare Festival did have in creating an authentic venue for playing Shakespeare was a considerable theatrical tradition to build on. The Renaissance courtyard of the castle had already been reinvented as a summer theatre venue in 1964. Inspired by the Dubrovnik Summer Festival, István Miszlay, director of the Békéscsaba county theatre founded the Castle Theatre in Gyula, which was the first open-air summer theatre established in postwar Hungary (Zappe 2003). This followed the castle's renovation and the construction of a spa during a period in which cultural politics were relatively liberal and domestic tourism was increasingly incentivized (Zappe 2013). Although there has been a continuous presence of professional theatre since the 1860s, at that point, in 1964, Gyula had no theatre of its own. The Erkel-színkör – 'a wooden theatre which was to Gyula like the Globe to London' – built by local craftsmen in 1901 and named after the famous son of the town, the renowned nineteenth-century composer of national operas, Ferenc Erkel, had been demolished in 1959 (Árpási 2014). The administration of Gyula therefore welcomed the idea of a summer theatre to compensate for the loss of its local theatrical life as well as for the loss of the county seat to Békéscsaba (Árpási 2014).

Given that 1964 was the 400th anniversary of Shakespeare's birth, it might have been fitting to inaugurate the new theatre with one of his plays, but that honour went to a production of Victor Hugo's *Hernani*. Critic András Rajk, a supporter of Miszlay's initiative, defended the non-Shakespearean choice: while some might think that '*Hamlet* would have been more appropriate, there is no rule that we must be playing "Elsinore" right at the start ... *Hamlet* would be put on in due course, even at times when it is generally not so much in the limelight' (1964: 2). Miszlay later on said that *Hernani* was ideal for an open-air performance and offered great roles for his actors at the Békéscsaba Theatre, but he also admitted to a more symbolic gesture (Zappe 2003). As *Hernani* was an important aesthetic and political battleground between conservatives and progressive romantics, Miszlay felt that it was a meaningful choice in the face of the animosity and scepticism met by the founders of the Gyula Castle Theatre (Zappe 2003). Between 1964 and 1990, Hungarian historical drama, by both contemporary and classic playwrights, was the most critically acclaimed element of the programme and the Castle Theatre became an important forum nationally for staging historical drama as a subterfuge for dealing with contemporary political issues (Zappe 2003; Shevtosva 2011).

In socialist Hungary, Shakespeare was an important vehicle for discussing such issues, especially through the problem plays (Schandl 2008). Shakespeare, however, was conspicuously missing from the programme in the first phase of the Castle Theatre's history (1964–73), whereas the theatre in Békéscsaba, to which the Gyula Castle Theatre belonged at the time, put on Shakespeare productions on a regular basis, almost annually between 1958 and 1975.[3] Yet the choice of *Hernani* might point to the importance of Shakespeare's afterlife and the long-standing influence of his works on Hungarian drama, starting with the Romantic movement. Hugo himself was a great admirer of Shakespeare, and *Hernani*, a historical play set in sixteenth-century Spain, was greatly influenced by Romantic Shakespearean aesthetics as well as by Hugo's spectating experience of English guest performances of Shakespeare's plays in Paris.

It was only after the political changes that a Shakespeare Cycle consisting of four plays (*Antony and Cleopatra*, *Macbeth*, *Hamlet*, *King Lear*) was staged between 1991 and 1994 by Ferenc Sík, managing director of the Castle Theatre and later of the National Theatre in Budapest (Elek 2003; Zappe 2013). Shakespeare became part of the new profile of the Castle Theatre, which moved away from contemporary drama to classical plays and operas as part of a new concept emerging in the early 1990s (Thuróczy 2003). This shift can be explained by the political and cultural context in the early years of the market economy in Hungary: a theatre acclaimed primarily for its contemporary dramatic repertory moved towards an eclectic multi-arts cultural event with an emphasis on festival elements (Elek 2003). From 1999 on, Shakespeare has been an annual presence in Gyula, but it was Gedeon's idea of a Shakespeare Festival that has condensed Shakespeare into one theatrical metaphor: by showing productions ranging from small independent companies to world-class names, indigenous and international, from monodramas to large-scale stadium performances, from popular street art forms to conceptual high-brow theatre, from children's theatre to educational projects, by offering theatrical experiences through music and dance performances to curious locals and summer spa audiences, as well as for scholars and theatre makers.

Gedeon, a native of Gyula, became the managing director of the Castle Theatre in 1995, marking the beginning of a new phase. He got involved in the life of the theatre in his teenage years as a halberdier and torch bearer in 1972 and later as an extra on stage (Balogh 2013). Working as a teacher at a local school, he was very active in organizing the town's cultural life and after 1991 worked in cultural affairs for the Gyula municipal council (Balogh 2013). There had already been festivals organized around a single art theme or genre (early music, jazz, folk, puppet theatre, poetry) as part of the summer programme since the mid-1970s, including a jazz festival which was also Gedeon's brainchild. But it was he who thought of the six-week summer programme as one big festival, inaugurating it with a folk festival (*Kőrös-völgyi Sokadalom*) in 2000, reminiscent of the ones on market days and holidays set up on fairgrounds, which was to embrace high and popular culture, theatre and the town. When the castle's renovation was finished in 2005, the idea of a two-week international Shakespeare Festival was born (Koltai 2013). It was the first major festival programme in

2005/6 which followed the official opening of the Castle Theatre's summer festival during the *Kőrös-völgyi Sokadalom*. Shakespeare became a celebration of theatre in Gyula.

The first production in 2005 was the epitome of this concept. The inaugural performance of the Shakespeare Festival, *Shakespeare's Laurel Wreath – Theatre, Theatre, Theatre*, the Castle Theatre's own production, extended well beyond the courtyard stage and made use of both the castle and its surroundings. Written by Ernő Verebes and directed by Attila Vidnyánszky, the play relied mainly on *Hamlet*, *Macbeth* and *Romeo and Juliet*, with occasional allusions to *Richard III*, *A Midsummer Night's Dream*, *The Merchant of Venice*, *As You Like It*, *King Lear* and *The Tempest* (Darvasi 2006). The production also called upon notions of *commedia dell'arte* in its use of improvisation, interaction with members of the audience, criers and the world of strolling players, enhancing the idea of Shakespeare as part of popular culture. The actors, while waiting for their cues, were cooking Hungarian goulash soup by the outer wall of the castle (Marik 2005). The production abounded in grotesque and bawdy scenes, music, circus and dance, and the finale included scenes with fire and a water fountain (Marik 2005). Although there is no surviving record of local theatre in medieval or early modern times, Gedeon believed that one should imagine the first theatrical activities in Gyula as medieval, when strolling players used to entertain people on market days (Szpenátyi 2009).

The marketplace-styled dramatic exposition of Vidnyánszky's production led to the next sequence, a mock-trial of Shakespeare: the prosecutor was Leo Tolstoy, looking like Death from the morality play tradition, who condemned Shakespeare as a bad and immoral writer; the defense attorney was Don Quixote, taking immense pleasure in Shakespeare's imaginary world. At the end, the floating stage turned into an island, while the audience watched the emerging shadows of Shakespearean characters on the wall of the castle: Shakespeare was saved from death – Tolstoy failed to set him on fire (Marik 2005). By using the various spaces within and around the Castle Theatre and by stressing the importance of the audience's role in the 'here and now' of the community created by the performance, *Shakespeare's Laurel Wreath* set a distinctive tone for the new Shakespeare Festival in Gyula. It relied on the prestigious status of the canonical author, but it also made room for irony and even doubt, inviting the audience to be aware of their status as judges, a status reflected in the dramaturgy of the trial-within-the-play.

Reaching out to audiences both in and out of the theatre was an important feature of the festival at several levels. The goal of broadening his audience base locally was very close to Gedeon's heart (Shevtosva 2011). Street performances and puppet shows, for example, have been regularly part of the programme to include those who might not attend the theatre. Ticket prices for productions were kept down to make them accessible to lower-income groups. This mission of showing high-quality theatre at an affordable price has been supported by state funding. Gedeon kept looking for ways of developing interest and discernment in serious theatre, especially among the young (Shevtosva 2011). Close links with schools during winter provided him with a direct route to them, followed up in the summer by such ventures as an interactive *Romeo and Juliet* in 2011, and, for younger children, *Stories from Shakespeare* (Shevtsova 2011).

However, Gedeon's goal was fraught with difficulties: many of his targeted spectators, particularly for the Shakespeare Festival, believed they would not understand productions of Shakespeare in Hungarian, let alone in a foreign language (Shevtsova 2011). After seeing the first edition, critic Tamás Jászay expressed his concern that Gedeon's Shakespeare Festival would struggle to find an audience besides critics and theatre people, and questioned whether it was not a luxury to have renowned international productions playing to half-empty houses (Jászay 2005). Figures from 2011 show that for six weeks during the summer, the Castle Theatre Festival attracted around twenty-five thousand people, and the Shakespeare Festival about four thousand (Shevtsova 2011). Its audience was made up of 30 per cent locals, another 30–40 per cent from the area and the rest from the capital and abroad (Shevtsova 2011). As László Zappe concluded in 2013, despite initial concerns and the fact that the productions did not always attract full houses, the Shakespeare Festival took root in Gyula (Zappe 2013).

A new period in the history of the Shakespeare Festival started in 2017, following Gedeon's death in 2016. The new director, Tibor Elek, a literature historian and editor, has lived and worked in Gyula for many decades. He used to be one of Gedeon's curators, and has organized the literary festival of humour as part of the Castle Theatre festival programme since 2003. As part of the

Shakespeare Festival's programme, he has, since 2007, hosted a series of conversations with contemporary Hungarian writers about their experiences of Shakespeare. He firmly believes in the tradition of the multi-arts festival format combined with the ethos of quality productions at the Castle Theatre (Elek 2003). But Elek is also wary of the Castle Theatre becoming overly synonymous with Shakespeare: 'It is problematic that the Gyula Castle Theatre, for a lot of people ... meant merely Shakespeare' (Marton 2018). Elek hinted, in the same interview, that productions that appealed to cultural tourists were not always welcomed by the locals. He also referenced a fatigue with regards to the Shakespeare Festival, partly because of the lack of support from the local community and partly due to growing competition posed by other international theatre festivals in Hungary, primarily by MITEM, the international theatre festival hosted by the Hungarian National Theatre, founded by Attila Vidnyánszky in 2014 (Marton 2018).

The waning importance of the Shakespeare Festival under the new leadership of Elek is manifest, reflected by different priorities. The Shakespeare Festival, which had been the first major theatre event to start the Castle Theatre's summer festival from 2005 to 2016, has been preceded by a two- to three-day festival dedicated to the works of Hungarian authors in 2018 and 2019. As new festival elements have been introduced, such as the Transylvanian Week,[4] the Shakespeare Festival was shortened from ten days in 2016 to one week in 2018. In 2020, the programme of the international Shakespeare Festival was to be a 'Hungarian Shakespeare edition' showing only Hungarian-language productions.[5] The idea of a 'Hungarian Shakespeare edition' may have been related to the commemorative events of the 100th anniversary of the Treaty of Versailles and the national trauma of the breakup of the Hungarian Kingdom, resulting in a major loss of territory and the dispersal of many ethnic Hungarians to neighbouring countries, a theme embraced by the Castle Theatre's programme for 2020. In the end, Covid-19 did not curtail the 2020 festival season at the Castle Theatre, but Elek had to let go of several Shakespeare productions because of Covid-related restrictions on indoor performances.[6] Altogether, there were four Shakespeare performances: a production of *The Comedy of Errors* (dir. Dániel Dicső) on 4 July, two other performances on 5 July[7] and the Castle Theatre's own production of *Hamlet* (dir. Péter Telihay) in co-production with the Szigligeti

Theatre in Oradea, Romania, on 29 August. Although some critics referred to it, wishfully, as a Shakespeare Festival (Almási 2020), there is no reference to a 'Shakespeare Festival' in the theatre's programme booklet and Elek himself called it a 'Shakespeare weekend' in a radio interview.[8] On the other hand, other festivals, such as the Transylvanian Festival, the Jazz Festival, Folk and World Music Festival, Sándor Márai Days, went ahead as planned, retaining their festival label.

A European festival

Even if productions outside of Europe have been included in the programme from the third edition on, the importance of the Shakespeare Festival in Gyula has been defined as a symbol of the European orientation in Hungarian theatrical culture (Karsai György qtd in Koltai 2013). Although the Gyula Shakespeare Festival is by no means a regional festival, it has shown a strong interest in Eastern Europe (Koltai 2013), especially in exploring its twentieth-century post-Soviet past. The festival programme brought internationally renowned directors to Gyula engaging with new forms of theatrical creativity, seemingly irrespective of their nationalities. But many world-renowned directors, whose productions were present at the festival, were from the region: the Lithuanian *A Midsummer Night's Dream,* directed by Oskaras Koršunovas, the Romanian *Twelfth Night,* directed by Silviu Purcărete, in the first edition, and another Lithuanian icon Eimuntas Nekrošius and Georgian director Robert Sturua (both producing *Hamlet* in subsequent editions) have set the stage for a negotiation of Shakespearean meaning embedded in a Europe east of the Elbe or, more recently, east of the Berlin Wall.

A pivotal performance in the festival's history representing the common past, vision and values of East and Central Europe was Oskaras Koršunovas *Miranda, After W. Shakespeare's 'The Tempest'*. This production, with its world premiere in Gyula in 2011, was the first one to be funded by the European Shakespeare Festivals Network (ESFN) and the first world premiere by an internationally renowned director in Hungary (Koltai 2013). Subsequently, it travelled to other Shakespeare Festivals, including Gdańsk and Craiova, receiving high critical acclaim and collecting prestigious awards. In this version of *The Tempest,* Prospero enacted Shakespeare's play to his disabled daughter, Miranda. While Prospero doubled as virtually all the other characters, Miranda doubled as Ariel. The action took place in a communist-era looking bedsit, cluttered from floor to ceiling. The fact that this Prospero had a drinking problem and turned into Caliban had sinister implications in the doubling. At the same time, some critics felt that the play shaped another alternative reality through theatre. Prospero's books were juxtaposed with Miranda's ballet as metaphors of artistic freedom, as well as freedom to act (Shevtsova 2011). According to a Hungarian critic's review of the premiere, the director's vision presented two threads competing with each other: the magical albeit melancholy view of *The Tempest* as opposed to the suffocating Soviet atmosphere in which reality is denied (Csáki 2011). In the director's interpretation, Miranda was Prospero's soul, while Prospero's books evoked the possibility for spiritual resistance against an oppressive regime on an island where people, also from the liberal professions, and regarded as inconvenient by the authorities, could look for spiritual freedom. The creation of artistic and propagandistic visions, often entangled, was foregrounded later by a Romanian production of *Richard III* in Hungarian directed by Gábor Tompa, which premiered in Gyula in 2008 (Matuska 2012). There is a special East-Central-European aspect to this. In countries which used to be theatricalized in a negative sense by an ideologically projected version of reality for decades – a reality that felt untrue to identify with – the importance of the power of a community to overwrite it with *their* theatre, their choice of shaping social reality, is an especially meaningful option.

Another important aspect of Europeanness for the festival has been cross-border cooperation both as a way of sharing performances and performance cultures, and as a way of connecting communities often plagued by ethnic tensions. Inviting productions from Hungarian minority theatres in neighbouring countries has been a long-standing tradition in Gyula, and the Shakespeare Festival was a means to embrace this. Attila Vidnyánszky's Hungarian-language theatre from Berehove, in Ukraine, which inaugurated the Shakespeare Festival, performed in Gyula before and after 2005 (Balogh 2013: 19). The Hungarian-language theatre company from Subotica, Serbia, has also had a regular presence at the festival, with productions such as *Twelfth Night* (2008), *Macbeth* (2014) and *The*

Tempest (2019). But, as the festival programmes attest throughout the years, the strongest international presence at the festival has been Romanian, including directors Silviu Purcărete and Andrei Șerban, who earned their international fame in France and the USA. Emil Boroghină, actor and director of the Craiova International Shakespeare Festival, has also been a special guest at the Gyula conference on Shakespearean monologues and gave a performance based on the soliloquies in 2013.[9] Hungarian-language productions from Romania were a regular presence at the festival, whether directed by new talents or by internationally famous names, such as László Bocsárdi from Sfântu Gheorghe or Gábor Tompa from Cluj. Gedeon's interest in Romanian theatre dates back to the late 1990s, and his thinking about theatre had been deeply influenced by it (Balogh 2013). He regularly visited Romanian theatre festivals, including Craiova, from 1997 onwards (Balogh 2013).

As a border town, Gyula has traditionally been well positioned to engage in such activity. Following the historical drama period of the Castle Theatre in the 1960s, the management's interest turned to contemporary Hungarian plays in the mid-1970s and 1980s under the leadership of Ferenc Sík, and the Castle Theatre became a centre for cooperation with Hungarian playwrights from Romania, its programme also including several theatre companies from minority cultures in neighbouring countries. The Shakespeare Festival, by regularly inviting theatre companies from minority Hungarian communities, has become part of this acclaimed tradition at the Castle Theatre. The Shakespeare Festival had also been an important instrument in showcasing Hungarian minority theatres at the Castle Theatre before Elek founded the 'Transylvanian Week' in 2018.

Hungary's accession to the EU in 2004 has played an important role in the festival's development both in symbolic and in material terms, in giving a new frame to the traditional priorities of the Castle Theatre and in developing new ideas. Gyula was one of the founding members of the European Shakespeare Festival Network in 2006. Several members of the network took part in various projects funded by the EU's Culture Programme (2007–13), coordinated by Theatrum Gedanense Foundation in Gdansk. The Gyula Shakespeare Festival participated in 'Beyond the stage – new trends in European theatre' (2009/10), an interdisciplinary project on theatre that combined art, theory and education; 'Shake-in the City. The art of inclusion' (2010/11) which involved especially young people in making theatre as part of their communities; and 'Discovering Theatrelands' (2012) which explored ideas of travelling players. As part of 'Shake-in the City. The art of inclusion' (2010/11), theatre students associated with the county's permanent theatre in Békéscsaba formed a street theatre troupe named Puck's Society (Hieropolitańska and Rola 2013). Referring to the popular culture figure who connects the fairy dream-world with mortals in *A Midsummer Night's Dream*, the theatre group brought a carnivalesque street performance of a Shakespearean *mélange* to the streets of Gyula and to smaller communities in the area (Mészáros 2010), involving places and people usually without much access either to theatre of any kind or to experiences of community engagement.

Global Shakespeare

From its inception in 2005, Gyula has welcomed what might be called 'Global' Shakespearean productions, many of which are designed for multi-festival circulation. Many world-class productions have been presented in Gyula, including some of those staged at the Globe to Globe Festival, dubbed the pinnacle of globalized Shakespeare (Kennedy 2017), such as a Lithuanian *Hamlet*, dir. Eimuntas Nekrošius (2006); a Zimbabwean *Two Gentlemen of Verona* (2010), dir. Arne Pohlmeier; a South Korean *A Midsummer Night's Dream*, dir. Jung-Ung Yang (2011); and a Russian *Measure for Measure*, dir. Yuri Butusov (2013). If we accept Eric Cohen's notion that authenticity is not a fixed state but a socially constructed concept, then these productions have different authentic meanings when presented to different (national or global) audiences (Kennedy 1998). Yohangza Theatre's *A Midsummer Night's Dream* (dir. Jung-Ung Yang), for example, was supposed to be a popular curiosity in Gyula, but it became a unique theatrical experience (Koltai 2013). As Ian Herbert wrote in the *Stage*, in Gyula it was a very different production and its magic came alive not only on the courtyard stage but on the castle walls, too (qtd in Koltai 2013). It has been suggested by some critics that the courtyard stage works best at the Shakespeare Festival when it becomes part of the action (Cseicsner 2008; Paraizs 2014).

But another globalized way of producing Shakespeare has also appeared in Gyula in the form of intercultural performance. Played by a multicultural cast, using non-Western theatrical traditions, intercultural performance can occupy several positions in the spectrum of globalized performance (Worthen 2003). Many intercultural performances are commodities, products in the world of globalized theatre, while others, even while using elements of an increasingly globalized theatrical repertoire, clearly arise as local practice (Worthen 2003). The production commissioned by the Castle Theatre for the 2019 edition, Pino Di Buduo's *Cheerful Shakespeare*, based on *Much Ado*, used many elements of intercultural performance. The production's main actors came from two theatre companies and two acting traditions: Buduo's Teatro Potlach from Italy and the Indian Fanatika Theatre. Local artists from Gyula and Békéscsaba – actors, folk musicians and folk dancers – were also involved. The production's languages were Italian, English and Hungarian, while Hungarian subtitles and occasional oral translation by a Hungarian member of Teatro Potlach were also provided. Critics praised the performance for bringing about an atmosphere of festivity overall (Fodor 2019) or, at least, in some parts of the show (Bóta 2019b). But according to Bóta, *Cheerful Shakespeare* was no more than a *mélange* without any overarching idea (Bóta 2019b). Di Buduo's own explanation for the production evokes ideas foregrounding the theatricality (Fodor 2019) that has underlain the festival from its outset, but in this production it was reduced to pure spectacle. This was most apparent in the production's handling of local culture as folk musicians, dancers and horse riders from Gyula and Békéscsaba merely served as a musical and visual background to the main action performed by the Italian and Indian companies.

In 2005 Gedeon founded an international Shakespeare festival: the first edition was made up of international productions (which included two world-class productions as well as Hungarian-language productions from neighbouring countries) and one production produced by the Castle Theatre, directed by Vidnyásnszky, from Berehove, Ukraine. Gedeon's aim was to show the richness and variety present in contemporary theatre through Shakespeare. From the second edition on, the national uses of Shakespeare have been made more explicit by inviting two or three of the best productions in the country alongside international productions and the Castle

Theatre's own premiere. The presence of national, Hungarian Shakespeare has become a vital part of the international Gyula festival as it has provided an opportunity to showcase and examine Hungarian theatrical activity in an international context. It has also enabled a number of Hungarian performances to become part of the international Shakespeare festival circuit. In Hungary, this kind of venture – surveying national theatrical activity in the context of international trends – is properly the function of a National Theatre, with all the structural and financial support this implies. And indeed this international platform emerged when Attila Vidnyánszky (director of the Hungarian National Theatre) founded MITEM in 2014, the International Theatre Festival of the National Theatre. Despite Gyula being superseded by MITEM in this regard by now, Gedeon's achievement was rewarded by the prestigious Sándor Hevesi Award in 2013 for promoting Hungarian theatre internationally.

József Gedeon was key to the success of the Shakespeare Festival. He managed to invite many of the best internationally known directors thanks, probably, to his charismatic personality, his love of theatre, his professionalism, his resilience in the face of adversity and his ability to unite people from all walks of life behind his vision (Bóta 2019a). He was always open to experiments (Shevtsova 2011) and to other cultures. Having worked as a teacher and public educator, he valued curiosity and learning in both life and theatre. His visits to various theatres in the UK, ranging from big London theatres to amateur companies, and his interest in Romanian theatre life (Balogh 2013) must have played a formative role in his theatrical taste, his theatre management skills and networking. There were other figures in the background (namely, his body of curators), but it was much like a one-man show (Bóta 2019a).

In the past three years, Elek has continued many long-standing traditions of the Gyula Castle Theatre: he believes in the importance of staging historical drama and contemporary Hungarian plays, in the presence of Hungarian minority theatres, in cooperation with the National Theatre and in the multi-arts festival format. But the Shakespeare Festival has less significance in his efforts to strengthen the position of Hungarian drama and minority theatres in the programme. The Shakespeare Festival used to be an important vehicle for representing minority theatres, but this function has now been superseded most notably by the newly founded Transylvanian

Week. Although, in the end, the Shakespeare Festival did not take place in 2020, the originally planned idea of a 'Hungarian edition' suggests an important conceptual change: the Shakespeare Festival is no longer a vital instrument in negotiating the meaning of European cultural heritage and the place of Hungarian theatrical creativity within it. If the international context feels relevant at all, Shakespeare ceased to provide it.

The future of the Gyula Shakespeare Festival is uncertain. But it has built an impressive legacy over fifteen years: in creating a unique hub for theatre companies, artists, directors, schoolchildren, scholars, locals and tourists on vacation, a forward-looking and inspiring vision was established. During the time of the six-week summer festival, Gedeon made an attempt to involve a wide range of audiences in various forms of performance, showing the relevance of theatre as a metaphor of life through Shakespeare. A Hungarian town with a multi-ethnic background was reinvented, its various public spaces engaged in new, performative ways, while its theatre's reputation – at least for the first fifteen years – has been enhanced to an international level.

Notes

1. All translations from the Hungarian are the authors', unless specified.
2. See Urszula Kizelbach and Jacek Fabiszak's chapter on the Gdańsk Shakespeare Festival in the present volume.
3. International drama was represented mainly by Spanish, French and Italian classics (e.g. Calderón, Racine and Goldoni).
4. Tibor Elek founded the 'Transylvanian Week' in 2018, showcasing productions by minority Hungarian artists from Romania representing a wide range of arts, including contemporary drama by Hungarian and Romanian authors.
5. Before Covid-19 hit Hungary, Elek spoke about his plans on the local television channel on 22 January 2020 for staging only Hungarian productions at the Shakespeare Festival. Available online: https://www.gyulatelevizio.hu/2020/01/22/csak-magyar-nyelvu-eloadasokat-mutatnak-be-a-shakespeare-fesztivalon/ (accessed 28 September 2020).
6. Gábor Bóta's interview with Tibor Elek in Művészbejáró, Klubrádió, 28 June 2020. Available online: https://www.klubradio.hu/archivum/muveszbejaro-2020-junius-28-vasarnap-1600-11428 (accessed 28 September 2020).

7   A performance combining music and dance inspired by *Othello* and a concert of English Renaissance music with extracts from Shakespeare's sonnets and plays.
8   Gábor Bóta's interview with Tibor Elek in Művészbejáró, Klubrádió, 28 June 2020. Available online: https://www.klubradio.hu/archivum/ muveszbejaro-2020-junius-28-vasarnap-1600-11428 (accessed 28 September 2020).
9   See Nicoleta Cinpoeş' chapter on the Craiova Shakespeare Festival in the present volume.

References

Almási, Zsolt (2020), 'Shakespeare járvány idején: Gyulai Shakesepare Fesztivál 2020' [Shakespeare in the Time of Pandemic: Gyula Shakespeare Festival 2020], *Prae*, 16 July. Available online: https:// www.prae.hu/article/11665-shakespeare-jarvany-idejen/ (accessed 28 September 2020).

Árpási, Zoltán (2014), *Gyula könyv* [The Gyula Book], Gyula: Iniciálé-Lap Bt.

Balogh, Tibor (2013), 'A magyar kultúra elkötelezettje – nemzetközi kitekintéssel, Jubileumi beszélgetés Gedeon Józseffel, a Gyulai Várszínház igazgatójával' [A Man Dedicated to Hungarian Culture – with an International Outlook, An Interview with József Gedeon, Director of the Gyula Castle Theatre on the Occasion of the Jubilee], in Balogh Tibor (ed.), *50 évad a Gyulai Várszínházban* [50 Seasons at the Gyula Castle Theatre], 14–23, Gyula: Gyulai Várszínház.

Bóta, Gábor (2019a), 'Shakespeare Shakespeare-rel' [Shakespeare and Shakespeare], *Népszava*, 20 July. Available online: https://nepszava. hu/3043782_bota-gabor-shakespeare-shakespeare-rel (accessed 28 September 2020).

Bóta, Gábor (2019b), 'Vidám Shakespeare, Gyulai Várszínház' [Merry Shakespeare, Gyula Castle Theatre], *Pesti Műsor* 74 (8): 41.

Csáki, Judit (2006), 'Hamlet állva hal meg. Gyula II. Shakespeare-fesztivál' [Hamlet Died Standing. Gyula Castle Theatre 2nd Edition of the Shakespeare Festival], *Színház* 39 (9): 35–8.

Csáki, Judit (2011), 'Vihar egy szobában' [Tempest in a Room], *Magyar Narancs*, 28 July. Available online: https://magyarnarancs.hu/zene2/ szinhaz_-_vihar_egy_szobaban_-_miranda_-_oskaras_korsunovas_ rendezese_gyulan-76605 (accessed 28 September 2020).

Cseicsner, Otília (2008), 'Gyula, fesztiválváros, Shakespeare-hagyomány, Rajongó útinapló' [Gyula, Festival Town, Shakespeare Traditions, The Travel Diary of a Fan], *Prae*. Available online: https://www.prae.hu/

article/1300-gyula-fesztivalvaros-shakespeare-hagyomany (accessed 28 September 2020).
Darvasi, Ferenc (2006), 'Vád alól felmentve, Shakespeare koszorú – Illyés Gyula Nemzeti Színház, Beregszász; Gyulai Várszínház' [Acquitted, Shakespeare's Laurel Wreath – Gyula Illyés National Theatre, Berehove, The Gyula Castle Theatre], *Ellenfény*, 3. Available online: http://www.ellenfeny.hu/archivum/2006/3/1758-vad-alol-felmentve?layout=offline (accessed 28 September 2020).
Elek, Tibor (2003), 'A minőségi színházi és összművészeti szórakoztatás fellegvára: A Gyulai Várszínház 1995–2003' [The Place of High Quality Theatre and Multi-Art Entertainment: The Gyula Castle Theatre 1995–2003], *Bárka* 11 (6): 92–5. Available online: http://www.barkaonline.hu/archivum/barka_200306.pdf (accessed 28 September 2020).
Fodor, György (2019), 'Un po' di Shakespeare' [A Little Bit of Shakespeare], *Gyulai Hírlap*, 17 July. Available online: https://www.gyulaihirlap.hu/126437-un-po-di-shakespeare (accessed 1 September 2020).
Hieropolitańska, Anna, and Kamila Rola, eds (2013), *Closer Look: European Cultural Cooperation Networks in Practice*, Warsaw: Cultural Contact Point Poland, Adam Mickiewicz Institute. Available online: https://iro.teh.net/closer-look-2013-european-cultural-cooperation-networks-in-practice/?lang=en (accessed 28 September 2020).
Irmer, Thomas (2008), 'Klinische Visionen, offene Spielwelten' [Clinical Visions, Open Play Worlds], *Theater Heute* 62 (October).
Jászay, Tamás (2005), 'Kortársunk, Shakespeare. I. Nemzetközi Shakespeare Fesztivál, Gyula' [Shakespeare, Our Contemporary, First International Shakespeare Festival, Gyula], *Criticai Lapok Online*. Available online: https://www.criticailapok.hu/archivum?id=10227 (accessed 28 September 2020).
Kennedy, Dennis (1998), 'Shakespeare and Cultural Tourism', *Theatre Journal* 50 (2): 175–88.
Kennedy, Dennis (2017), 'Global Shakespeare and Globalized Performance', in J. C. Bullman (ed.), *The Oxford Handbook of Shakespeare and Performance*, 441–57, Oxford: Oxford University Press.
Koltai, Tamás (2013), 'Gyula: Shakespeare-fesztiválváros' [Gyula: Shakespeare Festival Town], in Balogh Tibor (ed.), *50 évad a Gyulai Várszínházban*, 14–23, Gyula: Gyulai Várszínház.
Marik, Noémi (2005), 'Beszél majd az utókor ... Shakespeare-koszorú-Gyulai Várszínház' [Posterity will say… Shakespeare's Laurel Wreath – Gyula Castle Theatre], *Criticai Lapok* 14 (7–8): 9–10.

Available online: http://www.criticailapok.hu/index.php?option=com_content&view=article&id=10228 (accessed 28 September 2020).
Marton, Éva (2018), 'Lenni vagy nem lenni' [To Be, or Not to Be], *Színház.net*, 29 August. Available online: http://szinhaz.net/2018/08/29/marton-eva-lenni-vagy-nem-lenni/ (accessed 28 September 2020).
Matuska, Ágnes (2012), 'Shaping the Spectacle: Faking, Making and Performing Reality through Shakespeare', in Rui Carvalho Homem (ed.), *Relational Designs in Literature and the Arts*, 43–56, Amsterdam and New York: Brill/Rodopi.
Mészáros, Csilla (2010), 'Közhelyeken nem közhelyesen, avagy utcára tett Puck Társulás' [Performing at Common Places, but not Commonplaces, or the Puck Society in the streets], *Bárka Online*, July. Available online: http://www.barkaonline.hu/szinhazak/1527-gyulai-varszinhaz-oesszes (accessed 28 September 2020).
Paraizs, Júlia (2014), 'Gyula és Shakespeare: a 10. Nemzetközi Shakespeare Fesztivál a Gyulai Várszínházban' [Gyula and Shakespeare: The Tenth Edition of the International Shakespeare Festival at the Gyula Castle Theatre], *Prae.hu*, 25 June. Available online: https://www.prae.hu/article/7547-gyula-es-shakespeare/ (accessed 28 September 2020).
Rajk, András (1964), 'Hernani a gyulai várudvaron' [Hernani in the Courtyard of Gyula], *Népszava* 92 (176): 2.
Schandl, Veronika (2008), *Socialist Shakespeare Productions in Kádár-regime Hungary*, Lewiston: Edwin Mellen Press.
Shevtsova, Maria (2011), 'The Gyula Shakespeare Festival 2011', *New Theatre Quarterly* 27 (4): 386–94.
Szpenátyi, Katalin (2009), 'Az Hernanitól a Psychéig, Beszélgetés Gedeon Józseffel a Gyulai Várszínház múltjáról és jelenéről' [From Hernani to Psyche, an Interview with József Gedeon on the Past and Present of the Gyula Castle Theatre], *Bárka* 17 (3). Available online: http://www.barkaonline.hu/component/content/article/34-szinhazi-programok/1034-beszelgetes-gedeon-jozseffel (accessed 28 September 2020).
Thuróczy, Katalin (2003), 'A Gyulai Várszínház "Sík-korszaka" (1973–94)' [The Sík Era at the Gyula Castle Theatre (1973–94)], *Bárka* 11 (6): 78–91.
Worthen, William B. (2003), *Shakespeare and the Force of Modern Performance*, Cambridge: Cambridge University Press.
Zappe, László (2003), 'A Gyulai Várszínház és a szabadtéri színjátszás. Az első tíz év, 1964–1973' [The Gyula Castle Theatre and Open-air Performance. The First Ten Years, 1964–1973], *Bárka* 11 (6): 71–7.
Zappe, László (2013), 'Korszakok tükre' [A Mirror of the Times], *Színház*, November. Available online: http://szinhaz.net/2013/11/11/zappe-laszlo-korszakok-tukre/ (accessed 28 September 2020).

11

Unhomely Shakespeares: Interculturalism and diplomacy in Elsinore

Anne Sophie Refskou

For more than a hundred years, the august walls and tall towers of Kronborg castle in Helsingør (Elsinore) have formed a backdrop for theatre productions of *Hamlet* and other Shakespearean plays performed in the summer by Danish and international companies in this atmospheric place. Today, an annual theatre festival is run at the castle by HamletScenen, a state-supported theatre established in 2008 by the Municipality of Elsinore and the Danish Ministry of Culture to continue the tradition of hosting companies from abroad and to stage its own productions.[1] HamletScenen is housed in 'the old infirmary', one of the handsome yellow and ochre nineteenth-century military buildings on the castle's west side, but the festival, which runs for the first three weeks of August, is open-air.[2] Until 2017, most performances took place on a platform stage temporarily erected in the castle courtyard, but larger and more technologically sophisticated performing conditions have been achieved with the construction of a new platform stage across the moat, which makes the most of summer evening sunsets and the light-and-shadow reflections of the moat water on the bastion wall.[3]

Kronborg overlooks the narrow strait of Øresund that separates the Danish and Swedish coastlines. The magnificent Renaissance

FIGURE 11.1 *The new stage construction during the theatre concert* Searching for William *by Christian Friedel and Woods of Birnam (HamletScenen, Shakespeare Festival 2018). Photograph by permission of Bo Nymann.*

fortified castle – since 2000 a UNESCO World Heritage site – was built by King Frederik II in the 1580s on the medieval foundations of another fortress: Krogen, which, like the later castle, ensured that all passing ships using the strait as a passage to the Baltic would stop and pay the notorious 'Sound Dues' to the Danish Crown. This lucrative arrangement for Denmark also meant that the town of Elsinore – situated approximately 40 km north of Copenhagen – became prosperous and cosmopolitan to an unusual degree and gained an international reputation, which perhaps contributed to Shakespeare choosing it as the setting for his most famous play: to this day, Elsinore and Copenhagen are the only Danish cities to boast an English version of their names.

However, the ostensible lack of a material connection with Shakespeare – the fact that he is unlikely to ever have visited Denmark and that his plays were not performed there during his lifetime – makes it difficult for anyone who wishes to see Kronborg as anything other than what Alexa Alice Joubin has called an 'authentically fake site' (2007: 22). Describing Kronborg as at once 'fake' and 'authentic' is fitting in the sense that its claim to Shakespearean fame is, of course, quite openly based on fiction.[4] Joubin makes a helpful comparison with other cultural touristic venues that are 'manufactured and consumed in cycles of fictionalization' and 'now exist simultaneously on different temporal and spatial dimensions in the fictional and real worlds' (2007: 42).[5] Clearly the idea of authenticity – when couched in terms of materiality or originality – is misapplied when speaking of Kronborg and Elsinore as Shakespearean sites. However, the theatre festival and its history are real enough, and it would therefore perhaps be more productive to define the authenticity of Kronborg and Elsinore's Shakespearean heritage in terms of afterlife, plurality and difference, as I hope this chapter will demonstrate.

It is debatable exactly when the theatre tradition at Kronborg became a festival, and (as usual) it depends on the definition of the word and concept. Part of its 'festive' element could be said to begin with the commemorative celebration of the tercentenary of Shakespeare's death in the summer of 1916, when the Danish Writers' Association organized an open-air performance of extracts from *Hamlet* in collaboration with the Danish Royal Theatre in Copenhagen. This was followed in 1926 by a lavish production of *The Taming of the Shrew*, also by actors from the Danish Royal Theatre, in the context of Elsinore's 500th anniversary as a trading town. Both events demonstrate a local awareness of the Shakespearean connection as implicit to the construction and celebration of the town's identity. There is also evidence of Kronborg having at that time already received a substantial share of Shakespearean tourism and pilgrimage. One of the organizers of the 1916 celebration, the writer and dramatist Sophus Michaëlis, refers in a contemporary theatre journal to 'all the foreigners who visit Elsinore for the sake of Hamlet' (1916: 138).

In 1937, the Danish Tourist Association and Elsinore's newly established 'National Open-air Theatre' invited the first international production to perform at the castle. This was the Old Vic's *Hamlet*, directed by Tyrone Guthrie and starring Laurence Olivier and Vivien Leigh.[6] The intention was to establish an annual tradition of hosting prominent theatre companies from abroad, initially with a view to supporting Danish trade relations and tourism, but, not surprisingly given the political tensions in Europe, diplomatic messages also found their way into the conversations between host and visitors. The patrons in 1937 were a combination of high-profile Danish and British politicians (including the newly retired British PM Stanley Baldwin and cabinet minister Winston Churchill), as well as royals, lords and ladies, famous actors and corporate directors. The programme for the production included a message from the Danish prime minister, T. H. Stauning, supporting the artistic exchange 'especially with a country which has such a close relation to us as England', and hoping that this occasion would inspire bonds between peoples and further exchanges 'with all countries and nations in the interest of peace'.[7]

The Old Vic's visit in 1937 was followed by other British productions, as well as productions from Germany (Gustaf Gründgens' acclaimed *Hamlet* which had Hermann Göring in the audience), the Nordic countries, Ireland and the US, and the tradition became known as *Festspillene på Kronborg* ('Festive Plays at Kronborg'). However, insofar as a festival is usually expected to include several different productions, the tradition of hosting a single annual production does not quite fit. In the twenty-first century, the tradition did begin to include several productions (including plays other than *Hamlet*) and from a wider range of countries. What became a festival in the quantitative sense of the term was mainly run by the organization Hamlet Sommer ('Hamlet Summer'), until HamletScenen was established and began to run festivals under the name of the 'Shakespeare Festival at Hamlet's Castle'. However, throughout this chapter I use the term 'festival' to refer to the whole history of Shakespearean performances at Kronborg, despite the difference between the twentieth and twenty-first centuries.

Despite the castle's 'fake authenticity' in strict Shakespearean terms – or, perhaps better, *because* of it – any *Hamlet* production playing at Kronborg is necessarily haunted by a strong element of site-specificity. The history of the festival arguably represents an ongoing negotiation of signifiers between the play, the performance and the location. Even when performances do not use site-specificity as an explicit gesture, the location inevitably asserts itself – sometimes in prosaically practical ways, for example weather conditions, but always as the material manifestation of (or contrast to) the fictive Elsinore in the play and in the minds of audience members.

Certain dramaturgies and scenographies have been deliberately created for the topography of the castle, such as Singaporean director Ong Keng Sen's seminal intercultural experiment

Search:Hamlet in 2002, to which I will return later in this chapter. In describing the devising process for this production, which took place inside and outside the castle, Ong says that it was from what he calls 'these excruciating spaces ... that the artists scraped different emotions from the walls, the floors, the perspectives, the shadows, the stillness, the air, the echoes, the ghosts of Kronborg' (2002: 21). Ong's description adds a haunting quality to the site-specificity of Kronborg or, I would suggest, presents site-specificity in terms of present absences. Marcus Tan, drawing on the Derridean hauntology of present absences in *Specters of Marx* (1993), also notes this quality about Kronborg. Analysing the explorative use of site-specificity in *Search:Hamlet*, Tan claims that

> there is no Kronborg without Shakespeare (and no Kronborg in Shakespeare's *Hamlet* without the historical locale). The site-specific use of the castle in Elsinore then reifies that (inter)play of presence and absence established in the performance. Kronborg is both present and absent as Shakespeare haunts Kronborg.
>
> (2016: 8)

The point is that what Tan calls '(inter)play of presence and absence' offers plenty of artistic scope, as Ong's description also implies. Performances in Elsinore can capitalize on a location in continuous negotiation with its fictive double by utilizing the powerful defamiliarizing factor this provides. At the very least, it will produce a gratuitous heightened awareness in the audience or amplify the effects of meta-theatre already implied by the play. Moreover, the fact that most productions over the years have been international is a significant additional element in this context. Since the first international productions began to take place at the site in the late 1930s, local Danish festival audiences have seen representations of an Elsinore whose (already unstable) 'Danishness' is defamiliarized, first by Shakespeare, and subsequently by whichever cultural reconceptualizing of *Hamlet* is utilized by the visiting production.[8] Thus audiences may find themselves simultaneously inhabiting two 'Elsinores': one that feels homely and familiar, and one that feels distinctly other. An additional aspect of uncanniness is triggered given the relentless repetition of (usually) the same play, year after year, which can feel almost like a distillation of Marvin Carlson's claim that theatre – with its déjà-vu-like quality – is always already ghostly (2001: 1–2). To local audiences in Elsinore, the memory of previous *Hamlets* would be very fresh, with hardly any time to settle *as* memory, before it is repeated.

Not surprisingly, reviews and reports from festival years indicate appreciative, fascinated and anxious reactions to this experience. The town of Elsinore may have branded and promoted itself as the 'Home of Hamlet', but performances at the festival continue to produce 'unhomely' encounters that implicitly challenge the ideas of origin, stability or familiarity that are inevitably associated with such a brand name.[9] However, the point remains that such encounters, because of their potential unease, become more fertile from an artistic perspective, facilitating a complex and potentially rewarding (inter)cultural engagement.

Generally, intercultural performance in a globalized world inevitably offers potential for both creating and confronting anxieties. As Richard Schechner puts it: 'In a world where people of different cultures are in strong contact with each other, there also arise misunderstandings, distrust, ruptures and conflicts. These, too, are the themes of intercultural performance' (2002: 32). In Elsinore, such themes are arguably incorporated into the unavoidable site-specific circumstances – present as well as absent – of the festival performances. Furthermore, and importantly, some festival years and productions have made conscious efforts to confront Danish engagement with foreignness and xenophobia in a larger, political sense. Peter Langdal and Henrik Hartmann, the former co-directors of Betty Nansen Teatret in Copenhagen (a long-established theatre that regularly produces radical Shakespearean performances), who helped bring Ong Keng Sen's *Search:Hamlet* to Denmark, made an explicit statement in the Danish programme for the production:

> The aim is to put foreign voices on the Danish stage. The project is born out of a political question: why do 75% of the Danish population vote for 3 major parties, whose goal is to send the 2% that are of non-European heritage out of Denmark? What makes us so afraid of foreigners that we do not want them to be in our country? We want to use our theatre space to find the answer to this question.
>
> (2002: 6)[10]

Elsinore provides an apposite site for asking such questions, because, even when the performance or its context are not made explicitly political, the festival's unhomely encounters offer glimpses of the perhaps unexpected subtleties of xenophobia. Or, as Julia Kristeva asks, 'are we nevertheless so sure that the "political" feelings of xenophobia do not include, often unconsciously, that agony of frightened joyfulness that has been called *unheimlich*, that in English is *uncanny*, and the Greeks quite simply call *xenos*, "foreign"' (1991: 191).

However, before turning to more performance examples central to this discussion, it is also important to note how defamiliarization and the unhomely run parallel to another key feature of the festival, namely its close relationship with arts diplomacy, or 'soft power'.[11] As I have already indicated, some explicit instances of the harnessing of theatre for the sake of political and economic alliances took place in relation to visiting *Hamlet* productions in the 1930s and 1940s, and the festival's diplomatic strand is worthy of substantial treatment in its own right, but for my current purposes I want to draw it into the discussion for comparative reasons. Whilst performance-based processes of othering bring out and accentuate difference, arts diplomacy often relies on projections of universalism and on cultural familiarity rather than its opposite. In the case of Elsinore, this involves projecting Shakespeare as the means to finding cultural commonalities, shared beliefs and values and hence building (in the usual diplomatic cliché) bridges of understanding and trust, processes considered valuable from the perspectives of international diplomacy and trade.[12] In this sense, therefore, two of the most distinctive characteristics of the festival pull in different directions. When the intercultural approach of a production such as *Search:Hamlet* is concerned with producing what Joubin terms '*difference* and fertile novelty to comment on the ethics of cosmopolitanism' (2007: 40), other visiting productions are tasked with showcasing examples of monocultural expression to serve the purposes of international cooperation. The latter may involve presenting a version of cultural difference but under a banner of eventual sameness and circumventing the kinds of encounter that create (productive) tension. In this sense, the universalist premise of arts diplomacy, not very surprisingly, risks missing out on the opportunities for real dialogue that come with recognizing cultural collision as part of the process. And because collision is almost a given at Elsinore, performing for diplomacy here runs the double risk of self-contradiction.

One of the first productions in the history of the festival to demonstrate this problem – within a single theatre production – was a 1949 US *Hamlet* directed by and starring Robert Breen as Hamlet. As the seventieth anniversary of NATO in 2019 has prompted both celebration and unease for the organization's future, the politics surrounding the 1949 US *Hamlet* in Elsinore provide an intriguing reminder of NATO's equally uneasy beginnings, in a combination of postwar optimism and cold-war anxiety.

An American *Hamlet* and a 'gramophony' ghost

In the postwar world, it had become imperative for the USA to find multiple strategies to support its well-known policy of containment, seeking to isolate and prevent the spread of Soviet influence. Charlotte C. Canning describes the United States' increasing awareness that it would have to promote its national values, image and prestige as well as wielding its military power, and she refers to the 1949 *Hamlet* production, which was performed both in Elsinore and for American troops stationed in Germany, as a significant case study within this context. As Canning writes: 'government officials had come to understand … that art had a unique ability to represent cultural narratives that were seemingly independent from government intentions' (2011: 154). For Denmark, with the Nazi occupation freshly in mind, this meant making decisive moves to become part of a Western alliance that offered protection against the territorial ambitions of the Soviet Union. In the programme for the 1949 production, the Danish Minister of Education hailed the US production as 'the cultural embodiment of our great liberator', and the fact that the theatre company was flown to Denmark by the United States Air Force would undoubtedly have strengthened this impression.[13]

Robert Breen had fought in the war, and when he returned to the US, he became involved with ANTA (the American National Theatre and Academy). He helped turn this philanthropic organization, which had existed (without much success) since 1935, into a vehicle for supplying theatre for a US government increasingly keen to demonstrate and underwrite its world power through culture and the arts (see Canning 2011: 154–5). Hence the description in the programme for the Elsinore *Hamlet* of ANTA – of which Breen had become executive secretary – as an organization taking 'an active and purposeful interest in international current affairs'.[14] Overall, the many statements in the programme by officials on both sides underwrite what was clearly the political agenda of the visit (it also includes an approving salute from President Truman along with his photograph). An additional example of the determination of the artistic team behind the *Hamlet* production to serve the political agenda is apparent in a statement in the programme from Clarence Derwent, the actor who played Polonius (an unfortunate fact in context, arguably), and was also president of the Actors Equity Association. Derwent expressed his earnest wish for ongoing international artistic exchange and proposed that 'artists have an important role to play in the attainment of the idea that we all seek: the great goal of one world'.[15]

At the same time, Breen's *Hamlet* was one of the first productions visiting Elsinore explicitly to acknowledge its role as promoter of its sponsor country's national image by way of Shakespeare. 'Let's make it American, at least', the producer Blevin Davis told *The Kansas City Star*. 'Nobody wants to see us aping what the courtyard has seen before' (qtd in Canning 2011: 157). The set, designed specifically for the castle courtyard by Nat Karson, produced a powerful impression of US technological capacity, featuring six twenty-foot statues in a semi-circle, which also served to mask six tall standing projectors for lights. As Rosamond Gilder would later report in the 'International Notes' of a 1951 volume of *Shakespeare Survey*:

> The first American *Hamlet* to be shown in Hamlet's own historic Elsinore caused a great deal of comment for its unconventionality, for the striking effects of its staging and lighting and for its generally unusual presentation. The Danish criticisms ranged from warm enthusiasm to horrified commentaries for such impieties as beginning the play with the council room instead of the parapet scene, for allowing pistols, historically possible but definitely not standard practice, to be carried by Rosencrantz and Guildenstern, for a Ghost whose recorded voice emanated from a loud speaker.
>
> (1951: 124)

According to Nat Karson's notes in the programme, the statues served to represent Hamlet's ancestors and to establish a continuity between the set design and the castle architecture, but they arguably also produced a deliberate counterpoint to the more overtly modern aspects of the production and introduced ideas of shared European-American ancestry. Yet, if it was clear that the intention of Breen's *Hamlet* was to impress audiences with both artistic and technological skill, while also suggesting affinity and shared values, it is equally clear that some of the production's cultural foreignness backfired, as is also apparent from Gilder's comments. The local Elsinore newspaper – *Helsingør Dagbladet* – referred derogatively to Breen's guns and gramophone the following year, when praising what it considered a more palatable staging of *Hamlet* by The Old Vic, starring Michael Redgrave (Ørnø 1996: 51). Canning also refers to one Danish critic lamenting the use of the gramophone, who added that 'on the other hand, it seems very natural in our mechanized times to change this spirit voice into a voice from the immeasurable space – and they obviously like that better in America' (qtd in Canning 2015: 146).

It is not surprising that Danish audiences would have reacted to the unfamiliarity of what they would have thought of as Americanisms but, at the same time, it seems curious that a postwar European audience would react so strongly to the sight of American guns, or indeed to a disembodied voice, alienated by technology, and it is tempting to look at this response as more than a case of what the *Helsingør Dagblad* itself admitted was a form of theatrical conservatism (qtd in Ørnø 1996: 51). Historically speaking, neither guns nor recorded ghost ought to have felt in any way unfamiliar at the time, but their strong rejection by reviewers could equally have had something to do with traumatic familiarity made unfamiliar by the theatrical context. At the same time, the effect of the highly developed set design would have been all the more overwhelming, given that local audiences were used to experiencing far more traditional productions in the castle's familiar courtyard, thereby in all likelihood adding to their apparent sense of alienation. What is clear is that the 1949 US *Hamlet*, despite its pretensions to universality and familiarity, provides a key early example of an unhomely encounter with an(other) 'Elsinore' in the history of the festival.

Search:Hamlet and the unease of defamiliarization

Analysing the visit by the 1949 US *Hamlet* in the context of unhomeliness also highlights a missed opportunity to engage in a more nuanced intercultural exchange that might have addressed the tensions that lead to stereotypical perception and misunderstanding. When Ong Keng Sen set out to create a site-specific *Hamlet* production for Elsinore some fifty years later, he approached the task with a series of questions that demonstrated the need to negotiate signifiers in continuous dialogue with the location and its audiences. As he wrote in the programme notes for *Search:Hamlet*, 'Locating [the performance] at Kronborg would raise all sorts of cultural issues such as cultural authenticity and possession. Does Kronborg belong to Denmark or to the world? What is Asian, what is European, what is Danish?' (2002: 18). The first notably radical factor in the production was Ong's decision to remove the character of Hamlet from the performance, and instead create an uncannily present absence by representing 'Hamlet' with a spotlight[16] – hence the search for 'Hamlet' in the title, which turned the character into, as Ong says, 'a symbol and metaphor' and a vehicle for performers (and audiences) to look for 'Hamlet' within their separate and overlapping cultural contexts. On one level, Ong's absent Hamlet, represented by way of technology, echoes the 1949 US production's recorded voice for the Ghost: both seemed to operate somewhere between the familiar and the unfamiliar. Ong's spotlight was inspired by a tradition in Danish theatre which uses a similar device to commemorate the death of a well-known performer, and thus shows his ability to take a culturally specific element and re-contextualize it within an intercultural collage. Similarly, Ong made the deliberate decision to root the production at Kronborg, using the castle's architecture on several levels throughout the devising process and performance, but, whilst doing so, he also re-created – or indeed defamiliarized – the site and *re*-presented it to audiences in an unfamiliar form. As Danish reviewer Henrik Lyding wrote, 'we have never seen Kronborg like this before' (2002).

Yet Lyding's review combined delighted descriptions of the transformation of the castle into a multi-sensorial environment, emphasizing Ong's powerful visuals and atmospheres, with a more reserved reaction to the supposed search for a 'Hamlet' within this environment. Lyding wrote, for example, that the section of the site-specific performance which took part in the so-called 'casemates' (subterranean tunnels beneath the castle) was dwarfed by what he calls the 'sombre authenticity' of this space. Furthermore, he claimed that the 'search' was – for his own part, at least – inconclusive: he did not find a recognizable version of Hamlet. It is debatable whether Ong ever intended the 'search' to be conclusive; the emphasis, according to his statements, was more on a continuous and open-ended exploration, and indeed the point was to look for other than immediately recognizable Hamlets. But it is curious to see the Danish reviewer introducing a notion of authenticity, in what can almost be read as a reclaiming of Kronborg, by referring to both the material and intangible experience of a familiar space such as the casemates. Thus, a certain resistance to the defamiliarization processes at work in an intercultural reimagining of 'Elsinore', such as Ong's, may be sensed, along with simultaneous fascination and appreciation. Yet such a reaction arguably does not diminish the success of Ong's experiment, but rather demonstrates how a highly sensitive and investigative theatre project may highlight and accentuate the unhomely effect of performing at Elsinore, thereby bringing out some subtle responses to the culturally unfamiliar.

In 2005 and 2006, respectively, Lyding also reviewed two equally radical reimaginings of *Hamlet* at Elsinore, namely the multicultural adaptation *Ur-Hamlet* (based on the 'Amleth' tale in Saxo Grammaticus' *Gesta Danorum*, rather than Shakespeare's play) by Eugenio Barba and Odin Teatret, and Sulayman Al-Bassam's internationally celebrated *Al-Hamlet Summit*. Lyding's review of *Ur-Hamlet* was unequivocally sceptical of what he sees as an ethnographic display that largely 'forgets the story of Hamlet', but he praised Al-Bassam's production as being original and very timely, clearly appreciating its nuanced analysis of contemporary politics in the Arab world. As coincidence would have it, *Jyllands-Posten*, the newspaper that employed Lyding as a reviewer, would spark an international diplomatic crisis for Denmark, by publishing cartoon-like illustrations of the Prophet Mohammed, only a few months after Al-Bassam's performances at Elsinore. Although unconnected, the combination of the two events so soon after each other indicates another missed opportunity for dialogue in the history of the festival, especially when one compares Al-Bassam's endeavour to avoid polemics by way of what he calls 'a concrete and poetic formulation of Arab Viewpoints' in his programme notes with the arguably less nuanced approach taken by *Jyllands-Posten*. These examples form part of a much larger tapestry of events that links Elsinore performances to the questions about Danish perceptions and misperceptions of foreignness asked by Langdal and Hartmann in relation to *Search:Hamlet* in 2002. But they also serve to demonstrate the continued potential for nuanced intercultural engagement underwritten by the unhomely encounters inevitably produced at Kronborg. The potential lies in performers' and audiences' willingness to negotiate these encounters and inhabit both the familiar and the unfamiliar 'Elsinores'. As Kristeva writes, 'to worry or to smile, such is the choice when we are assailed by the strange; our decision depends on how familiar we are with our own ghosts' (1994: 191). Similarly, the ghosts of Kronborg and Elsinore are already on site, regardless of their perceived otherness.

Notes

1 Much of the research for this chapter draws on HamletScenen's large collection of historical materials – including theatre programmes, correspondence, photographs and video recordings – which I am grateful to have unlimited access to. I am also grateful to artistic director of HamletScenen, Lars Romann Engel, for many informative and inspiring conversations.
2 Kronborg was used as a Danish military base for several centuries, which resulted in the building of the several barrack buildings, some of which now house art galleries, cafés, shops and independent businesses. Today the buildings are known as Kronværksbyen and function as a small urban centre with its own sense of identity and activity, especially in the summer, when the town and castle are visited by a large number of tourists.
3 A few performances throughout the years have taken place inside the castle itself – usually in the 60-metre-long ballroom – including Shakespeare's Globe-to-Globe *Hamlet* production, which had its penultimate performance at Kronborg in April 2016 before returning to London. At the moment of writing, HamletScenen is in the process of renovating another of the larger barrack buildings, which will hold a small indoor theatre for all-year-round use and house the theatre's

new education programme in collaboration with regional sixth form colleges.
4 Apart from the oft-quoted visit to the court of Frederik II in 1586 by Will Kemp, George Bryan and Thomas Pope, who were later to become Shakespeare's colleagues in The Lord Chamberlain's Men (see Gurr 2011: 49).
5 I have explored some of the cultural and complicated identity of Kronborg as a simultaneously fictive and material site elsewhere (Refskou 2017).
6 For a detailed account of this production, see Shaughnessy (2002), Falocco (2010) and Sawyer (2019). I also explore some of the early-twentieth-century visiting productions and their context in Refskou (2017).
7 All quotes from theatre programmes are from originals in HamletScenen's collection.
8 An early example in the history of the festival of how Danish audiences might have felt both a sense of familiarity and alienation in relation to the play is the poetic 'Prolog til Hamlet, Prince of Denmark' by the Danish author and critic Tom Kristensen (alternately in Danish and English as the title indicates) for the visit of John Gielgud's 1939 *Hamlet* production. A section in the poem reads: 'Hvor kan vi vide, / hvordan vi er, hvordan vi taler, handler, / og hvad vi Danske ikke kan og kan? / Det blev fortalt os af en fremmed Mand' ('How can we know what we are, how we speak, how we act, and what we Danes can, and cannot do? This was told to us by a foreigner') (my translation).
9 The 'Home of Hamlet' brand was created in 2016 by Elsinore and several Danish organizations, including VisitDenmark.
10 Politically, the situation has changed since Langdal and Hartmann wrote this in 2002. The recent Danish elections in 2019 saw a decrease in votes for parties representing a hard-line stance on immigration numbers, but xenophobic rhetoric across most of the political spectrum has by no means halted.
11 Joseph Nye's concept of 'soft power', introduced in 1990, explains aspects of foreign policy strategies that rely on presenting a favourable national image abroad, using, among other elements, culture and the arts.
12 Bird, Eliadis and Scriven, describing the strategic contexts to recent use of Shakespeare for 'soft power' purposes, refer to trust as crucial to international investment and argue that '[i]n building trust for the long term, it is familiarity – and typically cultural familiarity – that is essential' (2016: 149).
13 Nor was it a coincidence that the invitation from Elsinore to the Americans came only a few months after the Berlin Airlift during

which US airplanes had supplied the Western controlled sectors of Berlin with food and coal, after the Soviets had blocked them off on the ground.
14 The description was by the chairman of the US National Commission for UNESCO, Milton S. Eisenhower.
15 Historically, too, there is some sad irony in Derwent's readiness to please the state, which underlines how the production occupied a moment of anxiety as well as optimism. As Canning notes, Derwent, who was a British subject and long-term resident in the US, was upon the return of the company detained by Immigration and Naturalization for six hours to be interrogated about communist affiliations, the reason apparently being that he had taken a trip to Prague the previous year as a US observer at the inaugural meeting of the International Theatre Institute under UNESCO.
16 See also Tan's extensive performance analysis (2016).

References

Al-Bassam, Sulayman (2005), 'Hamlet as an Expression of Politics … ', *Shakespeare på Kronborg Slot 2005*, Programme Notes, Elsinore, Denmark: Hamlet Sommer.

Bird, Conrad, Jason Eliadis and Harvey Scriven (2016), 'Shakespeare is "GREAT"', in Dominic Shellard and Siobhan Keenan (eds), *Shakespeare's Cultural Capital: His Economic Impact from the Sixteenth to the Twenty-first Century*, 148–62, London: Palgrave Macmillan.

Canning, Charlotte M. (2011), 'Teaching Theatre as Diplomacy: A US Hamlet in the European Court', *Theatre Topics* 21 (2): 151–62.

Canning, Charlotte M. (2015), *On the Performance Front: US Theatre and Internationalism*, Houndmills, UK: Palgrave Macmillan.

Carlson, Marvin (2001), *The Haunted Stage: The Theatre as Memory Machine*, Ann Arbor, MI: University of Michigan Press.

Derwent, Clarence (1949), 'A World Stage', *Hamlet Festival 1949*, Programme Notes, Elsinore, Denmark: *Festspillene paa Kronborg*, 17.

Falocco, Joe (2010), *Reimagining Shakespeare's Playhouse: Early Modern Staging Conventions in the Twentieth Century*, Cambridge: D.S. Brewer.

Gilder, Rosamond (1951), 'USA: Shakespeare Leads the Way', 'International Notes', *Shakespeare Survey* 4: 123–5.

Gurr, Andrew (2011), *The Shakespearean Stage 1574–1642*, Cambridge: Cambridge University Press.

Joubin (Huang), Alexa Alice (2007), 'Site-specific Hamlets and Reconfigured Localities: Jiang'an, Singapore, Elsinore', in Graham

Bradshaw, Tom Bishop and Tetsuo Kishi (eds), *The Shakespearean International Yearbook 7: Special Section, Updating Shakespeare*, 22–48, Aldershot and Burlington: Ashgate.

Karson, Nat (1949), 'Design for Hamlet', *Hamlet Festival 1949*, Programme Notes, Elsinore, Denmark: Festspillene paa Kronborg, 33–5.

Kristensen, Tom (1939), 'Prolog til Hamlet, Prince of Denmark', *Hamlet Festival 1939*, Programme Notes, Elsinore, Denmark: Festspillene paa Kronborg, 20–2.

Kristeva, Julia (1991), *Strangers to Ourselves*, trans. Leon S. Roudiez, New York: Columbia University Press.

Langdal, Peter, and Hendrik Hartmann (2002), 'Betty Nansen Teatret', *Search: Hamlet*, Programme Notes, Elsinore, Denmark: Hamlet Sommer, 6.

Lyding, Henrik (2002), 'Kronborg Slot: *Search: Hamlet*', *Jyllands-Posten* (review), 18 August. Available online: https://jyllands-posten.dk/kultur/teater/ECE3415915/Kronborg-Slot-SEARCH-HAMLET/ (accessed 6 July 2020).

Lyding, Henrik (2005), 'Terroristen Hamlet: Shakespeares klassiker originalt og spændende omsat til arabisk diktaturstat i borgerkrig', *Jyllands-Posten* (review), 13 August. Available online: https://jyllands-posten.dk/gamletillaeg/kulturweekend/ECE5067173/Terroristen-Hamlet/ (accessed 6 July 2020).

Lyding, Hendrik (2006), 'Slotsgården, Kronborg: Ur-Hamlet', *Jyllands-Posten* (review), 5 August. Available online: https://jyllands-posten.dk/kultur/teater/article3342152.ece/ (accessed 6 July 2020).

Michaëlis, Sophus (1916), 'Shakespearefesten paa Kronborg', *Teatret* 15 (18): 138–42.

Nye, Joseph (1990), *Bound to Lead: The Changing Nature of American Power*, New York: Basic Books.

Ong Keng Sen (2002), '*Search: Hamlet* – a dance-theatre Event, a free interpretation of Shakespeare's Play', *Search: Hamlet*, Programme Notes, Elsinore, Denmark: Hamlet Sommer, 18–21.

Ørnø, Sven (1996), *Godnat, Min Prins: Hamlet, Kronborg 1816–1996*, Elsinore, Denmark: Elsinore Municipality.

Refskou, Anne Sophie (2017), 'Whose Castle is it Anyway?: Local/Global Negotiations of a Shakespearean Location', *Multicultural Shakespeare* 15 (30): 121–32.

Sawyer, Robert (2019), *Shakespeare Between the World Wars: The Anglo-American Sphere*, New York: Palgrave Macmillan.

Schechner, Richard (2002), 'The "Yes", "No", and "But" of Intercultural Performance', *Search:Hamlet*, Programme Notes, Elsinore, Denmark: Hamlet Sommer, 32–5.

Shaughnessy, Robert (2002), *The Shakespeare Effect: A History of Twentieth-Century Performance*, Houndmills, UK and New York: Palgrave Macmillan.

Stauning, T. H. (1937), 'Til Kronborg', Programme Notes, Elsinore, Denmark: Festspillene paa Kronborg.

Tan, Marcus (2016), 'Spectres of Shakespeare: Ong Keng Sen's *Search: Hamlet* and the Intercultural Myth', *Cahiers Élisabéthains* 90 (1): 1–12.

12

Shakespeare's Globe in Inđija: A portrait of Itaka Shakespeare Festival (Serbia)

Alexandra Portmann

A mild summer evening. Several coaches from Belgrade and Novi Sad drive to the quiet village of Čortanovci in the Vojvodina region in Serbia and head up the small hill where Villa Stanković is located.[1] Built in 1930 as his personal residence by Dr Radenko Stanković, the founder and professor of the medical faculty in Serbia, the villa resembles a medieval castle. In the quiet evening and the light breeze, the view extends and the eye takes in the Danube and wild forests around the river bank. The experience continues for the willing travellers: they take the narrow stairs, climb the towers of the villa, take selfies and lose themselves in its garden. There is an atmosphere of expectation, anticipation and excitement. Shortly before dark, the numerous guests who have roamed the picturesque property are asked to descend two narrow stairs and take their seats in the grandstand. The villa itself becomes a stage for numerous artists and their Shakespeare performances.

The place described above is the main location of the Itaka Shakespeare Festival, which takes place annually at the end of June or the beginning of July, a time when the open-air theatre at Villa Stanković provides a picturesque stage for Shakespeare. Since 2014, it has become an attractive tourist destination and an established landmark for Serbia's cultural tourism. Nikita Milivojević, the founding and continuing artistic director of this international festival, named it after Odysseus' island Ithaca. Establishing the festival in Čortanovci, near his hometown Inđija, Milivojević's choice of name with its symbolism of homecoming after a long journey connects the festival to his own journey as a travelling and internationally operating artist and director (who has worked regularly in Greece). The overt allusion to Homer's *Odyssey* also points to the central role of so-called classics in the festival. The in-depth examination of early modern dramatic texts and of what role they can play for our present day are of primary interest for this artistic director. Informed by an interview with Nikita Milivojević, this chapter offers the broader historical context for the Itaka international Shakespeare Festival within the festival landscape of Serbia, its connection to the 2012 Globe to Globe Festival in London, and provides an insight into the curatorial strategies and criteria of this particular thematic festival dedicated to the work of William Shakespeare.[2]

Beginnings: from London to Inđija

Within the context of the 2012 Cultural Olympiad, Shakespeare's Globe in London launched an ambitious event: from 21 April to 9 June, the Globe's stage hosted productions of all of Shakespeare's plays performed by different theatre companies from around the world in more than forty different languages. Tom Bird and Dominic Dromgoole's challenging concept for the Globe to Globe Festival found its starting point in nine pre-existing productions, which were already known to the artistic team.[3] All other productions were specifically commissioned for the festival (Bennett and Carson 2013: 4), including all three parts of *Henry VI*, later labelled the 'Balkan Trilogy' (Bennett and Carson 2013: 161; Orford 2013: 79), which were performed by the ensembles of the National Theatre of Belgrade (Serbia), the National Theatre of Tirana (Albania) and the Macedonian National Theatre in Bitola. Nikita Milivojević, who went on to found the Itaka Shakespeare Festival in Serbia, was invited to direct *1 Henry VI* with the National Theatre in Belgrade for the Globe to Globe Festival.

This 2012 London-based festival not only influenced further debates on what was termed 'foreign Shakespeare' (Kennedy 1993), 'Shakespeare beyond English' (Bennett and Carson 2013), but also intercultural theatre practice, cultural representation as well as the multicultural city of London within the UK (Woods 2016). The festival, the online fora[4] and the follow-up publications have impacted not only on Shakespeare and festival research, but – I argue in the present chapter – prompted the establishment of several smaller Shakespeare festivals in southeastern Europe, in particular the Bitola Shakespeare Festival in Northern Macedonia (2013) and the Itaka Shakespeare Festival in Serbia (2014). Both these festivals use Shakespeare as a central premise to reflect on transcultural theatre and the role of the classics in contemporary regional and international theatre repertoires.

According to Milivojević, the experience of being part of the London Festival and the close collaboration with the artistic team of the Globe were ultimately decisive in locating the Itaka Shakespeare Festival, both formally and informally, within a broader network, such as the European Shakespeare Festivals Network (ESFN) which it joined in 2015.[5] These professional networks facilitated important knowledge exchange and helped simplify collaborations with international partners (for example, the organization of a European tour). The networks have also influenced the festival's offering, namely the selection of plays for the main programme as well as the conceptualization of the supporting and contextualizing side programme, thus anchoring the festival within the specific regional theatre system. In other words, while professional networks around festivals may have an influence on festival conception, in the case of the Itaka Shakespeare Festival these were crucial, and its existence must be viewed against the background of these formal and informal relationships.[6] Thus, Milivojević's close ties to the above-mentioned networks, his own artistic work and his interest in teaching and staging early modern drama have significantly shaped the festival since its inception and given it an unmistakable character. This also informs the particular institutional aesthetic, to borrow Balme's term (2019), of Itaka Shakespeare Festival. While Balme discusses the term institutional aesthetic in relation to theatres and leading figures such as artistic directors, I connect it also to festival dramaturgies which need to be discussed against the background of leading figures like artistic directors, curatorial commissions and the related professional networks. In the case of Itaka, I suggest that the institutional aesthetic refers to Milivojević's curatorial criteria, which relate to a specific artistic and intellectual understanding of Shakespeare's drama and which could be theoretically framed using William B. Worthen's concept of the agency. According to Worthen, the concept of agency can be understood as a framework for acting within given dramatic structures, such as particular scenes or the conceptions of certain dramatic figures. For this reason the agency of the dramatic text also promotes that of its performance (Worthen 2010: 82). In other words, agency sees itself as a dynamic interplay between text and its performance, which is itself shaped by a specific local staging tradition. This multi-layered conceptualization of agency (referring to both text and performance) can be understood as an approach to how the actuality and also the relevance of productions of so-called classical texts can be viewed from a theatre studies perspective. Although Worthen attributes agency to dramatic texts and their performance, this chapter argues that this specific understanding of the potential of staging early modern drama also informs curatorial criteria of thematic festivals.[7] Thus, it is Milivojević's specific understanding of dramatic texts that ultimately shapes the festival's institutional aesthetic and therefore positions Itaka uniquely within a specific theatre landscape of production houses, companies, festivals and audiences. Agency, therefore, plays a role on two different levels here: firstly, at the level of theatre production itself; secondly, at the level of institutional aesthetics and festival dramaturgies.

The Itaka Shakespeare Festival within Serbia's festival landscape

There are many theatre and cultural festivals in Serbia, including the long-standing and renowned Belgrade International Theatre Festival BITEF, which was established in 1967, and the prestigious national theatre festival for contemporary Serbian drama, Sterijno Pozorije, established in 1956. There are several other smaller international theatre festivals such as the Desiré Central Station Festival organized by the Hungarian Theatre Kosztolányi Dezső in Subotica. Although Serbia has had a lively theatre culture and a well-documented long-standing tradition of staging Shakespeare since the end of the nineteenth century (Popović 1928; Mihailović 1984), a regular Shakespeare festival in Serbia has never been part of this rich landscape. Occasionally, there have been thematic events dedicated to Shakespeare. One such event was the Shakespeare Fest organized by Ljubiša Ristić, the artistic director of the National Theatre in Subotica, in 1986. During the 1980s, Ristić launched various thematic seasons focused on different authors and topics, such as Molière (1987) or the theatre culture in Yugoslavia (1989). As artistic director of the National Theatre in Subotica and especially during these thematic summer seasons, he engaged with the multicultural region of Vojvodina and experimented with various theatre cultures, languages and aesthetic approaches.

In 1986, Ristić decided to curate a summer season completely devoted to Shakespeare's artistic work and its reception. During the Shakespeare Fest, which took place in Palić, outside Subotica, companies from all over Yugoslavia and Hungary were invited to present their then current work on Shakespeare. The festival programme was a mixture of genres, artistic approaches to dramatic theatre and a versatile supporting side program with thematic discussions and other contextualizing events. The festival opened with Giuseppe Verdi's opera *Macbeth*, staged by the Szeged National Theatre (Hungary), and was followed by performances of dramatic theatre, experimental dance, various exhibitions, concerts and public screenings of well-known Shakespeare films, such as Akira Kurosawa's *Hamlet* adaptation *The Bad Sleep Well* (1960) ('N.N.' 1986a). The programme included already existing touring productions invited to the event, such as *A Midsummer Night's Dream* by Skene Theatre from Budapest, as well as performances uniquely produced for the Shakespeare Fest in Subotica, such as *Titus Andronicus*, directed by Dušan Jovanović (Kopicl 1986), *Macbeth*, directed by Ljubiša Ristić, and *Othello*, directed and choreographed by Nada Kokotović ('N.N.' 1986b; Ruzman 1986b).[8] The entire festival was dedicated to cultural exchange between Yugoslavian and Hungarian theatre, which resonated with Ristić's engagement with the multi-ethnic character of Vojvodina (Marjanović 2001: 745). This became visible in other performances, too, such as the *Hamlet* production by Slovenian director Vito Taufer which was delivered in Hungarian (Lukić 1986; Ruzman 1986a). Even though the Shakespeare Fest within Subotica's summer season was considered a very successful event ('N.N.' 1986a, 1986b), it was a rather exceptional and exclusive occasion, embedded within Ristić's larger work as programmer and artistic director in Subotica.

During the 1980s, the National Theatre in Subotica became one of the most innovative modern stages in Serbia (Marjanović 2001: 745). The theatre was clearly influenced by Ristić's own interest in new approaches to dramatic theatre and new aesthetics in theatre and performance art (Dević 2018: 199–219). The Shakespeare Fest was, therefore, not only a presentation of contemporary work on Shakespeare but, clearly, also an investigation of the possibilities of dramatic theatre in general. This type of engagement with new approaches to the classics applies to the Itaka Shakespeare Festival in present-day Serbia. However, while the former was a one-off event, the latter was conceived to offer an annual creative platform to investigate the possibilities and agencies of dramatic theatre and international Shakespeare.

As a former artistic director of the BITEF festival, Milivojević is very familiar with the Serbian festival landscape and has a curatorial background and a transnational network, as well as a supportive, experienced professional team. Even while these important preconditions existed, the crucial element that turned his idea of a Shakespeare festival in Serbia into reality was, according to Milivojević, finding the perfect festival location: Villa Stanković. The director had already successfully directed *Love's Labour's Lost* there within the context of a summer festival, in 2007, as a co-production of the BITEF in Belgrade, the Cultural Centre in Tivat (Montenegro) and the Cultural Centre in Inđija (Levakov 2008: 22). Never opened to the public nor used as a theatrical venue before,[9] Villa Stanković provided an atmospheric setting well suited to outdoor staging.

Although a fairly small space (sitting 310) which requires the stage and the auditorium to be built for the period of the festival, according to Milivojević, the specific atmosphere of Villa Stanković provides an ideal platform to stage Shakespeare and to engage with experimental and innovative approaches to his plays. In the case of other European festivals engaging with Shakespeare, the performance space is often either site-specific, as for the Dubrovnik Summer Festival in Croatia, or the performance space is one of the major attractions, as for the Shakespeare Festival in Gdansk, which acquired in 2014 its own Shakespeare Theatre, a venue built

FIGURE 12.1 *Open-air stage, Itaka Shakespeare Festival. Photograph by permission of Jelena Ivanović.*

on the early modern footprint of the Fencing School, boasting a multifunctional stage and a multisensory roof, making the theatrical experience akin to the Elizabethan one.[10]

With the creative exchange between Bird and Milivojević continuing after the Globe to Globe Festival, Milivojević decided to use the tour of London's Globe *Hamlet* (2014) as an opportunity to launch his brainchild festival. This opening performance was followed by six different performances by international theatre companies from Finland, Greece, Slovenia, Georgia and Serbia.[11] Since then, Milivojević has curated a high-profile festival programme inviting international companies, among others the Globe Theatre (London),[12] the Company Theatre (Mumbai),[13] Tang Shu-wing Theatre Studio (Hong Kong)[14] and Catatonia Theatre Group (Tehran).[15] The festival has also hosted productions from the regions of former Yugoslavia, such as *The Taming of the Shrew*, performed by the Ljubljana City Theatre (2014), *Othello*, performed by the Macedonian National Theatre in Bitola (2015), *Titus Andronicus* by the Zagreb Youth Theatre (2018) and *Richard II* by the Gavella City Drama Theatre in Zagreb (2019). Within such diverse festival offerings, Milivojević has followed his interest in approaching the lesser-known plays of Shakespeare, which led to staging *Pericles* for the first time in Serbia, in 2015. In 2019, he produced a two-hour performance with the title *Moj Šekspir* (My Shakespeare), which dealt with the performance tradition of Shakespeare in the region of the former Yugoslavia. Within the production, various famous theatre and television actors exchanged their experiences of Shakespeare and the author's significance to their careers. Beyond private backstage stories from acting stars, such as Serbian Svetlana Bojković or Croatian Ozren Grabarić, the anecdotally structured evening also offered an insight into Shakespeare's versatile performance tradition in the entire region. For example, Bosnian actor, director and writer Zijah Sokolović recalled his experience of staging and performing his monodrama *Glumac ... je glumac ... je glumac* (Actor ... is an actor ... is an actor, 1978). In this one-man-show Sokolović used Shakespeare's plays (e.g. *Hamlet*) to reflect on theatre-making and acting in a witty and comical way. Stringing together different personal stories of theatre professionals from the entire region, fleeting snippets from individual productions and bringing together different generations of artists transformed the 2019 evening into a tour de force of ex-Yugoslav theatre history as a shared experience.

The main festival programme, consisting of invited transnational and regional performances, is usually accompanied by a supporting side programme of a variety of contextual events, artistic workshops and film screenings. For example, the festival organized an artistic workshop for directors, artists and actors entitled 'one-thought-one-action' which was led by the theatre and opera director Gia Forakis in 2014. The 2016 side programme engaged with Laurence Olivier's Shakespeare performances and offered public screenings of his *Hamlet* and *Richard III*. In 2017, Akira Kurosawa's work on Shakespeare was the main theme of the side programme. Furthermore, drama students from the Faculty of Dramatic Arts in Belgrade and Novi Sad have the opportunity to present their work on Shakespeare within this side framework.[16] The festival's programme over the last six years reveals that Itaka has become a crucial meeting ground for interregional and transnational companies performing Shakespeare, and therefore, clearly forms an important and unique landmark within the Serbian festival context. A survey of the wide-ranging programme shows that the festival has surpassed the mere presentation of regional and transnational

Shakespeare productions. The extensive side programme and broad networking with other regional cultural organizations (e.g. the Cultural Center in Indjia), universities (e.g. the Faculty of Dramatic Arts in Belgrade and Novi Sad) and theatres (e.g. the Serbian National Theatre in Novi Sad) indicate that the festival appears to be an important laboratory for exploring Worthen's notion of the agency of Shakespeare's plays for Serbia and the region.

Innovative approaches to Shakespeare as curatorial strategy

Aside from the appealing location, the festival promises a versatile programme of events and activities.[17] According to Milivojević, the transnational structure of the programme attracts a broad audience from all over Serbia that includes regular and less regular theatregoers from urban centres like Belgrade or Novi Sad, as well as from more rural areas across the country. Outside transnational festival events such as Itaka, there are very few opportunities for Serbian audiences to engage with different theatre cultures. Therefore, Milivojević considers the engagement with transnational theatre as a major indication of the festival's significant success. The second indication of success, according to Milivojević, is his interest in innovative approaches towards Shakespeare. He described his curatorial practice as follows:

> The invited performances should add something new to Shakespeare and engage with the theatrical potential of the dramatic text. In experimenting with a variety of approaches to the text, these performances are seeking to rediscover Shakespeare and make him relevant to the current social, political and cultural situation.
>
> (Milivojević 2017)

Unlike other theatre festivals, such as the BITEF, Itaka under Milivojević's artistic direction is not interested in new forms and tendencies in contemporary theatre, but rather in reviving the potential of dramatic texts. As he elaborates:

> In my view, Shakespeare is often performed in either a fairly old-fashioned manner or is estranged by [extraneous] theatrical experiments. Therefore, I want to invite productions which reveal something new, something surprising about Shakespeare while respecting the drama's message [...] Since Shakespeare is a stable part of the cultural repertoire and of school curricula, there are many opinions as to how Shakespeare should be staged. But this is a major problem because Shakespeare's dramas are complex and multifaced materials. For me it is most important to ask how to turn Shakespeare into something I can relate to, how to make Shakespeare my own experience.
>
> (Milivojević 2017)

Talking about his fascination with Shakespeare and the process of approaching early modern plays, he describes the tension between text and performance that Worthen conceptualizes as the place where a certain agency is inherent. Taking agency as the potential to actualize particular dramatic conflicts as well as the possibility to locate the performance within a wider serious performance tradition, this understanding of Shakespeare's drama also expresses his own curatorial strategy. Milivojević describes his curatorial practice at the Itaka Shakespeare Festival as an ongoing search for innovative, alternative approaches to Shakespeare's dramatic work. As an example, he mentions Maria João's production *Songs for Shakespeare*, which was invited to the festival in 2016. The well-known Portuguese jazz singer interpreted Shakespeare's sonnets by exploring the musicality of the early modern language. Another example is Milivojević's own production of *Pericles*, in which he approached Shakespeare's romance as a comedy, revealing new aspects of the dramatic text and its theatrical potential.

With his ambitious and successful Shakespeare Festival, Milivojević not only wants to explore innovative approaches towards dramatic texts, but also to increase the popularity of Shakespeare's dramatic work. Although there is a long-standing staging tradition of Shakespeare in Serbia, Milivojević recognizes there has been a shrinking audience for Shakespeare's plays over the last decade. Through the Itaka Shakespeare Festival, Milivojević wants to bring Shakespeare back into Serbia's theatre repertoires and to encourage young theatre-makers to engage with the classics anew. His two goals are visible in the selection of pieces for the main programme but also, and above all, in the supporting side programme. The entire festival, therefore, can be understood as a laboratory, as a search for Shakespeare's agency, where events such as workshops or artists' talks underpin this artistic and exploratory perspective. New plays in the main programme, such as *My Shakespeare* (2019), explicitly deal with the performance tradition of Shakespeare in the region, and serve to emphasize Shakespeare's agency, as well as to reflect on theatre history beyond the national borders. In this sense, the central principle of the Globe to Globe Festival can be seen here, too: to hold Shakespeare as a common language and, in the case of *My Shakespeare*, to refuse a purely national reception of theatre history of which Shakespeare is an integral part. This double perspective on the actualization and on the specific potential of theatre demands further investigation into the role of Shakespeare in theatrical repertoires in general and especially within a festival context.

Perspectives on the festival's ethos

To hold an international festival focused on new approaches to Shakespeare transforms drama into a communicative foil for transcultural exchanges and a fruitful platform for cultural, social and political questioning. Milivojević's own engagement with Shakespeare as a director of *1 Henry VI* at the Globe to Globe Festival is a good example of his approach to Shakespeare and his curatorial work for the Itaka Shakespeare Festival. The rarely played and lesser known play became an active reflection on rivalry and power relations. With minimalist scenography consisting of a metal round table and chairs, historical but simple costumes resembling the fifteenth century of Henry VI's England, and an ensemble of twelve actors, Milivojević rediscovered the theatricality of the play and offered a tragi-comic reading of the English-French war in the fifteenth century. He experimented with Shakespeare's language by using rhythmic elements such as percussions on stage, choric speech and musical motifs throughout the performance. He also used the rivalry between the French and the English to allude to Serbian history and the rival noble families Obrenović and Karađorđević. The emphasis on the play's inherent theatricality was acknowledged by critic Peter Orford, who highlighted Milivojević's comic approach to the play and praised the rediscovery of the traditionally overlooked characters of Vernon and Basset (Orford 2013). By using the playscript as material for a modern performance, Milivojević regarded Shakespeare as a contemporary author, who not only has the potential to allude to various cultural questions beyond time, but whose dramatic oeuvre is, above all, turned into an approachable and attractive material for emerging theatre-makers.

Another example of this potential for actualization and engagement with contemporary political and cultural questions was *The Taming of the Shrew*, directed by Anja Suša, which premiered at the Ljubljana City Theatre in 2013, and was invited to the first season of the Itaka Shakespeare Festival in 2014.[18] Together with her dramaturg Petra Pogorevc, Suša used Shakespeare's dramatic foil and the highly problematic, misogynist attitudes of the text to reflect on gender roles and equality. Suša staged the play with an all-male cast; in addition, Suša and Pogorevc invited three contemporary female writers from the region of former Yugoslavia (Ivana Sejko, Maja Pelević, Simona Semenić) to write three new versions of the controversial soliloquy of the tamed Katherine.[19] The creative team utilized the performance to reflect on the theatrical space as a platform for such cultural negotiations and to engage with various audience opinions on the role of comedy. This involvement included interacting with and negotiating the specific structural condition of the Ljubljana City Theatre as an institution known for its comedy repertoire. This performance exemplifies how the agency of the playtext and its controversial discourses have the potential to be actualized: to turn the play into a useful tool for – in this case – feminist critique in contemporary theatre repertoires and negotiate the visibility of female authors and directors within these institutions. This creative engagement with institutional frameworks could be considered as a form of constructive institutional criticism, an engagement described by Chantal Mouffe as intervention (Mouffe 2013: 66). In this regard, the agency of the classic text also has the potential to bridge the dichotomy between an old-fashioned version of theatre and contemporary performance at an institutional level. It is precisely this threefold agency (text, performance, institution) that legitimizes the staging of this highly controversial text and makes the appropriation of Shakespeare a contemporary experience. In Suša's case, this was well ahead of the

#MeToo movement and the criticism of institutional frameworks in the conventional performing art industries.

The two examples above emphasize how the understanding of agency here not only informs the performances invited to or produced for the festival, but also the curatorial strategy and the festival dramaturgy itself. With his curatorial claim to turn Shakespeare into a 'contemporary experience to which we can relate to' (2017), Milivojević continues to work on making the Itaka Shakespeare Festival a prosperous meeting point for audiences, theatre-makers and academics, a place to question anew the relevance of Shakespeare and the potential of theatre in general. Thus, the reflection on dramatic agency in the case of this festival clearly moves towards an institutional aesthetics, which both locates it within a wider theatre and festival landscape, and also expresses a certain reading of Shakespeare by using a contextualizing side programme to provide opportunies for knowledge exchange as well as a platform for networking. This multidimensional perception of agency emphasizes how the Itaka Shakespeare Festival positions itself within the regional and international theatre landscape and may be the momentum for the festival's rapid rise to prominence on the festival scene.

Notes

1 The region of Vojvodina belonged to the Austria-Hungarian Empire until 1918, and then became part of the Kingdom of Serbs, Croats and Slovenes, later the kingdom of Yugoslavia. Although there is a majority of Serbians in Vojvodina, there is also a significant population of Hungarians, Croats, Slovaks and Romanians. The region had the status of autonomous province in the Socialist Federative Republic of Yugoslavia from 1974 until 1989. Since 2002, its nominal status of autonomy within Serbia has been restored (Allcock 2018).
2 I would like to thank Nikita Milivojević for our comprehensive interview, the collaboration and his support. This portrait of Itaka Shakespeare Festival was written during an Early Postdoctoral Mobility Fellowship on international festivals in 2017, founded by the Swiss National Science Foundation.
3 These pre-existing plays were Grupo Galpão's *Romeo and Juliet*, Bremer Shakespeare Company's *Timon of Athens*, Tang Shu-wing

Theatre Studio's *Titus Andronicus*, Two Gents' *Two Gentlemen of Verona*, Meno Fortas' *Hamlet*, Teatr im. Kochanowskiego Theatre's *Macbeth*, the Vakhtangov Theatre's *Measure for Measure*, Yonhangza Theatre Company's *A Midsummer Night's Dream* and Compagnie Hypermobile's *Much Ado About Nothing* (Bird 2013: 13–14).

4 See for example bloggingshakespeare.com and yearofshakespeare.com (Edmondson, Prescott and Sullivan 2013).
5 See Šekspir Festival [Shakespeare Festival], http://sekspirfestival.org/.
6 On the impact of professional networks around festivals, see Portmann (2020).
7 There are various forms of international theatre festivals, which are diverse in conception. I understand Shakespeare festivals as thematic festivals dedicated to the body of work of a certain author. The curatorial decision to deal only with the dramatic work of one person can be understood as the lowest common denominator that makes the different formats of thematic festivals comparable. In the case of the Itaka Shakespeare Festival discussed here, the focus on Shakespeare's plays can be understood as one curatorial criterion among others. For the differentiation of festival formats and concepts see, for example, *The Cambridge Companion to International Festivals*, edited by Ric Knowles (2020).
8 Dušan Jovanović, Ljubiša Ristić and Nada Kokotović were members of the theatre troupe KPGT in former Yugoslavia, whose name is an acronym consisting of the starting letters for theatre in the four Yugoslav languages. They were collaborating with each other since 1977 and continued to do so until the beginning of the 1990s. The company was a supranational collaborative network, which was not based in one specific place.
9 Before establishing the festival in 2014, with the exception of the city's summer festival in 2007, the villa was mainly used as a representative building of the Government of the Autonomous Province of Vojvodina for conferences and other government work with no public access allowed.
10 Although Dubrovnik is not a thematic festival dedicated to Shakespeare, the engagement with Shakespeare, especially with *Hamlet*, is well known and clearly connects the performance space to Shakespeare and early modern Europe, especially Dubrovnik's unique Renaissance history (e.g. Paljetak 1997; Senker 2006; Kunčević 2012).
11 They were: *As You Like It* directed by Levan Culadze (Drama Theatre Tiblis, Georgia), *The Taming of the Shrew* directed by Anja Suša (City Drama Theatre Ljubljana, Slovenia), *Romeo and Juliet for Two* (Paradise Bird, Greece), *Poor Poor Lear* directed by Katja Kron (Helsinki/LosAngeles) and *1 Henry VI* directed by Nikita Milivojević (National Theatre Belgrade, Serbia).

12 Aside from *Hamlet*, the Globe Theatre was invited in 2016 with *Two Gentlemen of Verona* directed by Nick Bagnall.
13 *A Midsummer Night's Dream* directed by Atul Kumar.
14 *Macbeth* directed by Tang Shu-wing in 2016.
15 *Macbeth* directed by Hossein Noshir in 2015.
16 This is a feature the festival shares with other ESFN members.
17 The festival has become a major cultural attraction during the summer months, and since 2014 has been on the journalist agency BETA's top-ten list of major tourist attractions in Serbia.
18 I would like to thank Petra Pogorevc, who presented and discussed this performance within the panel discussion 'Will this thing appear again tonight? – Shakespeare adaptations in the 21st century' at the ESRA conference in Gdansk 2017.
19 See for example Tadel (2013).

References

Allcock, John B. (2018), 'Vojvodina. Autonomous Province Serbia'. Available online: https://www.britannica.com/place/Vojvodina (accessed 6 July 2020).

Balme, Christopher (2019), 'Institutional Aesthetics', in Peter Eckershall and Helena Grenhan (eds), *The Routledge Companion to Theatre and Politics*, 169–72, London and New York: Routledge.

Bennett, Susan, and Christie Carson, eds (2013), *Shakespeare Beyond English: A Global Experiment*, Cambridge: Cambridge University Press.

Bird, Tom (2013), 'The Globe to Globe Festival: An Introduction', in S. Bennett and C. Carson (eds), *Shakespeare Beyond English: A Global Experiment*, 13–17, Cambridge: Cambridge University Press.

Dević, Ana (2018), 'Theatre of Diversity and Avant-Garde in Late Socialist Yugoslavia and Beyond: Paradoxes of the Disintegration and Cultural Subversion', in J. Dolečki, S. Halilbašić and S. Hulfeld (eds), *Theatre in the Context of Yugoslav Wars*, 199–219, Cham: Palgrave Macmillan.

Dundjerović, Aleksandar Saša (2013), 'Inter-Theatrical Reading: Theatrical and Multicultural Appropriations of 1–3 Henry VI as Balkan Trilogy', in Susan Bennett and Christie Carson (eds), *Shakespeare Beyond English: A Global Experiment*, 161–70, Cambridge: Cambridge University Press.

Edmondson, Paul, Paul Prescott and Erin Sullivan, eds (2013), *A Year of Shakespeare: Re-living the World Shakespeare Festival*, London: Bloomsbury Arden Shakespeare.

Henry VI, Part 1 (2012), [Film] Dir. Nikita Milivojević, National Theatre Belgrade at the Globe to Globe Festival 2012.

Kennedy, Dennis (1993), *Foreign Shakespeare: Contemporary Performances*, Cambridge: Cambridge University Press.
Kopicl, Vladimir (1986), 'Zid smrti' [The Wall of Death], *Dnevnik Novi Sad*, 10 July.
Kunčević, Ivica (2012), *Ambijentalnost na Dubrovačku* [Dubrovnik Ambiente], Zagreb: Biblioteka Mansioni.
Levakov, Biljana (2008), *Godišnjak Pozorišta Srbije 2006/2007* [Yearbook of Serbian Theatre 2006/2007], Novi Sad: Sterijno Pozorje.
Lukić, Darko (1986), 'Gord, putena i virtualna Ofelija' [The Bitter, Sweet and Virtuoso Ophelia], *Olsobođenje Sarajevo*, 21 July.
Marjanović, Petar (2001), 'Serbia and Montenegro', in Don Rubin, Peter Nagy and Philippe Rouyer (eds), *The World Encyclopedia of Contemporary Theatre, Vol. 1: Europe*, 739–54, London and New York: Routledge.
Martin, Randall (2013), 'This is our modern history: The Balkans Henry VI', in Susan Bennett and Christie Carson (eds), *Shakespeare Beyond English: A Global Experiment*, 170–9, Cambridge: Cambridge University Press.
Mihailović, Dušan (1984), *Šekspir i srpska drama u XIX. Stoleću* [Shakespeare and Serbian Drama in the 19th Century], Belgrade: Univerzitet umetnosti u Beogradu.
Milivojević, Nikitia (2017), Personal interview with the director, 28 July.
Mouffe, Chantal (2013), 'Institutions as Sites of Agonistic Intervention', in Pascal Gielen (ed.), *Institutional Attitudes: Instituting Art in a Flat World*, 63–77, Amsterdam: Valiz.
'N.N.' (1986a), 'Analiza Šekspir-Festa' [The Analysis of Shakespeare Fest], *Dnevnik Novi Sad*, 18 September.
'N.N.' (1986b), 'Zašto je šekspir letovao u jugoslaviji?' [Why was Shakespeare on Vacation in Yugoslavia?], *NIN*, 24 August.
Orford, Peter (2013), 'Henry IV Part 1', in Paul Edmondson, Paul Prescott and Erin Sullivan (eds), *A Year of Shakespeare: Re-living the World Shakespeare Festival*, 76–9, London: Bloomsbury Arden Shakespeare.
Paljetak, Luko (1997), *Engleske teme* [English Topics], Rijeka: Izdavački Centar Rijeka.
Pervić, Muharem (1995), *Volja za promenom*: BITEF 1967–1980, Belgrade: Muzej Pozorišne Umetnosti.
Pogorevc, Petra (2017), 'Will this thing appear again tonight? – Shakespeare adaptations in the 21st century', unpublished conference presentation at the European Shakespeare Research Assocation conference in Gdansk.
Popović, Vladeta (1928), *Shakespeare in Serbia*, London: Milford.
Portmann, Alexandra (2020), 'International Festivals, the Practice of Coproduction, and the Challenges for Documentation in a Digital Age',

in Ric Knowles (ed.), *The Cambridge Companion to International Festivals*, 36–53, Cambridge: Cambridge University Press.
Prescott, Paul, and Erin Sullivan, eds (2015), *Shakespeare on the Global Stage Performance and Festivity in the Olympic Year*, London: Bloomsbury Arden Shakespeare.
Ristić, Maja (2014), 'Romeo and Juliet connects Belgrade and Prishtina'. Available online: https://balkaninsight.com/2014/04/14/romeo-and-juliet-connects-belgrade-and-pristina (accessed 6 July 2020).
Ruzman, R. (1986a), 'Gde su Gledaoci' [Where is the Audience], *Večernje Novosti*, 5 July.
Ruzman, R. (1986b), 'Jugoslovenski teatar u malom' [Yugoslavian Theatre in Miniature], *Borba Beograd*, 23 July.
Senker, Boris (2006), *Bard u Iliriji. Shakespeare u hrvatskom kazalištu* [The Bard in Iliria: Shakespeare in Croatian Theatre], Zagreb: Disput.
Stamenković, Vladimir (2012), *Dijalog sa tradicijom* [Dialogue with Tradition] – *BITEF 1967–2006*, Belgrade: Delfi.
Tadel, Vesna Jurica (2013), 'Neukročena Trmoglavka' [Untamed Stubborn]. Available online: https://pogledi.delo.si/kritike/neukrocena-trmoglavka (accessed 28 August 2020).
Vagapova, Natalia (2010), *Pozorište. Festival. Život*, Belgrade: Bitef Alerta.
Woods, Penelope (2016), 'Shakespeare's Globe Audiences: Old and New', in Bruce R. Smith and Katherine Rowe (eds), *The Cambridge Guide to the Worlds of Shakespeare, Vol. 2: The World's Shakespeare, 1660 to the present*, 1538–44, Cambridge: Cambridge University Press.
Worthen, William (2010), *Drama: Between Text and Performance*, Malden, MA: Wiley-Blackwell.

INDEX

Note: due to limitations of space, we only list proper names of places and people if they appear more than once in the book. The various titles of stage adaptations are also too numerous to index. We take the view that all productions – in whatever language – are adaptive, so a wide range of adaptations can be found under the entry for the Shakespeare play on which they are based.

adaptation *see under* Shakespeare, William
agency 13, 21, 109, 111, 112, 216, 221–5
Al-Bassam, Sulayman 206–7
Almagro Festival (Spain) 4, 10, 12, 37–54
amateurism 26, 27, 72, 157–74, 189
anniversaries 24, 41, 42, 57, 59, 64, 68, 75, 78, 97, 130, 139, 159, 168, 175, 176, 179, 183, 197, 202
Arco, Miguel del 39, 43, 46
audiences 9, 18, 21, 22, 23, 28, 30, 31, 33, 34, 39, 51, 60, 62, 63, 64, 66, 67, 75, 78, 79, 80, 84, 87, 88–9, 93, 94, 95, 96, 102, 109–11, 112, 124, 127, 128–32, 139, 140–1, 142, 144, 145–53, 159, 160, 161, 163, 164–5, 167, **169**, 170, 180, 182, 190, 198, 199, 208, 221, 222
auteur(-ial, -ship) 93, 105
authenticity 11, 38, 133, 177–8, 187, 196–7, 198, 205, 206
Avignon Festival (France) 4, 7, 11, 12, 13, 17–36, 39, 40, 47, 49, 50, 94, 113, 171

Banu, George 103, 114 n6
Barthes, Roland 4, 32
Békéscsaba Theatre 178, 179, 187
Berlin Wall 95, 178, 184
Bitola Shakespeare Festival 5, 8
Boroghină, Emil 94, 98, 104, 106, 186
branding 10, 104, 162, 200, 208
Breen, Robert 202–4
Bremer Shakespeare Company 77–8, 81, 87
Brook, Irina 17, 21, 22, 27, 34
Brook, Peter 21, 90, 108, 114, 120, 152
Bucharest 97, 99, 100, 102, 103, 104, 105, 108

Calderón de la Barca, Pedro 37, 41, 42, 44, 50, 190
Calvi, Lisanna 133 n2, 132 n7, 133 n9, 134
Canning, Charlotte C. 202–4
Carlson, Marvin 38, 122, 131, 199
Carrière, Jean-Claude 30, 34, 120
Ceaușescu, Nicolae/Ceaușescus 94–6
Cervantes, Miguel de 42, 130
Cheek by Jowl, theatre company 41, 99, 153

INDEX

Cinpoeș, Nicoleta 8, 13, 94, 96, 97, 100, 105, 107, 109, 110, 112, 115 n3, 116, 191 n9
Cold War 8, 9, 28, 202
Communism 8, 9, 55, 59–60, 61, 65, 94, 96, 101, 112, 161, 170
  neo-communism 94, 101
  post-communism 170
  post-1989 7, 60, 96
community 4, 7, 8, 18, 19, 22, 27, 29, 34, 39, 59, 84, 95, 96, 102, 110, 111, 112, 131, 158, 160, 161, 162, 170, 171, 181, 183, 185, 187
Corral de Comedias 10, 37, 38, 40
Covid-19 pandemic 3, 6, 14, 17, 18, 63, 68, 70–1, 112, 153, 170, 183, 190
Craiova (International) Shakespeare Festival (Romania) 4, 7, 9, 12, 13, 93–118, 171, 184, 186
Crocq, André 21, 26, 27
cross-national 9, 95
curation 4, 46, 104, 105, 109, 145, 176, 182, 189, 215–19, 221–3, 225

decentralization 20–22, 28, 131
  centralization 96
democratic theatre 4, 7, 17, 19, 26, 28, 30, 33, 41, 55, 56, 60, 65, 70, 129
destination festival 10, 22, 95, 104, 109, 111, 158, 159, 160, 171, 213
dissidence 9, 65, 96
Dodin, Lev 105, 152
Donnellan, Declan 106, 114, 143
Drábek, Pavel 57, 59, 60, 63, 72

Dubrovnik Summer Festival 5, 148, 178, 218, 226

Eastern Bloc 94, 95
  Soviet bloc countries 8
Eastern Europe 8, 9, 28, 73, 92, 101, 155
education 6, 21, 22, 27, 29, 76, 81, 86, 87, 88–9, 91 n13, 102, 104, 109, 131, 133 n13, 138, 140, 146–9, 152, 154 n1, 161, 171 n2, 180, 186, 202, 208 n3
Edinburgh International Festival (Scotland) 7, 8, 20, 39, 40, 49, 50, 93, 94, 98, 113
Elek, Tibor 182–4, 190
Elsinore (Denmark) *see* Helsingør
ESFN (European Shakespeare Festivals Network) 5, 22, 49, 84, 91, 95, 109, 154, 184, 186, 215
European Union 3, 159, 177
eventification 98, 100

Fabiszak, Jacek 144, 149, 155, 156, 190 n2
festivalization 10, 19, 22, 27, 95, 111, 119, 127, 131, 132 n1
Festivo Shakespeariano (Verona, Italy) 7, 10, 13, 94, 113, 119–36
Foucault, Michel 33, 127
Four Castles Shakespeare Festival (Czech and Slovak Republics) 4, 9, 10, 55–74
Franco, Francisco 40, 50, 53
fringe or 'off' festival 12, 18, 19, 21, 33, 38, 39, 42–3, 47, 48, 49–50, 140–1, 144–6
funding and sponsorship 84, 85, 91, 97, 100, 102, 103, 106, 114, 137, 141, 153, 154, 159, 160, 161, 182

Gdańsk Shakespeare Theatre and Festival (Poland) 1, 4, 7, 9, 11, 12, 14, 76, 94, 101, 102, 106, 109, 113, 137–56, 171, 178, 184, 186, 219
Gedeon, József 175, 176, 177, 178, 180, 181, 182, 186, 188, 189, 190
Gémier, Firmin 25, 28, 29, 31
Globe to Globe Festival (London 2012) 82, 91 n9, 141, 187, 207 n3, 214, 219, 223
Golden Yorick competition 140, 144, 150, 151
Guthrie, Tyrone 128, 197
Gyula Castle Theatre (Hungary) 11, 175, 176, 177, 178, 179, 180, 181, 182, 183, 186, 187, 188, 189, 191, 192, 193
Gyula Shakespeare Festival (Hungary) 4, 9, 10, 11, 13, 109, 175–93

HamletScenen (Elsinore Castle, Denmark) 195, **196**, 198, 207, 208
Hall, Edward 83, 86
Hartmann, Henrik 200, 207, 208
Havel, Václav 8–9, 55, 56, 60, 65
Helsingør/Elsinore (Denmark) 10, 12, 13, 138, 195–211
heritage 19, 22, 23, 25, 79, 76, 90, 96, 111, 125, 128, 131, 161, 176, 190, 196–7, 200
heterotopia 33, 128, 129
Hilský, Martin 64–7, 69–70, 72
Hoenselaars, Ton 3, 9
Huba, Martin 64–7
Hungarian National Theatre 180, 183, 189
hybridization 109, 110

inclusion, inclusiveness *see also* community 4, 13, 14, 23, 27, 28, 30, 31, 33, 95, 128, 131, 160, 162, 163, 186–7
indoctrination 96, 112
interculturalism 12, 165, 167, 188, 195, 198, 200, 201, 205, 207, 215
internationalism and globalism 4, 6, 7, 8, 9, 13, 17, 19, 20, 22, 38, 39, 40, 47, 49, 50, 51, 63, 75, 76, 79, 81, 82, 83, 84, 86, 89, 90, 93, 94, 95, 97, 98, 99, 100, 104, 105, 108, 109, 113 n2, 120, 125, 128, 131, 138, 145, 148, 149, 158, 159, 160, 164, 165, 166, 175, 176, 177, 180, 182, 183, 184, 186, 188, 189, 190, 195, 196, 197, 199, 201, 203, 206, 208, 209, 214, 215, 216, 218, 219, 223, 225, 226
International Association of Theatre Critics (IACT) 100, 105
Itaka Shakespeare Festival (Indija, Serbia) 11, 13, 213–29

Jászay, Támas 176, 182, 192
Johansson, Marjana 10, 21, 94, 95, 111
Joubin, Alexa Alice 196–7, 201
Judt, Tony 4, 6

Kačer, Jan 55, 60
Kennedy, Dennis 9, 28, 125, 128, 187, 215
Kizelbach, Urszula 141, 155, 156, 190 n2
Klata, Jan 143, 149, 150, 151, 155
Kleczewska, Maja 140, 149, 150, 151, 155

INDEX

Knowles, Ric 6, 51
Koltai, Tamás 176, 180, 184, 187, 192
Koršunovas, Oskaras 105, 106, 152, 177, 184, 191
Kristeva, Julia 201, 207
Kvapil, Jaroslav 57, 58

Langdal, Peter 200, 207
Lehmann, Hans Thies 149, 155
Limon, Jerzy 14, 57, 73, 76, 92, 92, 138, 139
localism and regionalism 2, 6, 9, 19, 21–2, 29, 33, 49, 62, 99, 109, 111, 112, 120, 128–9, 138–40, 157–174, 175–194, 199–200
  regional 9, 12, 41, 99, 100, 109, 116, 168, 178, 184, 215, 220, 221, 225
Lyding, Henrik 205–6

March, Florence 13, 20, 22, 25, 26, 27, 29
Middleton, Thomas 83, 152
Miszlay, István 178, 179
Mnouchkine, Ariane 12, 25–6, 34
Molière, Jean-Baptiste Poquelin 21, 22, 23, 217

National Theatre in Nice (TNN) 17, 21, 22, 24
nationalism and national identity 4, 5, 7, 9, 57, 58, 61
Nekrošius, Eimuntas 105, 107, 114, 152, 184, 187
Neuss Globe (Germany) 4, 11, 13, 75–92, 109, 129
'new Europe' 95, 96, 115, 177

'original practices' 38, 61, 85, 87, 129

Palais des Papes / Popes' Palace (Avignon, France) 11, 18, 20, 23, 25, 30, 31, 32, 35, 52
Parr, Philip and Parrabbola 109, 110, 111, 145
participation 29, 95, 96, 111, 117, 179
Patalenitsa Shakespeare (Bulgaria) 4, 9, 10, 13, 157–74
Pennacchia, Maddalena 13, 109, 111, 117, 126, 129, 133 n12 n14, 135
Perceval, Luk 149, 152
pilgrimage 6, 197
Portmann, Alexandra 13, 226 n6, 228
Printemps des comédiens (Montpellier, France) 12, 17, 29, 33, 34
Pujante, Angel-Luis 3, 9
Purcărete, Silviu 93, 94, 98, 101, 105, 114, 184, 186

Q Brothers 86, 142

reconstruction 6, 7, 14, 19, 20, 24, 25, 92, 95
regeneration 13–4, 28, 40, 95, 111
resilience 14, 18, 112, 160, 170, 189
resistance 7, 59, 97, 170, 185, 206
revolution 6, 59, 93, 96, 100
Romanian Theatre Association (UNITER) 97, 98, 105
Ryutopia 86, 107

Schechner, Richard 107, 200
school festival *see* education
Sen, Ong Ken 12, 198–9, 205–7
Shake-Nice! (Nice, France) 12, 17, 19, 21, 22, 24, 27, 29
Shakespeare in Performance Seminar 108

Shakespeare, William
  adaptations of the Complete
    Works
    After Shakespeare 24
    *The Complete Works of
      William Shakespeare
      (Abridged)* 130
    Le Tour complet du cœur (A
      Complete Picture of the
      Heart) 22, 24
  adaptations of scenes from
    multiple Shakespeare plays
    Blázni, milenci a básníci
      (Madmen, Lovers, and
      Poets) 69
    Pocta Shakespearovi
      (Homage to Shakespeare)
      68–9
    Shakespearations 145
    Shakespeare Laboratory 144
    Shakespearovi šašci
      (Shakespeare's Fools) 69
    Stories from Shakespeare 182
    To Love or Not to Love 164
  plays in festival productions
    Antony and Cleopatra
      81, 180
    As You Like It 64, 83, 99,
      114, 145, 181, 226
    The Comedy of Errors 83,
      167, 183
    Hamlet 1, 5, 12, 15, 20, 39,
      43–8, 57, 58, 64, 65, 66,
      68, 70, 83, 91, 100, 105,
      106–8, 123, 141, 142,
      143–4, 145, 148, 150–2,
      153, 160, 164, 167, 170,
      177, 179, 180, 181, 183,
      184, 187, 195, 197–207,
      219
    Henry IV plays 23, 25, 64,
    Henry V 27, 32, 83, 145,
    Henry VI plays 30, 214, 223
    Henry VIII 83

Julius Caesar 47, 49, 122,
  125, 145
King Lear 51, 57, 65–7, 69,
  81, 83, 129, 150, 180,
  181,
Macbeth 23, 48–9, 57, 60,
  64, 65, 83, 93–4, 98,
  101, 129, 130, 145, 148,
  153, 177, 180, 181, 185,
  217
Measure for Measure 59,
  114, 143, 150, 170, 187,
  226
The Merchant of Venice 68,
  83, 123, 140, 168, 181
*The Merry Wives of
  Windsor* 62, 63, 68, 81,
  141, 153
*A Midsummer Night's
  Dream* 19, 21, 24, 26–7,
  34, 41, 55, 60, 63, 64,
  67–8, 70, 76, 77, 83,
  101, 110–11, **110**, 124,
  158, 164, 168–9, **169**,
  181, 184, 187, 217
Much Ado about Nothing
  63, 83, 113, 124, 130,
  144, 188
Othello 83, 105, 124, 141,
  191, 217, 219
Pericles 41, 165, 166, 220,
  222
Richard II 8, 12, 19, 20, 23,
  24, 25–6, 30, 34, 120,
  124, 219
Richard III 17, 32, 47, 59,
  63, 64, 66, 83, 99, 101,
  130, 181, 185, 220
Romeo and Juliet 48, 49,
  58, 64, 65, 68, 83, 99,
  108, 113, 120, 121–5,
  126, 129, 144, 145, 148,
  163–5, 170, 177, 181,
  182, 226

The Taming of the Shrew 69,
81, 83, 120, 144, 164,
167, 168, 197, 221, 223
The Tempest 19, 24, 27,
34, 37, 39, 41, 45–6, **66**,
67, 68, 81, 83, 99, 109,
120, 149, 166, 177, 181,
184–6
Timon of Athens 101, 225
Titus Andronicus 98, 99,
107, 150, 217, 219
Troilus and Cressida 113,
114
Twelfth Night 34, 64, 68, 83,
114, 120, 140, 184, 185
*The Two Gentlemen of
Verona* 145, 187, 226
The Winter's Tale 83, 99, 164
Shakespeare's Globe (London) 5,
38, 75, 77, 79, 80, 81, 86,
87, 89, 104, 125, 127, 128,
129, 131, 178
Shakespeare in Catalonia 5, 10
Shevtsova, Maria 94, 106, 107,
117, 182, 185, 189, 193
Sík, Ferenc 180, 186, 193
Silvano Toti Globe (Rome, Italy)
11, 13, 119–36
site-specific 13, 15, 20, 22, 95, 144,
198–9, 200, 205–6, 218
SKUTR (Martin Kukučka and
Lukáš Trpišovský) 67–8, 70
socialism 71, 96, 179, 193,
225 n1, 227
Sokolova, Boika 9, 13, 161, 171
n3, 173
soft power 201–3, 208
Spanish Golden Age drama 37,
38, 39, 40, 41, 42, 43, 49, 50
spectatorship (*see also* audiences)
3, 13, 90
Spottiswoode, Patrick 81, 87

Stavreva, Kirilka 13, 161, 171 n3,
173
street art/performance/theatre 107,
180, 182, 187
Sturua, Robert 152, 160, 184
surtitles, subtitles (in
performances) 50, 67, 188

Teatro Romano (Verona, Italy) 10,
119–36
Terezin (Theresienstad) 59, 71
Tompa, Gábor 100, 185, 186
tourism 1, 10, 13, 14, 39, 63, 78,
79, 82, 90, 95, 106, 109,
111, 115, 120, 128, 132,
139, 144, 159, 160, 178,
183, 190, 197, 207, 213, 227
circuit 14, 95, 105, 109, 128,
132, 176, 189
translation 3, 4, 13, 20, 25, 30, 49,
57, 65, 67, 69–70, 75, 81,
86, 90, 109, 115, 121, 123,
124, 129–30, 131, 188
Tříska, Jan 65–7, 69
TwO Windows Theatre 144, 145

universalism 7, 28, 139, 176, 201,
204
utopianism 7, 33, 127

Varela, Jean 18, 21
Vega, Lope de 37, 39, 41, 42, 44,
50, 52
Vilar, Jean 18, 19, 20, 23, 25, 26,
28, 29, 30, 31, 32, 33, 35, 36
Villa Stanković (Čortanovci,
Serbia) 11, 213, 218

Wanamaker, Sam 76–7, 81
Wiertz, Rainer 81, 82, 84, 85, 88
William Shakespeare Foundation
(Craiova) 99, 104, 108, 117

www.ingramcontent.com/pod-product-compliance
Lightning Source LLC
Chambersburg PA
CBHW062137300426
44115CB00012BA/1955